# Discover Your Purpose! Design Your Destiny! Direct Your Achievement!

Proven Strategies for a Productive, God-Centered Life!

William D. Greenman

Take note that the name satan and related names are not capitalized. We choose not to acknowledge him, even to the point of violating grammatical rules.

**Destiny Image® Publishers, Inc.**
**P.O. Box 310**
**Shippensburg, PA 17257-0310**

"Speaking to the Purposes of God for This Generation
and for the Generations to Come"

ISBN 0-7684-2009-1

For Worldwide Distribution
Printed in the U.S.A.

This book and all other Destiny Image, Revival Press,
and Treasure House books are available
at Christian bookstores and distributors worldwide.

For a U.S. bookstore nearest you, call **1-800-722-6774**.
For more information on foreign distributors, call **717-532-3040**.
Or reach us on the Internet: **http://www.reapernet.com**

# Dedication

This book is dedicated to several people who have been instrumental in molding my personality, emotions, and intellect in a manner that has been unique, loving, and sometimes painful. I love them with all my heart.

First and foremost, this book is dedicated to the Lord Jesus Christ. From Him I received my spiritual life, my inspiration, and the meaning of my life.

Second, it is dedicated to my beautiful and gifted wife, Meg, who has always believed in me and walked with me. I do not deserve her.

Third, I want to recognize my father, John H. Greenman, to whom I owe my physical life and from whom came my life's watchword, for he once told me that I "could do anything." This book is a part of his prophecy fulfilled.

Finally, there are my two most profound mentors to date. Dale Brooks gave me every part of his life and ministry to see to it that I succeeded in becoming a minister and a man of worth. Also, Jim Goll became my friend, teacher, and guide in new areas of ministry. He challenged me to minister when I thought I had nothing left to give.

I present this work with joy, love, and insufficient thanks in honor of these loved ones.

# Acknowledgments

Every completed worthwhile endeavor is the product of many interested minds, hearts, and hands. The talents and energies of many such folks have gone into the production of this book. The following individuals stand high above the rest:

- My wife, Meg, who had to listen to my doubts, my exultings, and my endless parade of ideas concerning how this book is going to be the beginning of the greatest movement since indoor plumbing. I love you, Meg.

- My children, who endured countless conversations with the back of my head while I sat riveted to my computer keyboard creating this work. Thanks Jennifer, Daniel, and Gloria—you are the greatest!

- My home fellowship group, who prayed for me all along the way as I wrote. Thanks and blessing to you Sam and Linda Caster, David and Carrie Colister, Steve and Wendy Hames, Don and Lydia Herndon, and Richard and Debra Howard! You're tremendous!

- My good friend, Steve Hames, who loaned me his Macintosh when mine died shortly after beginning this work. I promise I *will* bring it back, Steve.

- My new friend, John Simpson, who loaned me his laptop for a week and never saw it again. You're a great guy, John. God will bless you for it!

- My many friends who gave me constant, positive feedback about the content and need for this book.

- My many fellow airline passengers who I totally ignored while pounding out these chapters somewhere over North America.

- All those teachers and trainers whose books, tapes, and videos I have studied over the years. Thanks for letting me hitch a ride on your wisdom!

# Contents

## Endorsements

This book answers questions people are asking! It is very practical and readers will be encouraged to reach for the high calling of God for their lives.

T.D. Hall
Vice President, Successful Christian Living
Dallas

People without clarity and purpose are rudderless ships, planes without navigators. William's book comes to the rescue with practical insight to equip you to find and fulfill your purpose in spirit, soul, and body. The Body of Christ has been waiting a long time for this book!

Wesley Tullis
Director, The Jericho Center
Colorado Springs

William Greenman is a man of integrity and has his eyes focused on loving God with all his heart. This book will prove helpful to people who feel aimless and are desperately in need of a clearer focus in their lives.

Mike Bickle
Senior Pastor, Metro Christian Fellowship
Kansas City

William Greenman's book on purpose, destiny, and achievement is an excellent work filled with Christ-centered advice and practical "how-to's" for daily living. I feel that it is a masterpiece, and I recommend it wholeheartedly!

Dr. William Standish Reed, MD, MS
President, Christian Medical Foundation
Tampa

Where was this book when I desperately needed it as a young believer?! This is not a theoretical book, but one filled with practical, biblical, and relevant ideas and information. The truths presented in this book serve as a key to unlocking and understanding God's purpose for our lives. William Greenman has provided an invaluable service to God's people with this excellent work.

Dr. C. Douglas White
Senior Pastor, Restoration Church
Dallas/Fort Worth

As a national youth speaker, I am regularly asked how to discover one's purpose in life. William Greenman's book contains the solid principles necessary to discover and perform our purpose and destiny. Dig into it and enjoy this insightful journey in determining God's ordained plan for your life!

Rustin B. Carlson
President, Rock the Nations Student Ministries
Colorado Springs

Masterful! Practical! Inspiring! With the skill of an artist, William Greenman weaves together the necessity of having a "prophetic vision" for your life, while wedding it together with the practical steps for achieving it. All new believers should read this book to aid them in the building of their personal foundation in God, so their life can be launched.

Jim Goll
Founder/Director, Ministry to the Nations
Nashville

In a day when so many are asking, "Who am I?" and "Why am I here?" William Greenman provides sane and sensible answers, Better still, they're biblical answers.

Dr. Sam Storms
President, Grace Training Center
Author, *The Singing God*
Kansas City

# Foreword

The greatest tragedy in life is not death, but life without a reason. It is dangerous to be alive and not know why you were given life. One of the most frustrating experiences is to have time but not know why.

From the beginning of man's history as we know it, mankind has been grappling with the questions: Why am I here? What is the reason for my existence? What is the meaning of my life? Is there a reason for the universe, the creation, and man? These questions are universal. They lurk deep within the secret chambers of the hearts and minds of every human who has ever lived—regardless of race, color, ethnic heritage, socioeconomic status, or nationality. Philosophers such as Plato, Aristotle, Socrates, and others throughout the ages have attempted to explore these seemingly illusive questions. For the most part, their efforts have resulted in more questions than answers.

The deepest craving of the human spirit is to find a sense of significance and relevance. The search for relevance in life is the ultimate pursuit of man. Conscious or unconscious, admitted or unadmitted, this internal passion motivates and drives every human being. It directs his decisions, controls his behavior, and dictates his responses to his environment.

This need for significance is the cause of great tragedies. Many suicides and attempted suicides are due to this compelling need. Many mass murderers and serial killers confess the relationship of their antisocial behavior to their need to feel important or to experience a sense of self-worth.

This desperate desire to feel important and relevant to one's existence also causes the sacrifice of common sense, good judgment, moral standards, and basic human values. Many individuals have sacrificed excellent reputations and years of character-building lifestyles for the sake of advancement to a desired position or for a place of recognition and fame in society or in the workplace—all so they could feel important and worthwhile.

This passion for a sense of significance and meaning in life is also the fuel for most capitalist and progressive economies. There are millions of individuals who sacrifice their families, friends, and convictions in the pursuit of significance. Accumulating status symbols and material possessions is their means of seeking a position of importance and meaning.

In essence, this deep desire and drive for a sense of importance, significance, and relevance is the cause and motivator of all human behavior and conflict. This passion for significance knows no boundaries. Rich and poor are victims of its power. Kings and peasants alike suffer under its rule. Is this passion for meaningful life a negative craving? Absolutely not!

This yearning for relevance and significance is evidence of an internal vacuum in the nature of mankind that needs to be filled. This age-old passion is the pursuit of purpose, a relentless reaching for a reason for the gift of life.

William Greenman in his work, *Discover Your Purpose! Design Your Destiny! Direct Your Achievement!* provides practical, time-tested principles to help you capture your personal purpose for living. In his crisp, provocative style, he simplifies the complex, making it easy to understand the nature of destiny. I challenge you to read this book and keep it as a companion to your life. It has the tools you need to fix the confusion that comes with living in a world without meaning. Let this book help you discover your purpose, design your destiny, and direct your achievement!

Dr. Myles Munroe
Nassau, Bahamas

# Preface

## Three Questions

For several years, I was aware of a great need within the Body of Christ. I heard it echoed again and again by the hundreds of brethren I counseled across this continent. Each had a need to find the *reason* he or she is alive on planet earth: *Who* am I? What is *my* purpose? Why am *I* here?

### The Sad Truth

This prompted me to begin my own investigation as to just how widespread this heart-cry was. Since 1980, I've asked Christians the same two questions virtually everywhere I've spoken, and each time I've gathered the same unfortunate results. My questions are, 1) What is your God-ordained purpose in life? and 2) What is your long-term plan to live out that purpose?

The results show that less than five percent of American Christians (and I feel confident that this is true of most other nationalities as well) know their purpose and less than ten percent of those who do know have any sort of a written plan to bring it to pass!

As this survey brought in the same statistics time and again, I found a third question haunting me: How can the *Church* possibly fulfill its corporate destiny if it has no understanding or impetus to do so at the *individual* level?

## Will He Find Faith?

When Christ, our Lord and Savior, returns for His own, He will look straight at His Church and search for the faith that makes heroes out of ordinary people. He will seek that quality that causes them to forsake everything to perform His will. But, if we, His Church, have *failed* to discover our individual and therefore collective purpose in daily, practical life, will He be pleased with us? Is evangelism enough? Is giving to missions enough? Is going to the right church fellowship enough? Is marrying the right person enough? Is having or rejecting great wealth enough? Is being a martyr enough? Personally, I don't think so.

I believe most Christians are honest and sincere in seeking the Lord on this matter. They long to know the purpose for their lives and to perform the bidding of their King. My own desire led me to the discovery of the principles that revealed God's plan for my life. These principles are so practical that they can be applied to anyone's personal endeavor, whether it is a major life goal or a short-term project. For many years now, I have had the pleasure of sharing these same principles with tens of thousands of such seekers with great results.

## The Big Picture

Due to the fact that so few Christians have discovered their personal purpose and developed their divine destinies, the *overall* purpose and destiny of the Church has been stifled. When the members of a body have no idea of their specific place and function, the entire body is affected. Aimless hands and feet cannot direct the abilities of a body out of control. Only by dealing with the individual members can we hope to strengthen the power of the entire Church. This book is the beginning of our concentrated, focused vision to assist the Body of Christ in that effort.

But the need does not stop at the Church. The world is the real treasure we seek to place at the feet of our Lord. There are literally billions of godless people waiting for the Church of Jesus Christ to rise up in all its power and glory to rescue them. The Lord Jesus is the only hope for these starving multitudes, and the Church is the vehicle He has chosen to bring them that hope!

But the Church is individuals. It is individual believers who will save the lives of millions with the gospel of Jesus Christ. If those believers do not find their God-ordained place and live in it, the effectiveness of the Church to meet the world's need for life will be drastically diminished. We *must* enlighten individual believers, thereby enlightening the Church, which will, in turn, enlighten the darkening world!

## Simple Faith

When I began to search for my own purpose, I had no publication like this to turn to and few counselors to advise me. I felt terribly alone. I did possess one thing, however, which proved to be all I needed to get the ball rolling in the right direction. I had an unshakeable faith in God and His Word. It was pure, child-like faith that said, "My Dad can do anything, and He will take care of me." This faith allowed me to believe, without reservation, whatever I read in the Holy Scriptures. As I constantly attempted to put into practice that which I read or heard taught from the Bible, I just knew that the Lord would not let me down.

I remember reading John 10:27, which says that the Lord's sheep know His voice and follow Him. Knowing that word had to be true, I soon found myself praying,

> *Father, I'm not sure what Your voice sounds like, but I know that You said I would hear it, so I know that I will hear You when I listen. I want to follow You. So this is what I am going to do: When I pray and ask things of You, You had better be the first one to speak because that is the voice I will follow.*

That was not the prayer of a prideful or arrogant man. It was a prayer of simple faith. The Lord graciously honored my prayer. Soon He and I were conversing like old friends, and it has only gotten better over the years. During our times of communion, God has shared with me the detailed workings of His purpose and destiny for my life. This close relationship did not come overnight. It has taken years to receive such direction, and I am still receiving new instructions all the time.

I have learned the meaning of both the "still small voice" and the "thunder and lightning" of God's authority. He has become my best friend, teacher, counselor, and disciplinarian. He applauds my victories and comforts me in my setbacks. He consoles me when I make mistakes and punishes my disobedience. I have felt the might of His healing power flow through my touch and the gentleness of His compassion caress troubled hearts through my words. I have experienced God's supernatural power and His insight into my humanness.

I have a *real* relationship with the Almighty God who created me. He *truly* is my Father, just as truly as He is my God. He is my most valued possession. Do I know all about Him? Of course not! But I am content with the fact that He knows all about me and *still* chooses to love and use me to His glory.

### Final Thoughts

Of all I can teach anyone, one truth is essential: *A meaningful and intimate relationship with the Lord* ***must*** *be the ultimate goal of every life*. Only when we have acquired such a relationship can we hope to find and live out the purpose He has for our lives. That is my prayer for you. That is why I wrote this book. God bless you!

# Section One

## *Discover Your Purpose*

*"...to those who are called according to His purpose"* (Romans 8:28).

# Chapter 1

## Start Here!

*Commit your ways to the Lord, and your plans will be established* (Proverbs 16:3).

This chapter is the most important of any in this book. Why? Because if you do not understand this chapter, you will have a hard time correctly assimilating the rest of the information in this book.

*To be sure, there is no more desired understanding than that of our God-ordained purpose and destiny.* To have the God of creation lay out before you the eternal reason for your life is an awesome and inspiring thing. Grasping His purpose, His life lived through you in your unique way, is the essence of the God-seeking mechanism that is within every human heart. It is the "why" of this book.

I do not want anyone who reads this book to think for one minute that anything suggests you might simply tap your *human* potential and be right where you are supposed to be for the rest of your life. No! *My major goal is to instill within your spirit the knowledge that God has a specific purpose, a specific destiny, a specific achievement for your life.* No one else but you was created to perform it. We are after His Divine Will here, not mere accomplishments or triumphs of humanity that point to the finite deeds of mortal man.

God is the *center* of this work. God is the center of each page and line and letter. *God, through the power of His Son Jesus Christ of Nazareth, is* the *focus*. If you read this book and do not understand that your destiny is *His* to proclaim, to produce, and to prevail through you, then I have served you nothing of value. I will have merely added another lump of pulp to the shelves of spiritually empty libraries. I will have failed.

Therefore, as you read each line, each word, I want the thought, *"God is leading me,"* to resonate through your soul and spirit. I want each page to bring you new insight into how He will guide you and show you things to come. Each time you reread this work, I want you to know beyond a doubt that you have *no* value without Him and *no* worthwhile future beyond His revelation. *This is a book about how* ***God*** *directs His own—nothing less*. The practical helps and information must be fused permanently with the desire to fellowship with Christ throughout the journey of your personal purpose, destiny, and achievement. To *Start Here* means to know God, be strong, and do exploits. (See Daniel 11:32b KJV.)

**Let your exploits be His by design and yours by obedience.**
(W.G.)

Take the time to incorporate every aspect of hearing, communing, and waiting on Him into your daily life. Be firm and resolute that nothing and no one will keep you from spending time with Him. Know God! He will make you strong. You will do *His* exploits—*your* destiny!

### Who's Responsible?

The strange dichotomy of a God-led destiny is the fact that you and I are responsible for the outcome. Even though our lives can be *ordained* by the Lord, how we *execute* that ordination is in our hands for the most part. If it were not so, could we still have a *free* will after making Jesus Christ our Lord? I think not.

*Every step of the way along the achievement of our purpose and destiny will be decided not by God, but by us as we say yes to His leading*. Though this truth may give cause for trepidation, it actually is the impetus for the most exciting life imaginable! How can I say such a thing with our personal destinies looming ominously before us, written indelibly by the hands of frail humans such as ourselves? Easily! When we are *yielded* to the Lord, He becomes more than a guide—He becomes our protection through His grace and mercy.

Yes, we *will* make mistakes. Yes, we *will* get off course now and then. But He never leaves us, nor does He ever lack the resources necessary to care for our every misstep or course change. He is our Father, and His love will bring Him to our aid whenever we need Him. But make no mistake about it, if your destiny, your purpose, is to know the fruit of achievement—if it is to see completion—it is up to *you* and no one else.

## Special Items

There are a few special items I wish to point out to you concerning this book. First, you will find many references to the *Destiny Planner*® throughout this book. This is an invaluable tool for discovering, designing, and directing your life.

Second, utilize every strategy, form, and action you feel is pertinent to your achieving your designated purpose. Do *not* feel that you must employ every single tidbit of information found within. I know better than to think every reader must or will be able to use every suggestion or instruction. Use what fits and feel free to leave the rest for a later time when it may be more appropriate.

Third, if you think that this book is about a get-rich-quick formula or an easy path to success and prestige, *go get your money back right now*! This is about work. You'll find no shortcuts to wealth, fame, or recognition here. You *will* find easy-to-implement principles of life that will make you successful in the Kingdom of God, which usually brings other rewards with it in this life. However, your motives must be pure *first*.

## Final Thoughts

I feel fairly confident that you wouldn't be reading this book if you weren't serious about living exactly the way God intends you to. I'm just as confident you'll enjoy this journey we're about to take together. It's the most important journey any human being can begin. Everyone is longing to go, yet most never get started. Few even find the map. But you have not only found the map; you *will* complete the journey...the journey to your God-ordained purpose, destiny, and achievement.

**Take command of your life by giving God control of your life.**
(W.G.)

# Chapter 2

# You Were Born for a Purpose

### What Made the Difference?

Let me compare the first five years of my Christian life with the second five years. The contrast is startling. The first five years of my Christian life showed little fruit. I *was* radically changed in my spirit and attitude, but any noteworthy, outward signs were mostly nonexistent. I did manage to lead a few people to the Lord, and I was very vocal about Jesus being my personal Lord and Savior. However, I acquired little knowledge of God, His Kingdom, or His ways. I still drank a great deal of beer to the point of becoming drunk, and I engaged in other such sins. I attended church, but I had no contact with Christians except for Sunday services. I was even still wondering if the Bible really was the infallible Word of God!

The second five years of my Christian life were remarkably different. During that time I led thousands of people to Christ. I wrote a booklet on basic Christian principles. I traveled across North America ministering to tens of thousands of people. I created my own ministry organization and began to train members of my home church in ministry techniques. I was ordained as a minister. I was interviewed by radio, television, and newspapers concerning my ministry. I also helped other new ministries get started in their callings.

What was it that made such a profound difference in my life in such a short period of time? What changed? Was it God favoring me above others? Did I get some big break? Was it fate? The simple answer is that I *discovered* my purpose and made the *decision* to fulfill it! That decision led to my gaining the knowledge I needed to accomplish the ideas and plans the Lord shared with me. It was hard work. It was often lonely. But it was the most wonderful time of my life because I knew I was doing what I was created to do. I still know that. I want you to know it for *yourself* as well! I want you to discover *your* purpose.

**From the first Adam to the last man of time, each human being is created for a unique and profoundly important personal purpose. The task of life is to find that purpose and fulfill it with enthusiasm and great joy.** (W.G.)

## The Question

What is *my* life supposed to accomplish? That is the second most important question you must ever answer (the first question being: Who is Jesus Christ of Nazareth?). Once you have dealt with Christ, you must discover exactly what you were created to do for Him and for the furthering of His Kingdom. No Christian has the right to decide what he or she wishes to do in life. That right was handed over to the Lord God when he or she made Jesus the Master of his or her life and was born again. From the moment of our surrender to Him, our number one goal must be to find and fulfill our God-ordained purpose. To fail to do so is to invite an eternity of unrealized accomplishment. This is not to say that a Christian can't accomplish worthwhile goals merely because he desires to do them; but how worthwhile can they be if they never pertain to your ordained purpose?

Were you born in this century by chance? Were you born into your family by a fluke of nature? Your country, your race—is it all an accident? If you are a person who never knew your mother or father, or if you were born to parents who were not married, or if you are the offspring of a woman who was raped—does that make you *less* a creation of God? Can people create human spirits? Can anyone decide when and where and to whom he wants to be born? The answer to all these questions is no. No! You are *not* an accident or a product of chance. You were ordained of God to be born in your generation, and He knew that if you would give your life to Him, He would be able to use every good *and* bad part of your life to His glory and to the betterment of those around you. *You are totally unique!* You were born for a unique purpose!

The goal of this book is to convince you of that fact and to give you the tools you need to find and fulfill your ordained purpose. I want to help you discover exactly what you were created to do and then learn how to do it. I want to meet you in Heaven and hear how you became more than you ever thought possible and accomplished more than you ever dreamed you could. If you will be diligent to study and apply the principles and techniques found in the following pages, I *promise* you that your life will be exemplary, productive, and profound!

> *For this reason also, since the day we heard of it, we have not ceased to pray for you and to ask that you may be filled with the knowledge of His will in all spiritual wisdom and understanding, so that you may walk in a manner worthy of the Lord, to please Him in all respects, bearing fruit in every good work and increasing in the knowledge of God; strengthened with all power, according to His glorious might, for the attaining of all steadfastness and patience; joyously giving thanks to the Father, who has qualified us to share in the inheritance of the saints in light* (Colossians 1:9-12).

In his letter to the Colossians, the apostle Paul mentioned that he prayed this particular prayer continually for that body of believers. When I began my commitment to the Lordship of Christ, I took that prayer for my own. Daily as I read this prayer, I claimed its truth for my life, and I still do so today. As God's child, I wanted the perfect will of the Father to be at work in me, and I desired to be filled with His wisdom and plan for my entire life.

I recited that set of Scriptures many times each day, and before long, the revelation of its words became reality for me. Through my daily walk with the Lord, I came to know and formulate the information in these pages into powerful strategies for living. This information was the road to finding my life's ordained purpose. It has changed me from a seemingly directionless disciple into a useful, on-target member of the Body of Christ. I want (more than you can imagine!) for you to know that same change.

These same principles will work for you. Why? Because they are from God's Word and they have been proven over and over again in my own life and the lives of countless others. These are not hyper-spiritual or spooky rituals. They are just simple Bible truths meant for all of us to understand and walk in. They demand work on our part, to be sure, but God gives more than enough courage, energy, and desire to carry out the task. You can do it! You can reap these same rewards! They are yours for the taking.

**Great minds have purposes, others have wishes.**
(Washington Irving)

In Second Timothy chapter 4 we find Paul admonishing his beloved pupil Timothy to fulfill the ministry God has given him. Paul follows this instruction by stating that he himself has fulfilled his own God-given ministry, stating emphatically, "I have fought the good fight, I have finished the course, I have kept the faith" (2 Tim. 4:7). These are powerful words from a powerful man. If you are anything like me, and I am pretty sure you are, these words from the lips of Paul probably invoke a sense of envy. When it is our time to leave this life, we would all like to say that we have run the race the Lord set before us and that we did not faint along the way. Unfortunately, most of us are more apt to cry that we fought the fight, but our eyes were so swollen from the beating that we couldn't find the course with a seeing eye dog, let alone keep the faith! If you're like me and that sounds like your all-too-sad song, let me assure you that the Lord has a new tune for you to sing. Let's take a closer look at the apostle Paul and discover how he found his purpose.

Paul thought he was already doing the will of God for his life; he was persecuting and killing Christians. He operated in the authority of the most "spiritual" men in the world, and he had the papers to prove it. He was zealous for his work and exemplary in his efficiency. His name struck fear in the hearts of those who called Jesus their King. *But, he was totally wrong!* Yes, he loved God. Yes, he wanted to obey God. Yes, he performed every letter of the Law of God. Yet, he was WRONG! He was not fulfilling the will of God—he was fighting it! But the mercy of God was so strong toward Paul's sincerely wrong life that He gently showed the Pharisee his real purpose. Here's what Paul discovered about himself and God's will for him.

*While thus engaged as I was journeying to Damascus with the authority and commission of the chief priests, at midday, O King,*

*I saw on the way a light from heaven, brighter than the sun, shining all around me and those who were journeying with me. And when we had all fallen to the ground, I heard a voice saying to me in the Hebrew dialect, "Saul, Saul, why are you persecuting Me? It is hard for you to kick against the goads." And I said. "Who art Thou, Lord?" And the Lord said, "I am Jesus whom you are persecuting. But arise, and stand on your feet; for this purpose I have appeared to you, to appoint you a minister and a witness not only to the things which you have seen, but also to the things in which I will appear to you; delivering you from the Jewish people and from the Gentiles, to whom I am sending you, to open their eyes so that they may turn from darkness to light and from the dominion of Satan to God, in order that they may receive forgiveness of sins and an inheritance among those who have been sanctified by faith in Me." Consequently, King Agrippa, I did not prove disobedient to the heavenly vision* (Acts 26:12-19).

Paul had a purpose that demanded he go to the nations of the world, but as an apostolic teacher-preacher-mentor, not a murderer. Our zeal, like Paul's, is meaningless if it is misdirected. There will be people who will stand before the judgment seat of Christ thinking they have done a great job for the Lord during their life on earth, only to be told, "I never knew you." You see, it's not about how much we do, but about doing what He directs and ordains. It's about hearing the Lord say, "Well done, good and faithful servant...My son in whom I am well pleased!" That's what I want for *you*. That's the heartbeat of my work.

## Why a Purpose?

Before we begin to discover how to find your personal purpose in life, let's take a moment to establish the truth of why you *need* a purpose in the first place. During my years as an assistant pastor and church counselor, the questions most frequently asked of me in counseling sessions were, "Why am I here?"; "What is my purpose in life?"; and "What is it that God wants me to do?" Those sincere questions usually flowed from hearts in great turmoil because they did not know the answers, yet they understood the severity of that lack of understanding. The eternity in their hearts was convicting them of a deep-seated need, but their inability to answer made for stressful living.

Their pain is hauntingly foretold in the following verses, which explain that such turmoil will come upon any and all who do not know their purpose in life or have a vision for their future:

*Where there is no vision, the people perish* (Proverbs 29:18a KJV).

*My people are destroyed for lack of knowledge* (Hosea 4:6a).

Let's look specifically at Proverbs 29:18 first. The New American Standard Bible states, "Where there is no vision, the people are unrestrained...." The word *vision*, according to *Strong's Concordance*, means "mental sight or a revealed word from God." The word *unrestrained* denotes "the absence of clear guidance or definite direction." A restraint, as referred to in this verse, is like a bit in the mouth of a horse. The restraint is not used to bind the horse, but to direct him and his immense power. In other words, if you do not have a mental image—a revelation of God's personal purpose for your life—you will be without direction, having no means of receiving His guidance in the various areas of your life. You will be perishing in many ways. Your mind will not know its fullness. Your physical attributes will not be able to perform at their peak. Your emotions will lack proper strength. Your relationships may be wrong. Your finances may never reach their potential. On the other hand, if you *do* have a revealed word from God, you will be restrained. You will be guided. You will have purpose and direction. You will have abundant life in all areas!

**More men fail through lack of purpose than through lack of talent.**
(Billy Sunday)

God does not want us to perish. He does not want us to be destroyed just because we lack knowledge of His plan for our lives. In First Corinthians chapter 12, the Lord states that He not only has an assigned position for each one of His children, but He will *personally* place us in it: "But now God has placed the members, each one of them, in the body, just as He desired" (1 Cor. 12:18). If you have not yet discovered your God-ordained place in life, you will not have the ability to be fully directed by Him. You may have visions, dreams, and goals you want to attain, and they may motivate you. They may even give you purpose and direction for a time. But only God's purpose for you as an individual will bring you the abundant, meaningful life both you and He desire you to experience.

## My Own Discovery

In the naiveté of my early Christian life, I thought "fire insurance" was all there was to salvation. I continued to make plans according to *my* desires, *my* dreams, and the direction *I* wanted to take. I eventually became a full-time professional circus performer, thinking that fulfilling the dream of being a professional entertainer, which had been in my heart since I was a child, was success. After five long years as a Christian with *me* in control of my life instead of Christ, I found out differently.

I discovered that no matter how much we may proclaim the reality of Jesus as our *Savior*, our lives are empty without Jesus as our *Lord*. And I discovered the truth of Proverbs 29:18. Because I did not have a revealed word from God, I did not have God's guidance active in my life. Instead, I had my own dreams and was, therefore, perishing. There was a void in my life. Finally realizing my failure, I cried out to God in desperation, "Okay, Father, no longer my will, but Your will be done in my life!" It was then that both my spiritual and natural life became ignited.

Almost immediately, God planted His vision of a Christ-centered circus in my heart. That vision illuminated to me my purpose of being a minister of the gospel, which fulfilled me in a way no other dream had done before. I was totally directed by that vision. I was restrained, directed, and guided because of it. My total motivation stemmed from that vision because it was part of God's purpose and plan for my life. Now that Circus Alleluia Ministries has been laid to rest, I have been given the next phase of my purpose and destiny. This phase, though of a different expression, is in line with my life purpose of ministering the gospel of Christ and helping others to do the same. My motivation has not diminished; it has merely been redirected.

God has a vision—a purpose and plan—for your life. He desires to share it with you. That purpose and vision will restrain, lead, and guide you for the rest of your life. It will save you from destruction. That vision is not some weird, ultra-spiritual quest. It is God's perfect will for you personally. I guarantee you, there is no greater feeling of security in the entire world than living out His perfect will for your life. *Ultimate success is placing all that you are into God's hands, to do with as He pleases, and then working with Him to fulfill His will for you.* The day I made that decision was the day my life took off like a rocket! I believe yours will too. Find your purpose. Find direction. Find the destiny ordained for you! It's there waiting for you right now. I will help you discover it through the tools offered in this book.

## Your Place in the Son

You have a specific place in God's master plan, a place only you can fulfill—a place you will occupy to fulfill the destiny He ordained for you. It will satisfy the deepest longing of your being. In later chapters, we will discuss exactly how to discover and live out your personal purpose and destiny. But in this chapter, I wish to deal with the general vision the Lord has for you and every Christian. The Father has set certain things (from which none of us is exempt) before His Church to accomplish. These universal orders will not only cause the master plan of God to be realized by His Body but will also assist in the preparation of the individual believer to live out his or her purpose.

In John 15:16 and Matthew 5:14-16, the Lord Jesus makes the following bold and far-reaching proclamations to His followers:

> *You did not choose Me, but I chose you, and appointed you, that you should go and bear fruit, and that your fruit should remain...* (John 15:16).

> *You are the light of the world. A city set on a hill cannot be hidden. Nor do men light a lamp, and put it under the peck-measure, but on the lampstand; and it gives light to all who are in the house. Let your light shine before men in such a way that they* ***may see your good works, and glorify your Father who is in heaven*** (Matthew 5:14-16).

What a mandate! What a powerful commission! By making these statements, Jesus is equating His Church with Himself in its ability to bring God into a world that does not know Him. He is clearly saying, "I've been the light. You be that light now. Go and do what I did. Bear fruit with your spiritual labor, just as you have with your physical labor. Bear fruit that remains due to its ability to reproduce after its kind. Be a giver. Be a healer. Be a vessel for the power of God to flow through to meet the needs of people. Let your good deeds reflect the glory of God! Don't be afraid, and don't hide what I am giving you. Men in a dark place are drawn to the light. Be that light for them." What a thrilling privilege we are given in these verses!

**Purpose is the engine, the power that drives and directs our lives.** (John R. Noe)

As exciting as Christ's command is, much lies behind its seemingly simple message. Being the light of the world requires more than a directive from the lips of Jesus. If we fail to put wings to His words, they will never find reality in our lives. Notice the small but pivotal set of letters that spell the word *let* in Matthew 5:16. With that one word, Jesus unquestionably places the responsibility for attaining His words on the all-too-human shoulders of His Church. That choice is unequivocally ours.

## Values

It comes down to what you value most. If God is not the most important figure in your life, you will not be able to fulfill your personal purpose because He will *always* be in the center of any purpose He gives. He asks us to take care of people, thereby bringing glory to Him. But if we do not value people, we cannot glorify Him because helping people is the very avenue we must travel to bring Him glory.

**Our value is the sum of our values.** (Joe Batten)

Make no mistake about it, you will always do what you *value* most. In the long term, you cannot sustain a trumped-up love of people or a desire to point others to the goodness of God. You either mean it or you don't, and the truth always prevails.

There was a time when the Church chose to rebel against this order. That decision plunged this world into the most vile period of its existence, which we appropriately call the Dark Ages. During that time, the Word of God was almost lost. The candle of God's Church flickered as if it might go out forever. But the Lord always has a people chosen and appointed to bear His light, and they slowly emerged again to spread the good news of His love.

Perhaps you are in a "dark age," or have not yet discovered how to let your light shine. Maybe you still struggle with what you value most. Do you put people after things? Is God someone to be feared but not known? What do you value?

**Whatever we value most, we will rarely be willing to compromise.**
(W.G.)

True God-ordained purpose will never have such conflicts. God's values for us place Him first and other people second. He gives us clear-cut ways to accomplish this value system. The key is lining up with His values and then finding out how to live by them. If you have yet to discover the basics of how to live out this system, here are some simple steps you can take. They comprise the *universal purpose* God has for His children, and they are the *general marching orders* to be followed by *all* who call Him Lord.

### Commission #1: Maintain Lordship

Maintaining Lordship is the first part of this general purpose God has for His people. [See Figure #1 on page 24.] In Matthew 6:33 we find the famous passage, "But seek first His kingdom and His righteousness; and all these things shall be added to you." First of all, we must understand what is meant by the word *seek*. The Greek word in this verse is taken from the Hebrew word for *worship*. In fact, upon studying both the Old and New Testaments, I discovered five different words that have been translated into the English word *seek*. For all but one of those words, either the primary or secondary meaning is defined as worship or prayer, and for all, the root meaning is that of searching for something.

To *seek*, then, means to search for through prayer and worship. We need not dig into vast volumes of theological studies or climb pinnacled mountains to holy temples in search of the Lord or His Kingdom. We need only to lift our voices and bend our knees daily in worship and prayerful communion to seek Him and His Kingdom. The Bible is quite clear on this subject, as can be seen in the following verses:

> *Then Jesus said to him, "Begone, Satan! For it is written, 'YOU SHALL WORSHIP THE LORD YOUR GOD AND SERVE HIM ONLY'"* (Matthew 4:10).

> *I urge you therefore, brethren, by the mercies of God, to present your bodies a living and holy sacrifice, acceptable to God, which is your spiritual service of worship. And do not be conformed to this world, but be transformed by the renewing of your mind, that*

*you may prove what the will of God is, that which is good and acceptable and perfect* (Romans 12:1-2).

*The twenty-four elders will fall down before Him who sits on the throne, and will worship Him who lives forever and ever, and will cast their crowns before the throne...* (Revelation 4:10).

*Worship of the Lord is the first order of maintaining Lordship.* These verses state the Lord's view of such worship. Not only are we to worship the Lord God and Him only, but the Scriptures clearly state that Jesus is the recipient of our praises. Even our physical bodies are to be a form of worship. Check yourself right now on that one. Our Father leaves no room for speculation. He orders us to worship, then He explains to whom our worship is extended. Finally, He informs us how our worship is to be given—our very lives are to become worship unto the Lord.

*The second aspect of maintaining Lordship is the study of God's Word.* In Matthew 4:4, Jesus states the importance of the Word of God in the lives of His followers: "But He answered and said, 'It is written, "MAN SHALL NOT LIVE ON BREAD ALONE, BUT ON EVERY WORD THAT PROCEEDS OUT OF THE MOUTH OF GOD."'" God's Word is actually more important than food for our bodies. Not that we should neglect the replenishing of our physical form with proper foods, but we must realize that the Word of God is even more needed by our spirits. Why? The Scripture following gives us the answer. Food stuffs can only energize our bodies, but the Word can touch our entire being:

*All Scripture is inspired by God and profitable for teaching, for reproof, for correction, for training in righteousness; that the man of God may be adequate, equipped for every good work* (2 Timothy 3:16-17).

The Word of God is a multi-faceted instrument with which the Father can mold and shape us into the people we were meant to be. It can correct a fault, instruct in service, convict, or reprove. God's life-changing Word has the supernatural ability to turn total rebels into totally godly men and women. But as with anything in God's Kingdom, we have the final say in how much, if at all, His Word will affect us. We must make a daily effort to study and understand the Scriptures. The Holy Spirit is our teacher in this effort, for He will take what we are studying and reveal its full meaning to us. This knowledge is known as revelation and was announced by Christ as the rock upon which He would construct His Church. The Holy Spirit, however, can only reveal the Word that we put inside us. We must visit the equipment shed before the Equipper can give us the items we need. For that very reason, it is our duty to establish a solid relationship with God.

> *...Flesh and blood did not reveal this to you, but My Father who is in heaven. And I also say to you that you are Peter, and upon this rock I will build My church; and the gates of Hades shall not overpower it* (Matthew 16:17-18).

*The final necessary aspect of maintaining the Lordship of Christ in our lives is that of obedience.* Jesus did not mince words on the subject:

> *And why do you call Me, "Lord, Lord" and do not do what I say?* (Luke 6:46)

> *But prove yourselves doers of the word, and not merely hearers who delude themselves* (James 1:22).

Doing whatever the Holy Spirit reveals to you from the Word of God is mandatory if you are to fulfill your desire to serve Him. (We will discuss in later chapters how to hear and confirm God's voice in your personal prayer time.) Many people claim to be believers, but it is the *doer* who will stand strong and immovable when the floodwaters of life crash upon him or her. The point is that the storms of life will come against us regardless of how prepared we are. Digging deep into the solid rock of God's Word through the doing of the Word is the guaranteed method for preparing successfully.

## Commission #2: Local Living

Functioning in a local church body is the second part of our general commission. In First Corinthians chapter 12, we have a vivid description of how the Lord sees His Church. He likens it to the human body, which has many members that make up one whole. In verse 12, Paul asserts that we are all members of one Body, denoting the universal Body of believers. But the passage also mentions the local aspect of church membership, in verse 18. Here the writer states that God will personally place each of us in the specific section of His Body where we belong. Such precise placement can only be realized at a local church level. That spot, for which we are singularly molded and prepared, allows us and the body of which we are a part to operate at full capacity.

To help us further understand His view on this matter, God indicates that, as in the human body, there should be no divisiveness between members. No one believer is more important than any other. No member should either exalt himself or degrade others. Clearly spoken, we need one another:

> *If the foot should say, "Because I am not a hand, I am not a part of the body," it is not for this reason any the less a part of the body. And if the ear should say, "Because I am not an eye, I am not a part of the body," it is not for this reason any the less a part of the body. If the whole body were an eye, where would the hearing be? If the whole body were hearing, where would the sense of smell be? ... And if they were all one member, where would the body be? But now there are many members, but one body. And the eye cannot say to the hand, "I have no need of you"; or again the head to the feet, "I have no need of you." ...there should be no division in the body, but that the members should have the same care for one another. And if one member suffers, all the members suffer with it; if one member is honored, all the members rejoice with it. Now you are Christ's body, and individually members of it* (1 Corinthians 12:15-17,19-21,25-27).

This scriptural analogy is both informative and reassuring. But our God does not leave us without explicit instruction on how to daily and effectively live according to His exhortation. Within the pages of the New Testament are 30 specific orders directing believers on how to live as loving members of Christ's Church. It is only possible to follow these orders at the local level, where relationships have been firmly established. These relationships will require time and effort to build, which is impossible for a person who is constantly on the move from church to church. Again, obedience or rebellion are the only choices a believer has with this issue.

The following is what I call the Checklist of Relationship Success. If we can fulfill this list, we are well on our way to living the life Christ meant for each of us to experience and enjoy. I personally believe every Christian should be a part of a small home-based group of other believers with which he or she can live out the following list of relationship-oriented items. This allows for interaction, accountability, and unconditional love. I will not attempt to go farther than that in this book, but I challenge you to become part of such a meaningful group—for your sake and theirs. Even the thought of it may be hard for you, as it was for me for many years; push through your fears and dislikes and do it anyway. You will find a richer life and much closer friendships. Since 1973 the closest friends of my life have *all* stemmed from such groups.

**Checklist of Relationship Success**

1. Love one another (Jn. 13:34-35).
2. Be members of one another (Rom. 12:5).
3. Be devoted to one another (Rom. 12:10a).
4. Outdo one another in showing honor (Rom. 12:10b).
5. Rejoice with one another (Rom. 12:15a).
6. Weep with one another (Rom. 12:15b).
7. Have the same mind toward one another (Rom. 12:16).
8. Do not judge one another (Rom. 14:13).
9. Accept one another (Rom. 15:7).
10. Build up one another (Rom. 15:14).
11. Greet one another (Rom. 16:16).
12. Wait for one another (1 Cor. 11:33).
13. Care for one another (1 Cor. 12:25).
14. Serve one another (Gal. 5:13).
15. Bear one another's burdens (Gal. 6:2).
16. Be kind to one another (Eph. 4:32a).
17. Forgive one another (Eph. 4:32b).
18. Submit to one another (Eph. 5:21).
19. Counsel one another (Col. 3:13).
20. Bear with one another (1 Thess. 5:11a).
21. Encourage one another (1 Thess. 5:11b).
22. Stir up one another (Heb. 10:24).
23. Don't speak evil against one another (Jas. 4:11).
24. Don't grumble against one another (Jas. 5:9).
25. Confess your faults to one another (Jas. 5:16a).
26. Pray for one another (Jas. 5:16b).
27. Be hospitable to one another (1 Pet. 4:9).
28. Minister to one another (1 Pet. 4:10).
29. Be clothed with humility toward one another (1 Pet. 5:5).
30. Fellowship with one another (1 Jn. 1:7).

## Commission #3: Exposing the Light

The third and final part of the general commission to believers is that of sharing our new life with others who have never met Jesus. This is a major aspect of letting our light shine in a dark world. It is known as "being a witness." Jesus' final words before His ascension echoed this call:

> *And He said to them, "Go into all the world and preach the gospel to all creation. He who has believed and has been baptized shall be saved; but he who has disbelieved shall be condemned. And these signs will follow those who have believed: in My name they will cast out demons, they will speak with new tongues; they will pick up serpents, and if they drink any deadly poison, it shall not hurt them; they will lay hands on the sick, and they will recover* (Mark 16:15-18).

> *...All authority has been given to Me in heaven and on earth. Go therefore and make disciples of all the nations, baptizing them in the name of the Father and the Son and the Holy Spirit, teaching them to observe all that I have commanded you; and lo, I am with you always, even to the end of the age* (Matthew 28:18-20).

> *But you shall receive power when the Holy Spirit has come upon you; and you shall be My witnesses both in Jerusalem, and in all Judea and Samaria, and even to the remotest part of the earth* (Acts 1:8).

These verses explain the full intent of our Father in the area of witnessing for His Son, Jesus. We are to preach, teach, administer God's healing power, deliver the captives of satan, and baptize those who believe. This is no passive witness, but a very aggressive one—aggressive in the sense that we are to reach out boldly to people who are on their way to a Godless hell. We are not to wax fat and happy in our newfound glory in Christ. We are to give it away at every opportunity.

Billions of people are just like we were; they need what we have. Sharing our faith in Christ is our privilege and it is the main reason we are left on this planet after we receive Jesus as Lord and Master of our lives. Christ relinquished to His Church the task of informing people about Him, and He gave clear instructions on how it should be done. It is up to us and us alone. Only the living Church of Jesus Christ can be His witness:

> *For "WHOEVER WILL CALL UPON THE NAME OF THE LORD WILL BE SAVED." How then shall they call upon Him whom they have not believed? And how shall they believe in Him whom they have not heard? And how shall they hear without a preacher? And how shall they preach unless they are sent? Just as it is written, "HOW BEAUTIFUL ARE THE FEET OF THOSE WHO BRING GLAD TIDINGS OF GOOD THINGS!" However, they did not all heed the glad tidings; for Isaiah says, "LORD, WHO HAS BELIEVED OUR REPORT?" So faith comes from hearing, and hearing by the word of Christ* (Romans 10:13-17).

Countless books have been written about witnessing. Courses in personal evangelism abound. But if you want a clear, simple method of being a successful witness for Christ, remember this phrase: *Find a need and meet it.* With the power of God at your disposal, that statement transcends the impossible. All you need to do is apply it. Do everything within your ability to educate yourself on sharing the gospel and making disciples. Witnessing is the most exciting and rewarding element of the Christian life.

> *And Jesus said to him, "If You can! All things are possible to him who believes"* (Mark 9:23).

Letting your light shine before men is your fundamental purpose as a part of the universal Body of Christ. Each of us is to take that truth and apply it daily to an ever-darkening world. Through the constant monitoring of our lives, we can fulfill the commission left by Jesus and actually proclaim the good news in every country on earth. This requires each of us to buckle down to the task of maintaining the Lordship of Christ in our lives through daily worship, Bible study, and obedience. We need to discover our place in a local body of believers and live out our personal visions. Opening ourselves to the joys and heartaches of giving is mandatory. Our lives must become examples of living to give. And, of course, the very reason for the shining of our brilliant light is to witness about the glories of our God and King. Boldly, yet meekly, displaying Christ to a hurting world is God's anointed and unfathomable plan for us. And it will take each of us, to the person, to pull it off.

## Final Thoughts

I find it amazing that such an all-powerful God can trust such monumental and exacting tasks to such fragile and vulnerable creatures as men, women, and children. But that is the miracle of God, for He actually lives His life through us. Yes, the general purpose for Christ's Church is a mighty one. It is one every believer must accept if he or she is to find the peace and joy that comes with fulfilling the will of God. Your personal purpose in life will fit perfectly with the general purpose of the Church. In fact, the Lord will endow you with special gifts to assist you to that end.

# Figure #1

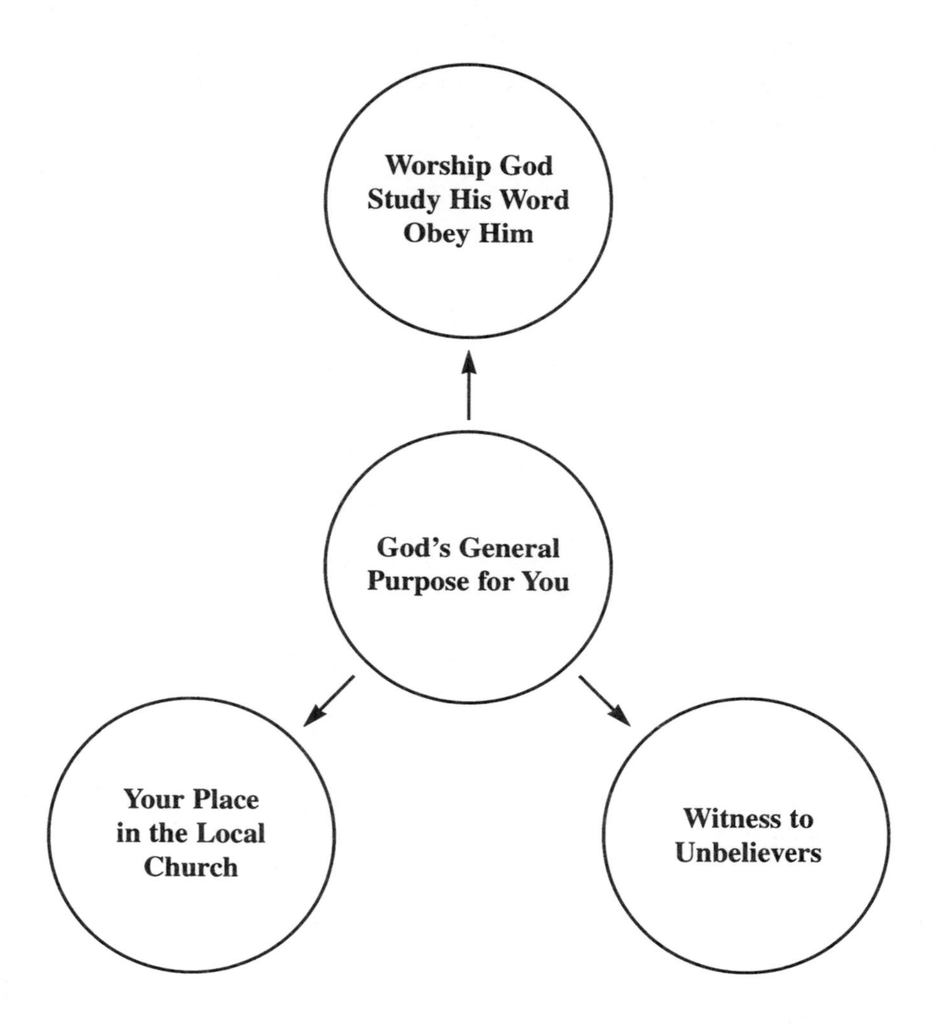
Worship God
Study His Word
Obey Him
God's General
Purpose for You
Your Place
in the Local
Church
Witness to
Unbelievers

# Chapter 3

## Gifts and Skills

*As each one has received a special gift, employ it in serving one another, as good stewards of the manifold grace of God* (Philippians 4:10).

The Lord in His infinite wisdom has chosen to endow every one of His children with certain gifts. Each gift has a specific function and place in the overall picture of His will for this age. These gifts are given to assist the individual believer in his or her attempt to live out God's ordained purpose for his or her life. The primary objective for these gifts is identified in His Word as that of ministering to the other members of His Body. In Paul's letter to the Romans, he reiterates this truth once again:

*For just as we have many members in one body and all the members do not have the same function, so we, who are many, are one body in Christ, and individually members one of another. And since we have gifts that differ according to the grace given unto us, let each exercise them accordingly...* (Romans 12:4-6).

According to these verses, the main reason individual members of the Church are given gifts is to serve one another. Our personal purpose will be enhanced by the gifts entrusted to us by our heavenly Father. By effectively operating in these gifts as singular believers, we will enhance the overall effectiveness of Christ's Body. The sharing of our gifts with one another will complete the Body of which we are to be a part.

My gifts will complement yours, and yours will complement mine. Although I am definitely not gifted in math, my wife is, and therefore she takes over the bookkeeping in my stead. Where she may lack understanding of the difference between transmission fluid and motor oil, I take over that chore. The Body of Christ is to function in a similar manner, with each person supplying the gift needed at the moment, as fits his or her giftings.

> *From whom the whole body, being fitted and held together by that which every joint supplies, according to the proper working of each individual part, causes the growth of the body for the building up of itself in love* (Ephesians 4:16).

Whether it be our natural gifts, our spiritual gifts, or even our intellectual ones, all are meant to enhance and complete the Body of Christ (of which we are to be useful and necessary parts). No gift is given to a believer solely for self-gratification. We are to share our gifts as freely as we have received them. The following Scripture makes that perfectly clear.

> *Heal the sick, raise the dead, cleanse the lepers, cast out demons; freely you received, freely give* (Matthew 10:8).

**The measure of life is not its duration, but its donation.**
(Peter Marshall)

### Make a List

Take the Gifts and Skills List from the Appendix of your *Destiny Planner*® and fill it out to the best of your ability before you read further in this chapter. If there are gifts you feel you possess that are not listed on the worksheet, by all means add them. This list will be crucial to your understanding and accomplishing the purpose and destiny God has prepared for you.

After you finish reading this chapter, go through the list again and see if your first list was accurate. Then return this sheet to the proper tabbed heading in your *Destiny Planner*® for future reference. If you do not have a *Destiny Planner*®, just use a clean sheet of paper and list every natural, spiritual, and other gift you feel you possess.

## Natural Gifts

Although this chapter will deal primarily with spiritual gifts, I will take a moment to discuss the field of natural gifts with which our Maker blesses us. This category of gifts includes the physical attributes of a human being. Physical gifts include talents that display expertise or above normal control of one's body. Such things as running, jumping, throwing, and swimming would be good examples. A gifted person would find such activities simple to learn and easy to perfect. You know the guy—the first time he picks up a baseball he's striking out major leaguers! Or the girl who buys a tennis racket one day, and by the following week she's on TV playing Wimbledon! Are these gross exaggerations? Certainly! But to someone who throws a frisbee like a shot put, it seems all too close to reality. A gifted athlete stands out among his teammates.

Not all natural gifts come under the heading of sports or athletics, however. Such gifts as singing, playing the piano or other musical instruments, drawing, sculpting, acting, and even mime may also fit under this heading. These gifts are also easily recognized. Many can sing, but few have a three or four octave range. A multitude may "tickle the ivories," but few pack Carnegie Hall for a concert. Again, a gifted person will be spotted easily among the average.

## Intellectual Gifts

Now, let's take a peek at the intellectual gifts. Intellectual gifts are primarily concerned with our mental faculties. By that I do not allude to the forms of mind-over-matter that seem to bend spoons and move small objects. That is purely demonic in origin and not worth explaining here. Mental gifts, as I will refer to them, relate to the above normal ability to understand and apply what we learn in the intellectual realm.

We all know someone who excels beyond reason in such areas as mathematics or physics. Perhaps you personally have the capacity to remember the minutest detail of a book you've read or some event you witnessed. Another person may understand the workings of electricity to the point that he thoroughly confuses most average listeners to whom he may try to explain it. Quite simply, we are talking about people who exemplify the word *genius* in one category of learning or another. They just have a knack for it; they are *gifted.*

I, myself, have never had a problem with memorizing anything. Most of my academic career was spent on the recreation fields instead of in the study hall because I could read something once or twice, and with a couple of minutes of review, I would remember most of it with ease. Although this was a valuable asset at exam time, it made my school years a bit boring. It's not much fun throwing a football to yourself while everyone else is pouring over the test materials.

But even with this enviable gift, I never became adept at some subjects. I was always frustrated by any math problem dealing with more than a plus, minus, division, or multiplication sign. Memorizing for exams was never a problem, but applying it in a check-out line—no way! (As I have already mentioned, having a wife who is pretty good at math definitely has its advantages.)

Let's face it, some have these specific gifts and some don't! But as we face that truth, let's also consider Romans 2:11 (KJV), which states that "there is no respect of persons with God." Simply put, this means that God does not covet my prayers above yours or your crystal-shattering voice above mine. The gifts He entrusts to us are not due to an unequal love, but to His wisdom in knowing what we each will be able to adequately handle. The Father knows exactly what course our lives will take, and He will hold us accountable only for the gifts He gives.

God is not a snaggle-toothed ogre waiting to strike His wards if they step out of line and operate in an area in which they are not gifted. Neither does He gleefully watch the despair of a well-meaning disciple attempting to sing a solo on Sunday morning with a voice meant only for the shower on Saturday night. He is a loving Father who cares deeply for His children. God bestows His gifts not only for the effective working of His will but also for our *pleasure*. I believe God enjoys a good swing on a trapeze or a stroll on the slackwire as much as I used to.

Think about it. What loving father has ever given a gift to one of his children without being filled with joy at the excitement that child experiences while using that gift to his or her own pleasure. If mere men can show such compassion and empathy, certainly the God who created them can as well. Although the Lord does not give us gifts solely for that reason, He does take delight in our pleasure.

So if you happen to be a singer, musician, carpenter, mechanic, artist, designer, tight end, outfielder, or certified public accountant, your natural gifts are to be a blessing to your local body of Christ. If they aren't, you are both robbing other believers of your God-given talent and missing out on receiving that completion in your own life. At the end of this chapter, we will take a close look at the consequences of the use and abuse of our gifts.

## Super Natural Gifts

A final thought on natural gifts: a person's natural gifts often are enlarged with his or her spiritual rebirth in Christ. For example, before I became a Christian I was interested in sports. I tried out for the football team, the basketball team, and the track team at my high school. I proved to be sometimes average, but more often mediocre. Organized sports and I gelled like water and oil. All I received for my pathetic high school athletic career was two points scored playing basketball, two wins out of 36 football games, a first and a few second and third place ribbons pole vaulting on the track team, two brain concussions (on the same brain of course), a cracked shin, a couple of broken fingers, and a hip-to-ankle cast for a broken knee! To say I was *not* gifted is to overstate the obvious.

But in 1971, a phenomenal thing began to occur. Shortly after giving my life to the Lord Jesus in the fall of that year, I took up karate. I excelled! Two years later, I joined the Florida State University Flying High Circus. Within a few short weeks I was performing publicly in several acts, including trapeze and the very difficult slackwire. My fellow circus performers were astounded by the ease with which I acquired such skills and with the rapid development of my chosen acts. I had become a top performer, and I went on to master almost every skill in the show from flying and catching on trapeze, to juggling, balancing on wire, and teeterboards.

What made the difference between the mediocrity of my high school years and the meteoric rise of my abilities in college? My only answer and my firm belief is that the Holy Spirit took my natural abilities and added supernatural abundance to them. Rest assured, His motives were not for my personal pleasure alone, but for the edification and strengthening of the Church and for ministry to unbelievers. Although it took me several years to realize this truth, I eventually aligned my motives to match His. This humbling gave birth and substance to God's purpose for me as He directed me to create a circus that would proclaim Jesus Christ as Lord. Your natural abilities, gifted and not, will find new power when Christ gains full control of your life.

## Spiritual Gifts

Spiritual gifts are those that are bestowed upon believers to assist them in the overall function of the entire Body of Christ. Does that sound like an echo of our discussion of natural gifts? Well, there is one major difference—the Holy Spirit. Natural gifts are affected by genetics, but spiritual gifts are specifically distributed by the Holy Spirit and are not bound by a person's physical background or ancestry. The only prerequisite for spiritual gifts *bestowed by the Holy Spirit of God* is that the person receiving them has been born again through the resurrection power of Jesus Christ. Until the Holy Spirit has been given opportunity to dwell within a person, He *cannot* dispense the spiritual gifts in the way He desires.

I believe that many people are given spiritual gifts at conception. But unless a person is born again by God's Holy Spirit, those gifts will become perverted and manipulated by the demonic, such as the "psychic" phenomenon that began receiving worldwide attention in the early 1990's. Although such gifted persons may be sincere in their desire to help others, they are merely taking the very people they wish to aid further from the Lord who can *truly* meet their needs. But rest assured, no such manipulated gifts will ever be a match for the true spiritual gifts created by God for His people.

The spiritual gifts that the Lord transmits to us actually have the power to transcend the laws and understanding of the natural world around us. They are given to allow the believer to perform specific acts and to live out otherwise impossible assignments dictated by their position in Christ's Body. These gifts are listed across several books of the New Testament. Not everyone will experience every gift, and some believers may possess more gifts than others, just as with natural gifts. The point, however, is not how many gifts one is given, but what we do with the gifts that we *have* received.

> *Now concerning spiritual gifts, brethren, I do not want you to be unaware* (1 Corinthians 12:1).

The apostle Paul expresses his concern that believers not be ignorant or unaware of the spiritual gifts God has entrusted to them. That includes you and me. The Lord, through Paul, goes on to illuminate several of the gifts to which He refers. The listed gifts fall into three distinct categories: the gifts of the Holy Spirit, the motivational gifts, and the ministerial gifts. The first category is so named because the Holy Spirit is specifically mentioned as He who decides when and through whom these gifts will be activated. Also, these particular gifts are purely *supernatural*; they are activated solely by the power of the Holy Spirit working through an individual. They are usually given at a specific moment to meet a particular need. This is in contrast to the motivational and ministerial gifts, which operate in an on-going fashion rather than at the timed discretion of the Lord.

The gifts of the Holy Spirit listed below, as well as those under the other two headings just mentioned, will be given only a small explanation here. My intention is not to expound greatly upon these gifts, but to share the basics of their workings so you may take this information and seek further insight on your own through other publications, meditation, and prayer. These brief summaries will, however, provide valuable insight into the spiritual gifts with which the Lord has blessed you. All the spiritual gifts listed here are, as I have mentioned, for sharing with others and not for self-gratification.

## Gifts of the Holy Spirit

These nine gifts are given by the Holy Spirit to whom He wills and when He wills. The key to operating in these gifts is to know how they are received. The obvious need then is to know when the gifts are present (no pun intended) and to utilize them. Although some people may experience certain *physical feelings* when the Holy Spirit is bestowing one of the following gifts upon them, such feelings are neither common nor necessary for the operation of one of these gifts.

The only way a believer can have a clear understanding that the Holy Spirit is moving upon him in the area of one of these gifts is to establish the two-way communication necessary for such reception. This communication is established only through daily time with God. (We will discuss the language of the Holy Spirit in a later chapter, for unless you understand His language, your learning to flow with the Holy Spirit in the area of these gifts will be greatly hindered.)

Having said that, I must also say that the Lord can drop any spiritual gift He likes upon anyone at anytime, regardless of whether the person has asked for the gift or has a clue how it works! I have met too many ministers and laymen who have extraordinary gifts of the Holy Spirit and never even knew there was such a thing until the gift suddenly "turned on" one day. Such is the exception and not the rule, however. Many of those who've experienced such deliveries have been forced to play "catch up," so their understanding and faith level might reach that of their newfound abilities. This seemed especially prevalent in the prophetic gifts during the late 1980's and early 1990's.

> *Now there are varieties of gifts, but the same Spirit. And there are varieties of ministries, and the same Lord. And there are varieties of effects, but the same God who works all things in all persons. But to each one is given the manifestation of the Spirit for the common good. For to one is given the word of wisdom through the Spirit, and to another the word of knowledge according to the same Spirit; to another faith by the same Spirit, and to another gifts of healing by the one Spirit, and to another the effecting of miracles, and to another prophecy, and to another the distinguishing of spirits, to another various kinds of tongues, and to another the interpretation of tongues. But one and the same Spirit works all these things, distributing to each one individually just as He wills* (1 Corinthians 12:4-11).

**Word of Wisdom**

Wisdom is the ability to use what we know to the fullest extent. This gift takes the knowledge at hand and couples it with the supernatural, overall understanding possessed by the Holy Spirit for meeting the particular need of the situation or individual. It is not dependent on our human areas of experience or knowledge. The many times I have been privileged to experience this gift have caused me to marvel at the words that came from my mouth for the people I was ministering to. There was no way I could have known or thought of the answers and solutions I was giving. It is a wonderful gift to see in operation, for it brings the perfect information to the need so swiftly and precisely.

## Word of Knowledge

A word of knowledge is specific information, which one has no natural way of knowing, that is revealed to the believer to meet a very specific need in the Body of Christ or in an individual's life. Often this gift is found working with the gifts of miracles and healing. The Holy Spirit has given me such words literally thousands of times over my ministerial career, and I find that it is a powerful blessing to the recipients. Once while praying for the sick after one of our circus performances, the words "cystic fibrosis" came to my mind. I had never heard those words before, but I knew it must be a disease of some sort. I called for anyone with such a disease to come forward, and only one young boy ventured forth from the audience of several hundred. When I rebuked the disease in the name of Jesus Christ, the Lord instantly healed the boy of cystic fibrosis and two more diseases as well, which was confirmed by his doctors. That word of knowledge was given to allow the gift of healing to be administered. It was wonderful!

## Faith

The gift of faith is the supernatural ability to believe beyond all doubt that the Lord will do as He said He would. This ability will allow the recipient to stand unflinchingly in the face of what, in the natural realm, seems to be unbeatable odds. It can be both long-range and short-range in its function. One morning I was awakened by my wife, Meg, to see a tornado heading straight for our house. While still shaking the daze of sleep from my head, I pointed my finger at the roaring giant and commanded it to pull back into the clouds and be gone. There was no fear or doubt on my part, and the tornado obeyed instantly! Meg added, "And you can't hurt anyone either!" The tornado touched down in a trailer park less than a mile away, but it only managed to tear down some trees and sheer off some siding. No one was injured in the slightest! From Bible study I knew that I possessed authority over the weather. The faith to remove that storm hinged on a knowledge of the Lord's Word that was already in my spirit. The power released came through the gift of enlarging my faith to the capacity necessary.

## Healing

The gift of healing flows through us to someone else. A person with this gift will actually be a vessel through whom the Lord will pour His power to heal someone else's physical body without natural aids (such as the boy mentioned above under *word of knowledge*). However, this gift can also be given directly to the person who needs it. There are no limits to the power of this gift to heal the human body and also the soul.

**Miracles**

This gift also turns the believer into a transmitter of God's power to meet a specific need. Miracles defy all natural laws and can actually change the structure or course of nature itself. The dismissal of the tornado mentioned above was the gift of miracles operating with the gift of faith. Often there is a form of creative power unleashed in the delivery of this gift, such as the regeneration of body parts or the raising of someone from the dead, but it can also pertain to material provision, such as the feeding of the 5,000 by Jesus. Miracles are normally associated with instantaneous results.

**Discerning of Spirits**

This gift enables the believer to know with certainty the type of spirit behind certain situations, behaviors, or actions. It is quite often employed to discern demonic activity, but it can also be used to confirm the presence and will of God. When referring to a demonic force, the actual name of the spirit may be given. At other times it may simply be a "yes or no" discernment of what the source or activity is. A few years ago a man came to the church where I was an associate pastor. From his talk, he sounded very spiritual. My spirit, however, was never comfortable around him. Many people thought he was a great humanitarian and servant, but I just couldn't buy it for some reason. Within a few weeks after his arrival, he began to spawn much hurt and division among our congregation. Eventually, he was asked to leave our fellowship because he would not submit to the eldership's authority and instruction concerning his conduct. My uneasiness was a form of discerning of spirits. The man was not motivated by the Lord, but by spirits of lust for control and power over others. The Holy Spirit revealed this to me through my uneasiness to confirm what was eventually brought to light. However, I have been a part of many counseling sessions where the Lord has told us specifically what demonic force we were dealing with, and this allowed us to remove the spirit every time.

### Tongues

The gift of tongues is given to a believer for use in a specific instance to bring a message to the church or an individual. It is a language the believer has never learned and does not understand, even when he speaks it. This gift of tongues is always to be followed by the gift of interpretation so that those present may receive the value of the message. This gift of tongues is not to be confused with the prayer language given to believers when they receive the Baptism in the Holy Spirit. That is a personal form of tongues, which can be utilized by the believer at any moment he desires without specific unction from the Holy Spirit. The gift of tongues mentioned in First Corinthians chapter 12 is a *specific* urging of the Holy Spirit for a *specific* reason at a *specific* time.

### Interpretation

This gift is given that one might interpret a message given in tongues into the language of those present. Paul clearly stated in First Corinthians chapter 14 that tongues without interpretation does the Body of Christ no good, even though it will edify the person who spoke merely because of his obedience. This interpretation will immediately follow the tongues given, and it may come through the same person who spoke the message in tongues, although that will not always be the case.

### Prophecy

The gift of prophecy is given to a believer to bring a specific word from the Lord concerning a specific event, situation, person, or group. It may be directive, corrective, or simply informative, but it will most often be exhortive, consoling, or comforting. It can be metaphoric or even pictorial in its delivery style. Normally there should be a confirmation and an acceptance of the prophecy by the spiritual leaders present, or it should be presented to such leaders before any action is taken concerning it.

## Motivational Gifts

The second gift category we will look at is that of motivational gifts. These are the gifts that spur Christians to action, usually in a service-oriented way. Motivational gifts tend to function on a daily basis, rather than at specific moments as directed by the Holy Spirit. All believers will have one or more of these gifts operating in their lives at one time or another. To list these motivational gifts we must look at First Corinthians chapter 12 and Romans chapter 12.

> *And since we have gifts that differ according to the grace given to us, let each exercise them accordingly: if prophecy, according to the proportion of his faith; if service, in his serving; or he who teaches in his teaching; or he who exhorts, in his exhortation; he who gives, with liberality; he who leads, with diligence; he who shows mercy, with cheerfulness* (Romans 12:6-8).

> *And God has appointed in the church, first apostles, second prophets, third teachers, then miracles, then gifts of healings, helps, administrations, various kinds of tongues* (1 Corinthians 12:28).

From the above references we discover the listing of the following motivational or action-initiating gifts.

**Prophecy**

This motivational gift is not to be confused with the Holy Spirit's gift of prophecy. Although the Holy Spirit's gift of prophecy that is mentioned in First Corinthians chapter 12 is bestowed for *specific* instances as the Spirit dictates, the motivational gift of prophecy is an on-going gift that is part of the person's spiritual life. As a part of the believer's personality, it is the ability to see into a situation or a person's life and bring forth an utterance from the Lord that pertains to a need or problem. It may also pertain to coming events. The person with this gift may not necessarily be a prophet, yet he or she can be just as accurate in his or her prophecies.

**Service**

This gift motivates the believer to serve his brethren in various practical ways. These people will always be the ones cleaning up after a group function or taking food to the needy. They are seemingly *driven* to serve in some way or another and are happiest when doing just that.

### Teaching

The gift of teaching causes the believer to be constantly looking for the exactness of truth in God's Word. The person with this gift desires to present the pure Word of God in a way that will benefit the Church. The ability to place things in a precept-by-precept, point-by-point outline is a good indication this gift is in operation within you. However, having this gift does not necessarily mean you are anointed with the ministry of the teacher, as will be explained under the next heading.

### Exhortation

A person with the gift of exhortation will uplift, comfort, excite, and motivate the Body of Christ. Believers with this gift will constantly be edifying others and encouraging them to do great things for the Lord.

### Giving

This gift motivates believers to give of their natural and material resources for the benefit of others. They enjoy giving in every area and desire to move others to do so. Quite often these people are adept at producing or raising finances for specific needs or ministries.

### Leadership

The gift of leadership enables the believer to organize and set goals for others and then direct those people in the accomplishment of those goals. This person will keep the ball rolling and will help everyone work together toward the common end. They will usually lead by example and not merely by giving orders.

### Mercy

This gift will move the believer with compassion and empathy toward those in great personal distress. They will perform the necessary tasks to help hurting people find relief. These people are very loving and self-sacrificing.

### Helps

The gift of helps motivates the believer to pour his time, efforts, gifts, and talents into the lives and ministries of others. They seek to assist someone else rather than themselves. The majority of believers are called to this gift, and all are to operate in it to some extent—even if just in the local church. (I have devoted an entire chapter in this book to this all-important gift because I feel there is not enough solid teaching being given on this subject. I hope you read that chapter many times!)

### Administrations

This gift equips the believer much like the gift of leadership. The person with this gift will understand the goals—both short-term and long-term—of a group and will be involved in their planning and execution at the leadership level. This is a much needed gift for the majority of ministries, for most are founded and headed by visionaries who have little taste for the tedious, detail-oriented planning that is necessary to fulfill their ministry objectives.

## Ministry Gifts

> *And He gave some as apostles, and some as prophets, and some as evangelists, and some as pastors and teachers, for the equipping of the saints for the work of service, to the building up of the body of Christ; until we all attain to the unity of the faith, and of the knowledge of the Son of God, to a mature man, to the measure of the stature which belongs to the fulness of Christ* (Ephesians 4:11-13).

The third category of spiritual gifts is often called the fivefold ministry gifts. These gifts are given to believers called by God into full-time ministry. Although attributes of these gifts may be enjoyed by many believers, this gift category is for those with a lifetime call. The ministry gifts, which are listed in the verses above, are specifically given for the "perfecting [equipping, NASB] of the *saints,* for the work of the ministry" (Eph. 4:12 KJV). Christians possessing these gifts are the trainers, coaches, and drill sergeants of God's army. The majority of Christ's Body will *not* be found endowed with these special gifts. If all were trainers, there would be no one to train and send out to battle. All believers, however, should have a knowledge of these five gifts so they can submit to and receive from anointed ministers who possess them. These godly men and women have been appointed to build up the Body of Christ and help all believers participate in performing the Lord's perfect will.

### Apostle

An apostle is an authoritative figure over several church bodies, rather than over one specific church. This person will plant churches and will both establish and oversee the spiritual workings of those local bodies. The apostle will remain a contributing factor in the actions of the leadership in those churches. The apostle is a strength to the entire Church, contributing an overall anointing, view, and understanding of the Lord's work and will throughout His universal Body.

### Prophet

This gift allows this spiritual leader to be the voice of God to His people in a profound and consistent way. The gift of prophecy will operate in his ministry with great accuracy, although New Testament instruction demands that even a prophet's words be judged by others (see 1 Cor. 14:29-33). A prophet speaks in a way that convicts as well as edifies. He may tell of future events concerning the world and the Church, and he may possibly reveal the meaning of past and present events. His attitude is usually one of absolute submission to God. He will be the messenger, but not necessarily the one to interpret the message or administer its fulfillment.

### Evangelist

This gift allows the believer to share the gospel with people under an anointing of God that often brings unusual conviction and conversion among the hearers. The evangelist will be successful in leading many to salvation in one-on-one settings and possibly in mass meeting situations. He will be consumed by the desire to tell people about Christ and to train and exhort others to do the same.

### Pastor

A pastor will become a shepherd to a specific group of brethren. He will have an on-going understanding of and concern for the needs in his church. The pastor will help teach, comfort, direct, and correct his congregation to meet those needs. This is usually a long-range position lived out with one church body, but not always.

### Teacher

This gift is different from the motivational gift of teaching in that it is a lifetime spiritual leadership calling, not a gift that is used occasionally. This gift enables the believer to acquire and then share in-depth truths of the Kingdom of God with the church in a systematic and logical way. His or her goal will be to ensure that those listening both learn and apply what is taught. He or she will delight in using every available circumstance as a tool or example to share a biblical truth with anyone who will listen. The teacher usually sees every revelation as one to be taught to the Body of Christ.

## Investing

Each of us has received one or more of the motivational and or ministry gifts listed in this chapter. The gifts of the Holy Spirit will be given at the discretion of the Lord for the specific time and event He so desires. But as with anything given us freely by the Lord, we must accept responsibility for the gift's exercise and must produce fruit thereby. God wants us to have an understanding of His spiritual gifts, as noted in First Corinthians 12:1: "Now concerning spiritual gifts, brethren, I do *not* want you to be unaware." Not only that, He expects us to cultivate a desire for them, actually striving to operate in those gifts considered greater than the others (see 1 Cor. 12:31–14:1).

Our heavenly Father even takes the point a step further by prodding us to stir up or rekindle the gifts within us that may have become dormant for any reason. (See Second Timothy 1:6.) And just in case there is a hardhead in the camp (such as yours truly!), First Timothy 4:14 contains an emphatic order that exhorts us to make sure that *neglect* of our gifts is *never* an option. As explained throughout the Epistles, the responsibility for using our gifts—be they spiritual or natural—quite plainly lies with us, not God.

Think about it. What giver is held responsible for the gift once it has been given? None, obviously. But also, what giver isn't frustrated when a gift is left unused or unemployed by the recipient? Clearly, the Father trusts His children to be "good stewards"!

Do we deserve such trust? I think not. For as Romans 12:6 instructs, it is God's grace that determines the gifts we receive. This truth should spur us on all the more to excel in the use of our gifts. God's grace was anything but cheap for Jesus Christ. The price of His death is justification enough for the consequences He places on those who are unwilling to use what He has imparted. The following passage clearly shows us the seriousness of those consequences:

> *For it is just like a man about to go on a journey, who called his own slaves, and entrusted his possessions to them. And to one he gave five talents, to another, two, and to another, one, each according to his own ability; and he went on his journey. Immediately the one who had received the five talents went and traded with them, and gained five more talents. In the same manner the one who had received the two talents gained two more. But he who received the one talent went away and dug in the ground, and hid his master's money.*
>
> *Now after a long time the master of the slaves came and settled accounts with them. And the one who had received the five talents came up and brought five more talents, saying, "Master, you entrusted five talents to me; see, I have gained five more talents." His master said to him, "Well done, good and faithful slave; you were faithful with a few things, I will put you in charge of many things, enter into the joy of your master." The one also who had received the two talents came up and said, "Master, you entrusted to me two talents; see, I have gained two more talents." His master said to him, "Well done, good and faithful slave; you were faithful with a few things, I will put you in charge of many things; enter into the joy of your master." And the one also who had received the one talent came up and said, "Master, I knew you to be a hard man, reaping where you did not sow, and gathering where you scattered no seed. And I was afraid, and went away and hid your talent in the ground; see, you have what is yours." But his master answered and said to him, "You wicked, lazy slave, you knew that I reap where I did not sow, and gather where I scattered no seed. Then you ought to have put my money in the bank, and on my arrival I would have received my money back with interest. Therefore take away the talent from him, and give it to the one who has the ten talents."*
>
> *For to everyone who has shall more be given, and he shall have an abundance; but from the one who does not have, even what he does*

*have shall be taken away. And cast out the worthless slave into the outer darkness; in that place there shall be weeping and gnashing of teeth* (Matthew 25:14-30).

This parable illustrates a powerful principle we must apply to our spiritual gifts, even though this passage is obviously speaking about the proper use of entrusted finances. I also wish to point out that we are *not* comparing God to this wealthy man. God's infinite mercy is a factor for a Christian that the fearful and foolish servant had no chance to enjoy.

It is not the *number* of gifts we possess that determines our reward, but what we *do* with what we are given. If we are faithful to achieve our utmost with our gifts, then there will be a reward of appropriate measure for us. In fact, equal proportional blessing was given to the two faithful slaves, even though the size of their initial gifts and respective increases was quite different. As it has been said, "the pay is the same" regardless of your assignment within God's Kingdom. It is the person who does *nothing* with the gift granted to him that will be found desperately wanting. If we fail to utilize our gift for the Kingdom of God, neither we nor those around us can enjoy the fullness of it. According to Christ's teaching mentioned above, to bury the gift is a *serious* offense.

An easy parallel to this principle of gift investment and return can be found in the developing and retaining of circus skills. I trained for years to acquire the skill necessary to climb a ladder while balancing it on a slackwire the thickness of a pencil. Lack of practice took its toll more than once through a misplaced step or an overcompensation in balance—usually with quite painful results. Just as my skills had to be kept sharp through investing time in rigorous practice sessions to avoid dangerous atrophy, so our spiritual gifts must be kept "in shape."

**Man discovers his own wealth when God comes to ask gifts of him.** (R. Tagore)

The gifts the Lord has endowed you with are for His glory and for meeting the needs of people, most often within His Body. As each of us finds our specific gifts and begins to live them out on a daily basis, the Church will be strengthened and the world will be forced to take notice. *These gifts are for giving away*. They are for each of us to use to assist one another in our purposes in life. As each strives to find and develop his or her individual purpose, his or her spiritual and natural gifts will come more and more into play to bring about its fulfillment. You *are* gifted!

## Skills

Let me share a word about the difference between gifts and skills. A skilled person may have little or no gifting in his or her skill area, and a gifted person may have little or no skill in the area of his or her gifting. This is apparent in sports, music, business, science, and the other natural gifting areas. We have all observed highly skilled athletes or performers who were cut from their team or group in the early years of their quest due to a lack of talent. And just as truly, we have seen gifted players who never rose to the heights they are capable of reaching because they did not discipline themselves to perfect their skill. Why are these observations true? The answer is *desire*.

Desire is the burning force within us that compels us to go on in the face of seemingly insurmountable odds. A man with desire will overcome every obstacle. Every conqueror, every inventor, every explorer has experienced this type of motivating force. When someone has a burning desire to learn, to excel, to go beyond the average and even beyond the limits of his or her own ability, that is where greatness is born. That is where desire shines brightest.

As of this writing I can think of no better example of such desire than basketball star Michael Jordan. Michael had a desire to be a great ball player from a young age. But he was so bad at the game that he was cut from his high school team in the tenth grade. He had a choice to make—give in to defeat or fuel the fire of desire even more. He chose the fire! His high school coach offered to train Michael before school every day so he could make the team in his junior year. From that point on, Michael never looked back. He went on to a renowned college career and then on to the pros. He has been voted the Most Valuable Player of the NBA. He has led his team to five world championships and garnered five NBA Finals MVP awards—one in each championship, two of them after returning from retirement!

Was Michael the most gifted? Many will debate that, including Michael. What is *not* up for debate is the intensity of the desire he has displayed throughout his career. He works harder to perfect his skills than almost any other player. His work ethic is unequaled. He is often the last man off the court during practice, leaving others to shake their heads at his desire to improve. He is the clear heart and soul of his team.

Skill is not *given* to anyone, it is acquired. It is not dependent upon gifting, but it is helped by it, to be sure. In my own life, I have found that skills come with the decision to gain them and the desire to attain them. I believe if a Christian is given a gift, it is his or her duty to turn that gift into a skill for the glory of God and the helping of others. I hope you agree with that. I hope you live it. (I will address the subject of skill in more detail in Chapter 14.)

## Final Thoughts

> *For I long to see you in order that I may* ***impart*** *some spiritual* ***gift*** *to you, that you may be* ***established*** (Romans 1:11).

During my study of spiritual gifts, I have come to understand the heartbeat of Paul's longing to impart such to the church in Rome. His desire wasn't so much for the gift itself, but that through the gift, those believers would be established in their faith. The learned apostle understood that the person who was in step with the gifts of God's Spirit would be firmly set in a position of victory. This is my prayer for you as well. For isn't the hand established in the body due to its unique abilities—likewise the eye, the ear, the heart? Every member of our human body is established by its special skill, firmly set in place, proven, and, of course, greatly needed.

When you, as a believer, discover and begin to live within the realm of the gifts God has entrusted to you, you will likewise become established within His Body. Through those gifts, you will be utilizing the very power of God to live out your particular purpose, thereby enhancing the overall purpose of your local church and the Body of Christ at large. Learn which are your personal gifts and discover how to use them practically in your daily life. You *are* gifted!

# Chapter 4

# Dynamic Desire

*Delight yourself in the Lord; and He will give you the desires of your heart* (Psalm 37:4).

*Desire* means "appetite, longing for, a craving." It is an inner motivating, propelling, energizing dynamo. As I mentioned in the last chapter in our discussion of skills, desire can drive men to accomplish greatness or to die in the attempt of reaching for something that may not even exist. The Scripture verse above shows us how desire relates to the nature of God. This verse implies that God will give us not only the desire by placing it in our hearts but also the ability to achieve and realize the fulfillment of those desires. It is a tall order, but God is up to the task. (We are the ones who seem to be lacking.) To give us the desires of our hearts is no small gift.

I have counseled and spoken with countless believers (and nonbelievers) who struggle greatly with this issue of desire. Obviously there are human desires for food and shelter—the instinct-oriented desires. But what about the desires for achievement or success? What about financial desires? Social desires? Material desires? Career, education, ministry, or family desires? My opinion is that the answer to all of these is found in the verse above. God wants us to have the desires of our hearts—as long as they are the desires *He* gives us.

**Lord, grant that I may always desire more than I can accomplish!** (Michelangelo)

God will never give you a desire that is not in line with His Word. He is not looking for opportunities to trip us up, but to set our feet on solid ground. He longs to give us what He knows will give us the most joy, just as any Father would. He wants us to enjoy our lives. He knows exactly what we can and cannot handle. So, the desires He places in us and then helps us to fulfill will be the best we could ever hope for. Please settle that issue in your mind now, for the rest of this chapter, and even the rest of this book, will be hard to believe until you do.

### The Dreams and Desires List

What would you love to do? What gives you the most joy? What is the most fulfilling and rewarding of all that you do? Is there something you really want to do but have never done? Do you love your job or is it just a paycheck? If you could work any job, what would you choose? What job would you do even if you did not get paid for it? What are your dreams? Do you believe God would let you do what you really want to do? Why haven't you done the things that you long to do?

If you have never asked yourself these questions, or have never answered them honestly, I challenge you to do so right now. In your *Destiny Planner*® there is a worksheet entitled Dreams and Desires. You will notice that I have listed six specific headings, which I call Life Areas, under which you may place your dreams and desires. These areas are the framework of your life, the pillars, if you will. Let me explain these areas a bit, for we will refer to them in almost every chapter from now on.

Each Life Area is a category within the threefold being of man—spirit, soul, and body. (Read 1 Thessalonians 5:21.) Although there are several subheadings under each of the six categories listed on the next page, I will save those for the chapter on goal-setting, where I will give you a more detailed explanation of how to cultivate a productive lifestyle in each of them. Look over this list and memorize it as best you can. Keep yourself tuned to just these six areas and you will maintain a very productive and powerful life and lifestyle. Know them and make them the *primary focus* of your daily disciplines.

1. **Spirit:** If you walk in the Spirit, you will not do the deeds of the flesh (see Gal. 5:16). This area covers everything connected with your growth as a Christian through your personal relationship with God.

2. **Intellect:** You have the mind of Christ (see 1 Cor. 2:16b) and are to be transformed by the renewing of your mind (see Rom. 12:1-3). This area concerns your mental capacities, such as learning, thinking, reasoning, knowledge, understanding, and wisdom.

3. **Personality:** "But the fruit of the Spirit is love, joy, peace, patience, kindness, goodness, faithfulness, gentleness, self control..." (Gal. 5:22-23). This area deals with who you are—your attitudes, emotions, act/react inclinations, confidence, fears, skills, gifts, and motivations.

4. **Physical:** Your body is the temple of the Holy Spirit (see 1 Cor. 6:19). "But I buffet my body and make it my slave..." (1 Cor. 9:27). This area speaks of your physical body—your health, your activities (such as sports or travel), and the care of your body.

5. **Social:** "Love one another, even as I have loved you" (Jn. 13:34). This area includes all your human relationships and related activities—family, spouse, co-workers, persons with whom you associate in organizations or in ministry to others, and those in your local church.

6. **Financial:** "Riches and honor are with me [wisdom], enduring wealth and righteousness" (Prov. 8:18). This area is that which has to do with money and your production, such as your career or occupation, and the expenditure, giving, and investment of money throughout your life.

Look at your Dreams and Desires Worksheet. Place each dream and desire of your heart in the appropriate Life Area. Record every dream and desire you've ever had that is legal within the Kingdom of God. (If you don't have a *Destiny Planner*®, use a clean sheet of paper and follow these instructions.) Do not hesitate, write down exactly what you *want* or have *dreamed* of doing at some time but have yet to achieve. Take all the time you need. Please do this before proceeding with this chapter.

Once you have listed your dreams and desires, you will have many of the aspects of your purpose and destiny in writing. I say "many" because you will undoubtedly have included some dreams and desires that are your own (not necessarily inspired by God). These may not be outside the will of God, yet they may be items you just feel you would like to do. It will be up to you to discover which are truly *His* will and which are your *own* ideas. Do not worry at this point which is which; you will know without a shadow of a doubt before this book is completed. (I have written an entire chapter in this book to help you learn how to confirm what is and is not God's will for you.)

**A passionate desire and an unwearied will can perform impossibilities.** (Sir John Simpson)

The purpose of this chapter is to instill in you the understanding that God *does* place specific desires within you. By writing down the desires you *already* possess, you will obviously unearth some that are His. Next you must believe that whatever desires He gives you will be *inside* His purpose for you, as a part of your destiny. The Lord did not give His life on a cruel cross only to keep you guessing about the life He has for you. And He will *not* take the chance of giving you a purpose and destiny so foreign to your own desires that you might say no to them!

Jesus gave away His life so we, in turn, could give away our lives, doing His will in the manner best suited to our personalities and backgrounds. That doesn't mean you will *not* be sent to a foreign field of missions or that you *will* live in plush surroundings your entire life, although either may be true. It does mean, however, that if you are to live in luxury or if you are to go to the African bush, you will be consumed with the desire to do so. He will give you the desires of your heart—first the desire, then the ability. If He wants you in Africa, you will *want* to go. This will be clearer to you as you read more of this book.

### Do What You Love!

I have always loved performing. It has been a consuming desire for my entire life. I love being before people to entertain, instruct, or minister. I fulfilled my wish to be a professional entertainer by entering professional circus after college (the last year of the first five years I mentioned in Chapter 2). But a year later I gave up the rights to my life and handed them to Jesus Christ, my Lord. I walked away from circus and vowed never to perform it again unless it was to His glory. It never occurred to me that He *wanted* me to do just that! Within a few months (within the first year of the second five years), the Lord was directing me to begin a circus that would proclaim Jesus as Lord. He was giving me back what I loved most. Actually it was what He had designed me for.

For ten years I did what I loved. It was so wonderful! The Lord showered me with blessings of anointing to win souls, heal the sick, and help people get free from the strongholds of satan. For ten years I had the time of my life doing the two things I loved most—circus and ministry. Then it ended. When God told me the circus was over, I was not upset or even remorseful; I was elated! Why? Because God then revealed to me the next step in my destiny, and I loved it just as much!

**Answer this question: Why aren't you doing what you love?**

The Lord led me into prophetic ministry. By the time He told me to make the change, I was more than ready for it because He had put the desire for it in my spirit. Within a few months after I had stepped away from circus, I was introduced to a prophetically gifted and humble group of ministers in Kansas City and was asked to join their staff. The Lord told me to serve these men and I did so—as a pastor—even though I felt I had neither the temperament nor the gifts for it. What I did have, though, was the desire to serve, which had been placed in my heart by God. The prophetic gifts God had instructed me to pursue were nurtured during my tenure as a pastor with these ministers.

Since that time I have gone through several more transitions in my destiny. I will undoubtedly take a few more turns before I finish my course. I've come to understand that changes are not something to be feared, but embraced. I'm totally confident that the Lord, my Father, will be sure to place the next desire in my heart before the change comes along. I'm looking forward to the coming changes because I know I will always be doing what I love, because I love Him and He loves me. It may take me some time to learn to love what He leads me into, but I know it will come.

## Focusing

Focusing on what you do best will bring a surge of self-confidence to you. (It's rare that anyone else gives us a boost in this area, so why *not* do it yourself?) You'll probably be surprised at just how close your gifts, skills, and desires are to your personal purpose. Take your Dreams and Desires List and mark the items you are the most passionate about with a highlighter or a red pen. What things really get your heart racing when you think about getting to do them? Mark the top five items in some way.

Next, take your Gifts and Skills List and place it next to your Dreams and Desires List. Now take the Focusing Worksheet from your *Destiny Planner®* (or a separate sheet of clean paper) and place it on the table next to the other worksheets. Your paper should have the following headings on it: Top Gifts, Top Skills, Top Desires. Your assignment is to place your highest gifts, skills, and desires in the proper categories. By filling out this worksheet, you will have a much clearer focus of what you are suited for. What you are suited for will very likely be a part of your purpose and destiny.

When I made this focus list, I was struck by how the top five items in each category were so complementary to each other. Each item on this list has been put into practice during the years I have been walking out my purpose with the Lord.

## Motivator or Hindrance

Another aspect of desire is its ability to motivate us. A white-hot desire to accomplish, learn, and become someone new supplies ample power to get it done, as we saw in the previous chapter concerning basketball star Michael Jordan. God is not ignorant of this. He has established a covenant with His people based upon extraordinary and bountiful promises. Isn't Heaven and the soon return of Christ a desire in our hearts? Don't we long for freedom? Aren't we consumed with doing the will of God? All of these are desires that spur us on to acts of courage and achievement. All give us cause for life.

That is the power of desire! God is very much able and willing to harness that power to help us become what He desires for us. Our job is to agree with those God-given desires and let them *drive* us forward into His waiting arms. Desires and dreams in the heart of a believer are usually *not* evil. For the dedicated Christian, most are inspired by God. But I have found that many believers are *paralyzed* in the pursuit of their dreams and desires by the *fear* that what they want to do is not in the will of God. Others think it is somehow *illegal* to even have such dreams and desires. I believe neither could be further from the truth!

**Whatever you like to do, just find a way to do it.**
**The biggest mistake people make in life is not trying to make a living at doing what they most enjoy.**
(Malcolm Forbes)

My dear friend, Chris Bonham, came to me with a dilemma while he was a member of our circus ministry. He was torn between what his heart was telling him and what he thought his parents wanted him to do. He longed to go into full-time ministry, but he was sure his parents wanted him to be a dentist. They were talking about pre-med classes and then dentistry school, while all he could think about was pastoring. His main problem was that he so respected his parents' authority and wisdom that he felt his desires couldn't be right. He was motivated to ministry, but he was hindered from pursuing that call through fear.

We solved this problem by having Chris first get totally honest with himself. He wanted to be a minister, and he admitted that he would be miserable as a dentist or anything else because of this truth. We then spoke with his parents and they were delighted at his desire to go into ministry! They were simply trying to help him choose something lest he choose nothing. Since his mother was in the dental field, their inclinations were naturally in that direction. Chris found that his fear was unwarranted. All his paralysis vanished!

Chris fulfilled his desire and has been in full-time pastoral work for many years. The bottom line to this story is that *God* gave Chris the desire for ministry. Chris thought the ministry desire had to be wrong because of his parents' leanings toward dentistry. In reality, the only illegal aspect to Chris' decision would have been to have chosen dentistry! Once Chris came to terms with what would really make his heart sing, there was no turning back. He knew it was in the will of God, and the Lord confirmed it many times over.

I believe that our God is a loving and caring Father who longs for each of us to be the happiest possible! How can we have good desires in our hearts, fear *having* such desires, and yet be happy at the same time? How can we say that God is our Father but not believe that He wants us to enjoy this life by doing that which we are most suited for and long to do? I don't believe this is God's way or will for anyone, least of all for His own children.

## Final Thoughts

The real issue here is not *having* a dream or desire; it's knowing that those dreams and desires are *not* going to get us in trouble with our Creator. There is only one way to stop that paralyzing, fear-spawned wonderment: *Ask Him.* I realize that many people are not sure how to do that or how to know with certainty that He has even given them an answer. I struggled with those questions for a few years myself. But then I discovered that the Lord had given His children several ways to rid themselves of this doubt and frustration. I will address both issues in the next two chapters, and before you are done with them, you will know not only *how* to ask, but *who* to ask. You will also have a foolproof system for confirming everything you feel God reveals to you. God *will* give you the desires of your heart!

# Chapter 5

# Helps Help

**Oh, the infinite value of the humble gospel helper.** (Godbey)

The ministry of helps is perhaps the most misunderstood ministry in the church world today, yet it is also the most widely needed. A powerfully anointed ministry gift, helps is listed along with such power offices as apostles and prophets! I believe many of you reading this chapter will find yourself and your purpose in its pages.

*And God has appointed in the church, first apostles, second prophets, third teachers, then miracles, then gifts of healings, helps, administrations, various kinds of tongues* (1 Corinthians 12:28).

Helps is not a gift to be taken lightly, but one that should be utilized by anyone with a designated purpose for his or her life. In Habakkuk 2:2 (which we will discuss at length in a later chapter), the Lord speaks of runners. Runners are those who operate in the ministry of helps to assist you with your purpose and destiny. We all need the ministry of helps. Actually, we all need to operate in this gift ourselves from time to time. Any purpose that God imparts to you will invariably be too big for you to handle alone. "Lone Ranger" Christianity is not God's idea of quality ministry. He will effect your need of others to help you, and He will call upon you to be such a helper for others.

## The Law of Reciprocity

This brings us to the most important principle in this book, that of sowing helps in order that you may reap helps. In Second Corinthians 9:6 we are told, "Now this I say, he who sows sparingly shall also reap sparingly; and he who sows bountifully will reap bountifully." Whatever we sow, we will reap. My suggestion to you is that you sow the ministry of helps bountifully into the lives and ministries of others who need assistance with their purpose and destiny. By so doing, you will have a bountiful harvest of such helps coming to you when your purpose and destiny expand to the point that you require more laborers.

**This is the miracle—the more we give away to others, the more we have.** (Anon.)

Let me give you an example from my own life and ministry. When the vision of Circus Alleluia was just a fire that was growing in my heart, the Lord led Meg and I to move to Tampa, Florida. Shortly after settling in, we began to attend Calvary Temple of Temple Terrace in the northeast section of town. I shared my vision with Dale Brooks, the pastor, and he immediately felt a witness in his spirit that it was from God. When he urged us to make Circus Alleluia a part of Calvary Temple, we took his advice. Almost immediately the Lord placed within my heart a desire to sow a major portion of my time and energy not into my new circus ministry, but into Dale's vision and purpose, the church.

I had experienced firsthand the realities of God's law of reciprocity—sowing and reaping. Some years earlier, Meg and I had employed this law to climb out of debt after quitting the professional circus world. I knew that it would work in this ministry of helps and that there would come a time in my ministry when I would be forced to enlist the support of many people. So I determined in my heart to obey this leading and sow the majority of my time and energy into my new pastor's vision.

I made myself available for whatever task was needed. At that time there were approximately 25 people attending the church services on Sunday, so volunteer help was at a premium. Meg and I cleaned the bathrooms, vacuumed the carpets, scrubbed the outdoor baptistry, and mowed the acreage. We poured in our time and labor, not for a few weeks, but for the first several years of our own ministry. We taught the youth group, ran the print shop, sang in the choir, and took cars to the repair shop. If it needed to be done, we did it and gladly.

Meg and I also looked for other major ministries into which we could sow our time and energies. Whenever a large convention came to town, I volunteered my services as an usher or counselor. I did this as an act of faith to sow excellent seeds of helps into these quality ministries. I sowed quality seed by giving them my *best*—the best of my abilities, the best of my time, and of course, the best of my finances—because I wanted the *best* to come back to me!

## The Ants Have It!

Proverbs 6:6-11 speaks of an industrious little ant. These creatures work hard through the summer to ensure a sufficient food supply during the winter months. This illustrates my need to sow the ministry of helps during the time when my own need was minimal. When my vision began to increase, I could reap the necessary harvest. That is exactly what happened. After several years of sowing the seeds of faith into my pastor's vision and the visions of other men and women of God, I began to see a bountiful harvest returning to me!

Even today, decades later, I still stand amazed at the ministry of helps that comes my way. The servant attitudes of others and their willingness to help with the purpose and destiny God has given us can be intimidating at times. The dedication of the people who have assisted us and even now are assisting us, astounds me. People from our church have volunteered to work with us not only in the spotlight but also behind the scenes where no one sees them. Many times they have volunteered without us *asking* them to help! One day I asked God why He was blessing us so wonderfully with these selfless people. He immediately reminded me of all the years we had spent sowing our time and efforts into other ministries. I was merely reaping the harvest.

**There is no more noble occupation in the world than to assist another human being—to help someone succeed.**
(Alan Loy McGinnis)

Whatever your vision or purpose may be, you should sow quality time as a minister of helps into someone else's purpose. In fact, I believe the majority of you will have a purpose that is the ministry of helps itself. Why? Because leaders are not in the majority; assistants are. Neither role is "better" or more important than the other; it's just that leaders are few in God's scheme of things. Therefore, it stands to reason that the majority of people will be ministers of helps to assist the leaders in their purposes and in the development of their destinies. If yours is a ministry of helps, what an exciting purpose God has given you—to hold up the arms of a Moses or to go before the Son of God to secure a place for the Last Supper.

## Final Thoughts

The ministry of helps is scattered across the pages of the Old and New Testaments. Even Jesus Himself operated in the ministry of helps when He fed the 5,000 and healed the multitudes. He was helping and assisting them to receive their needed supplies. In fact, I do not believe that God will give anyone a vision or purpose that does not in some way involve the ministry of giving and needing helps. Remember, any vision from God will always do two things: First, it will glorify God; second, it will help people. Visions, purposes, and destinies of mere *survival* are not in God's plan for His Church.

You *will* need people operating in the ministry of helps to further your vision from God. Therefore, before your need becomes too great, reach out and sow your time and effort as a minister of helps into someone else's vision. When you need it, your helps will be there.

**Success in life has nothing to do with**
**what you gain or accomplish for yourself.**
**It's what you do for others.** (Danny Thomas)

# Chapter 6

## Your Guide to Discovery

*But seek first His kingdom and His righteousness; and all these things shall be added to you (*Matthew 6:33).

Seeking the Kingdom of God is a command, not an option. If the Lord has a vision and plan for us, why would we believe that He would have any of His precious children operating outside of His Kingdom? Anything outside of God's Kingdom is inside satan's kingdom, and according to Colossians 1:13, we have been delivered from that kingdom of darkness. Our kingdom is the Kingdom of light. Our personal purposes will be found within the confines of the Kingdom within which we reside.

We are in this world, but not of it (see Jn. 15:19). As Christians, our actions help in the destruction of satan's kingdom on a daily basis. We tear down his strongholds and undo his works by the power of God working through us, doing all that Jesus did-and even greater (see Jn 14:12). Aspects of our ordained purpose will include such activities. Assuming you agree that the vision and purpose ordained for you by God is within the confines of His Kingdom, let's discover its more exact location. Once that location has been established, we can begin the task of transferring your purpose details into this natural world, where you can live out your purpose.

Jesus states in Luke 17:21, "Nor will they say, 'Look, here it is!' or, 'There it is!' For behold, the kingdom of God is in your midst." In the King James Version this verse reads, "...the kingdom of God is within you." The Lord explains here that the Kingdom of God is inside each person who calls Jesus, Lord. This can be easily understood by realizing that a king always lives within the borders of his kingdom. (Absentee kingship never proved to be a very worthwhile or long-lived state of authority.) When a person receives Christ as Lord, He immediately comes to live inside that person's spirit. Therefore, it is logical to assume that if Christ lives inside us, His Kingdom must also be inside us. Our lives become the borders of His Kingdom. If our purpose is found in His Kingdom and His Kingdom is inside us, then our purpose is inside us as well! (See Figure #2 on page 68.)

The God-ordained purpose for your life (including the entire plan for its completion that God has set forth) is inside you at this very moment! It is lodged in your spirit because that is where the Kingdom of God resides. Your purpose is a seed, and God's Kingdom is the shell in which it is tightly, yet lovingly held. But a purpose locked inside the Kingdom of God within you will be worthless. Neither you, the unsaved world, Christ's Church, nor the Lord Himself will ever receive its benefits. You must find the keys to release it.

## The Revealer

**Man's search for meaning is the primary motivation in his life.**
(Victor Frankl)

Once you have discovered where your purpose information lies, you must be sure to get the information from the right source. I realize that God the Father, God the Son, and God the Holy Spirit are all the same being, but He left us instructions and information that tell us exactly who will do the revealing to us concerning anything in our future (and it won't be dial-a-psychic hotline! God speaks direct!).

Have you ever become frustrated by calling a business and explaining to someone your need for help with a specific problem? You may give him all the details only to hear that he can't help you and that you need to speak with someone else! I hate that! The point is this: When you want results, speak with the right person. When you want the Lord to reveal your purpose to you, tune into the right source.

We said in an earlier chapter that when we receive a personal vision, a revealed word from God, it will restrain or guide us. The Holy Spirit of God will reveal our purpose to us so that purpose can lead and guide us for the rest of our lives. It is the Holy Spirit's assignment here on earth to lead us in such a revelatory way, as the following verses attest:

> *But when He, the Spirit of truth, comes, He will guide you into all the truth; for He will not speak on His own initiative, but whatever He hears, He will speak; and He will disclose to you what is to come. He shall glorify Me; for He shall take of Mine, and shall disclose it to you. All things that the Father has are Mine; therefore I said, that He takes of Mine, and will disclose it to you* (John 16:13-15).

Jesus clearly instructed here that the Holy Spirit will reveal to us all that is the Father's. *All* means "all inclusive." Such revealing *must*, therefore, include our personal purpose and destiny! The Holy Spirit will open to us the plan that our Father in Heaven has ordained for our lives. We can be assured that those plans will help people and will glorify the Lord. They will always be larger than we can personally perform and bigger than we can imagine. That is why we have been given the Revealer.

## The Language of the Holy Spirit

The Lord uttered a comforting, yet often frustrating promise when He proclaimed, "My sheep hear My voice, and I know them, and they follow Me" (Jn. 10:27). Jesus comforts us by stating that we, as His sheep, do hear His voice. His declaration that we will follow Him implies that we will understand His words when He speaks to us. Herein lies the agonizing frustration of many believers—learning to hear and understand so they may follow correctly and precisely.

Most of us believe that we can hear the Lord's voice; we're just not sure which voice is His. Is it Jesus, us, the devil, or the pizza we ate last night? To assist us in putting an end to such nerve-racking questions, the Lord set certain laws in motion, such as those we have just examined concerning the Holy Spirit as the Revealer of God's will. It is the Holy Spirit's job to speak to us in such a way that we can hear, understand, and follow. Our job is to learn and to listen to His communication.

In order to accomplish this, the Holy Spirit created His own unique language, a language composed of thoughts, ideas, visions, and dreams. He will plant these communications as seeds within the fertile soil of our spirits and minds. However, if we do not understand the language of the Holy Spirit, we will not hear and, therefore, will not be able to obey Him when He begins to reveal God's purpose and/or other commands to us. Let me illustrate.

To become a successful circus performer, I was forced to learn a new and unique language known only to those in the world of circus. Until I knew the names of the various pieces of rigging and the meaning of specific commands, it was virtually impossible for me to progress in the circus realm. As an unlearned beginner, I committed many errors due to my ignorance of the language (some were quite painful!). When someone ordered me to "take a foot on that block and set a bite," I was helpless to obey. It was frustrating for everyone involved. Not only was I continually embarrassed by the missed assignments, but my coaches and fellow performers were also often hindered in their efforts. When I finally mastered the language, however, I became capable of understanding instructions and carrying them out to the letter.

The parallel to our individual purpose should be obvious. If we don't understand the language of the Holy Spirit, we block both our own lives and the overall plan for the Lord's Church. We must acquire the exciting and revealing language of the Holy Spirit in order to accomplish our assigned tasks as individuals, thereby advancing the master work of God's people as well.

God's Word contains over 230 instances in which the Lord spoke to His people through visions and dreams. These visions and dreams are detailed in 32 separate books of the Bible, with 14 such occurrences in the Book of Acts alone. In fact, the entire last book of the Bible, The Revelation, is all one vision given to the apostle John in his twilight years. The extraordinary language of the Holy Spirit was regularly used to communicate God's purpose and plan for individuals and for His people as a nation. Moses saw a burning bush and heard the audible voice of God explain his life's purpose. The apostle Paul saw a bright light and heard a voice proclaiming what his purpose was to be.

We are not speaking only of these types of visions or awesome angelic appearances. Neither are we limiting this language to those dreams and visions you experience while you are asleep. The language of the Holy Spirit includes God-inspired thoughts and ideas. The Holy Spirit will skillfully insert His words and thoughts into your mind. You may never hear an audible voice. Most people never do. But daily, at any moment, God can flash His ideas across your brain. Sixty-five thousand images flow through the average person's mind each day. It would be ridiculous to think that God would not be a part of those ideas and thoughts. Throughout His Word, God proves again and again that this is a major avenue of His guidance for His people.

Jesus was led in this way during His life on earth. He was guided by the Father on a moment by moment basis, for He proclaimed:

> *...Truly, truly, I say to you, the Son can do nothing of Himself, unless it is something He sees the Father doing; for whatever the Father does, these things the Son also does in like manner. For the Father loves the Son, and shows Him all that He Himself is doing; and greater works than these will He show Him, that you may marvel ... I can do nothing on My own initiative. As I hear, I judge; and My judgment is just, because I do not seek My own will, but the will of Him who sent Me* (John 5:19-20,30).

Jesus was so in tune with the Father that He was able to receive exact instruction and never miss once in seeing, hearing, or doing His Father's will. These instructions probably came through the thoughts and ideas Christ received during His times of prayer, rather than through supernatural visions or audible voices. The New Testament records only one open vision that Jesus experienced during His tenure on earth. That vision was on the Mount of Transfiguration, when He was engulfed in the shining white glory of God as He conversed with Elijah and Moses. (I am not saying that God did not give Jesus *other* visions, dreams, or such, but that is the only one recorded.)

The Bible records two times that the Father spoke audibly to Jesus during His human life; both were merely to confirm the fact of Christ's Sonship—a fact Jesus was already well aware of. With this in mind, it is safe to assume that the Father spoke to Jesus through His thoughts—through His spirit—as Their regular, daily means of communication.

For example, how did Jesus know it was time to be baptized by John? By what means of communication did the Holy Spirit lead Him into the desert to be tempted by the devil? I believe it was through thoughts and ideas flowing across His mind. Many times in Scripture we are told that Jesus departed to a lonely place to pray. When He returned from the mountains or from the desert after those times of prayer, He would often perform great miracles. Why? Because during those seasons of communication with the heavenly Father, more of the purpose and plans for Jesus' life were revealed. God would speak to Him through the thoughts and images of His mind.

In John 12:49, Jesus stated that He did not speak on His own initiative, but that His words were given Him by God. How did those words come to Him? They came by thoughts and ideas crossing His mind. The Holy Spirit will speak to us in like manner concerning the purpose and destiny He has for our lives, thus fulfilling Jesus' promise that we would do the works He did and have hope for greater works.

I believe such inner guidance is a much higher form of receptiveness than physical communication from the Father (i.e., hearing an audible voice, seeing an angel, etc.) The ability to discern God's still, small voice with clarity and confidence is the result of a solid relationship between sender and receiver. (See First Kings 19:9-12). Such communication requires a deep, meaningful life of faith. Jesus obviously exemplified such faith for us to follow.

Remember also that *vision* means "mental sight." Many times the Holy Spirit will show you the actual images of those things He wants you to do. (Look again at John 5:19-20 and notice that the word *show* is used twice in conjunction with Christ's submission to the Father's will, implying sight of some sort.) The Holy Spirit plants pictures within us as He communicates God's will—our purpose—to us.

I believe that the Father did this for Jesus on a consistent basis. Jesus always spoke the answers to the problem—the finished product—rather than the problem or its steps to completion. The Father gave Jesus mental sight of the complete picture of His will. Be it healing a paralytic or raising the dead, Jesus saw the answer. If Jesus is our example—and He is—it is reasonable to believe that God will do the same for us.

## Listening to the Spirit

Over the past several years, I have grown accustomed to listening carefully to the wonderful language of the Holy Spirit. When I pray, I am actually surprised if He does not share with me a vision, a divine thought, or a mental image of some sort. As I intercede for someone or for a specific situation, I do so fully expecting the Holy Spirit to reveal to me, through His language, precisely how to meet the need. After all, He knows exactly what must be done. The Father desires to work through His children, of which I am one, so I should well expect Him to communicate the solution to me. That is not arrogance, it's Bible. And it works!

For instance, I was once praying for a young woman. She had come to me and pleaded, "I need direction in my life!" As I prayed for her, I saw a picture in my mind of that woman sitting in a large wing-backed chair, hunched over an old, dark-stained wooden desk. Standing on the upper right-hand corner of the desk was a tiny brass lamp with a delicate, milk-glass shade. The woman was busily writing something in a large, black, three-ring notebook. There were several other notebooks cluttering the desk's well-worn top. In the deep gray background of the dimly lit room, I could see a silver-haired old woman wrapped in a large-knit shawl, sitting silently in an old wooden rocking chair.

As the image disappeared, I realized that this was the Holy Spirit speaking to me about the direction He had for this woman's life. I interpreted the vision as the Holy Spirit inspired it to me and told the young lady what I had seen. The interpretation was basically this, "Whatever you were writing in that notebook, whatever you were working on at that moment, and whoever that old woman was in the background, that is your direction."

Her eyes widened as she listened to me speak. Then, somewhat awestruck, she revealed to me that just the night before she had been at a relative's house working at the very desk I had described. She had been studying and formulating plans to help her elderly grandmother, who was actually sitting in the room behind her at the time she was working. God had shown me, through the language of the Holy Spirit (which is thoughts, ideas, and visions), exactly what the woman had been doing the night before! She then acknowledged that she had always had a desire to help older people. I assured her that this desire was part of the Lord's direction for her life. The anxiety on her face suddenly lifted and was replaced by a noticeable expression of peace.

The Lord states again and again that He shows no partiality toward His people and will give us all that He has given to Christ. If Jesus knew the language of the Holy Spirit, then you and I also have that privilege. But we must strive daily to develop this divine form of communication. It demands much time spent in prayer and the worship of our Lord. It requires sacrifice. But the reward of such time and sacrifice is the priceless ability to be led and guided by the Creator of the universe! The cost versus the benefit is definitely in our favor.

## From Seed to Fruition

Take a moment now and look about the room in which you are seated. Every object you see, even the book you now hold in your hand, began as a mere idea, an inspired thought in someone's attentive mind. That thought or mental picture eventually became the physical reality you now experience. However, that idea did not simply leap from the person's creative mind into immediate physical reality. Instead, the idea underwent many phases of development before it materialized. Your own purpose will also be revealed and lived out in a step-by-step process. The steps of that process are *in* you right this very second!

When the Father reveals His purpose for your life to you, it will begin as one simple yet powerful thought or idea. That thought or idea is like a seed, having within itself the entire plan (your destiny) of how that purpose will come about. In every acorn is the plan for a mighty oak tree. Each kernel of corn contains the potential to become a stalk with many ears holding thousands of new kernels. Likewise, when God conceives the seed of your purpose in the womb of your spirit and mind, it will contain the complete plan and destiny for its achievement. Those detailed plans will be revealed to you continually in the same manner as the first thought or idea came to you—by the picturesque language of the Holy Spirit.

## Two Experiments

All this information is of great value, but if you cannot apply it in a practical way, it's merely ink on paper. I want you to know these truths personally. By performing the following experiments, you will open up some very real possibilities for experiencing the truths we have just discussed. One will be geared to quiet listening and the other toward specific thinking. You may wish to try both several times. I believe you will gain much insight from each exercise every time you attempt it. Be sure to have a pen and paper handy.

**Experiment #1**

Take a moment right now, or at your earliest possible convenience, and listen to the Holy Spirit's loving language. Ask the Lord to reveal to you in thoughts, pictures, and ideas concerning His purpose for your life. Do not tell Him how to speak to you, only ask Him to let you know with understanding what His will is for your life. As you listen, be ready to write down whatever comes to your mind. Do not disregard any thoughts you may think or pictures you may see in your imagination. Don't worry about whether or not you believe them, just write them down.

No one is going to hold you accountable for anything you receive. This is not for a grade. You are simply creating an opportunity for the Holy Spirit to speak to you. This is a faith exercise, for you are expecting the Holy Spirit to be the prominent voice within you. Give Him the okay to dominate your thinking and imagination. Be prepared to listen quietly for at least ten minutes.

**Be more impressed with ideas than you are with things or events!**
(W.G.)

When you have received some thoughts, ideas, or images and have written them down, look at them and ask yourself how they line up with what you really like to do. Remember, we are talking about a purpose here, not the actual plans and steps to walk it out. Then, without giving them a great deal of thought, jot down some simple answers to the questions below. These questions will help you to focus your thoughts about what you receive.

- Does it sound like you and your desires and dreams?
- Would you enjoy doing the things you heard for the rest of your life?
- Are they in line with your gifts?

No one but you will be able to answer these questions. They are merely to get you thinking about the possibilities that a purpose given only to you might offer. Again, no one will hold you to anything you write in these exercises, but it is likely you will get some very important information from the Lord during this experiment.

**Master your imagination, and you will never be its slave.** (W.G.)

**Experiment #2**

Now let's use your sanctified imagination for a moment. Ask the Holy Spirit to lead you through these questions using His wonderful language, painting the answers upon the canvas of your imagination—your thoughts. Do not spend a great deal of time on any one question, but try to let the answers flow quickly from the Lord. Be ready to write as you go.

Think for a moment about all your gifts, skills, and experiences.

- Where do they all seem to be pointing you right now?
- Is the direction you see one you feel good about?

Next, see yourself at the end of your life, having lived without any limitations of finances or ability.

- What do you want your obituary to say?
- What was your major focus of accomplishment?
- What kind of person were you?
- Who did you work with?
- Where did you go?
- Where did you live?
- How did you affect the world?
- Which of your accomplishments will continue to produce results that help people and bring glory to God after your death?
- How will you set that legacy in motion before you die?

This second experiment is my favorite because it allows us to think on a different plane than we normally let ourselves consider. We will discuss this type of thinking in greater detail in a later chapter, but I'm sure that this experiment either caused you to realize your limited ability to let even God enlarge your thinking in these areas or it enthralled and captivated you with what you saw. Either way, you took a major step forward in learning the language of the Holy Spirit, which is the main purpose of these experiments.

## Final Thoughts

As we go through this book together, we will expound on these and other questions that are vital to the achievement of a life-long purpose. And, if you tried these experiments and came up seemingly empty-minded, do not be dismayed. Remember the general orders given to all believers that we discussed in a previous chapter. They can fill your life with purpose and destiny the rest of your days! Also, you will receive some very specific information in the following chapters that will quickly fill the void and bring you great joy. And if you are wondering whether you actually heard from the Holy Spirit, rest easy. In the very next chapter I will give you a foolproof method for confirming such divine information.

# Figure #2

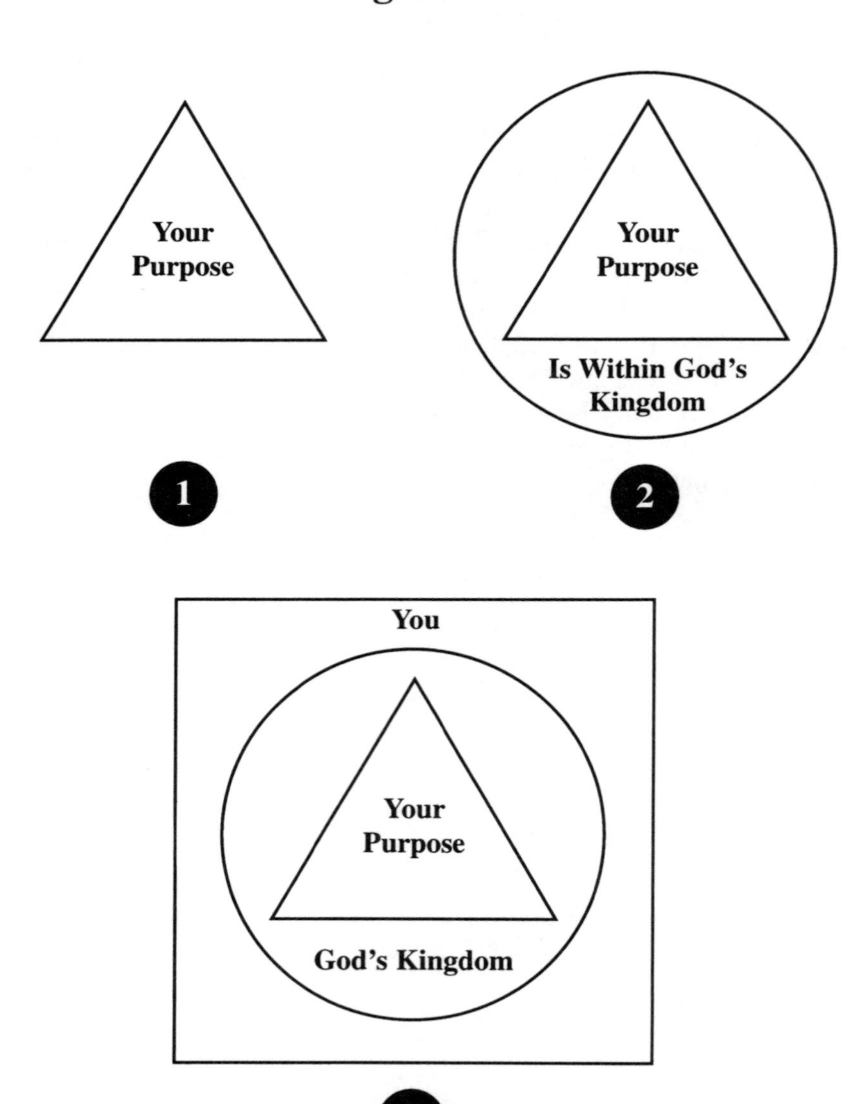
Your
Purpose
1
Your
Purpose
Is Within God's
Kingdom
2
You
Your
Purpose
God's Kingdom
3

# Chapter 7

# Absolute Confirmation

*EVERY FACT IS TO BE CONFIRMED BY THE TESTIMONY OF TWO OR THREE WITNESSES* (2 Corinthians 13:1b).

Once you begin to recognize the voice of the Holy Spirit, understand His language, and receive the purpose He has for your life, you must then confirm beyond a shadow of a doubt that what you are receiving is actually His instruction. Your enemy, the devil, will attempt to confuse and distract you. Friends and loved ones might not believe in your dreams. Even your own thoughts, imaginations, and ideas can rise up against you with doubts and fears. Therefore, to assist you in realizing your true purpose and the potential good it holds for all, the Lord has established several ways in which you may confirm His leading through His Word.

Before enlisting any of these steps of confirmation, you must affirm your total commitment to the Lord and His will for your life. You must be confident of a solid relationship with your heavenly Father. Such a relationship with Him will require much time spent in prayer, Bible study, and fellowship with other committed Christians, and in witnessing to those who have not heard about Christ. By establishing your relationship with the Lord, He can confirm His will to you much more easily because you will know His voice and ways. The more deeply you root that relationship, the more easily you will hear and understand the Holy Spirit's language and receive His leading.

Let me illustrate this. I have three children. When each was born, he or she was no more aware of me than of anyone else. They recognized neither my voice nor the touch of my hand. But as I spent time with them, they heard my voice, felt my touch, and saw my face again and again. Eventually, our relationship was established (at least as much as this is possible with newborns). When I spoke or simply entered the nursery, my child would instantly respond to me, even if others entered the room with me. As my children grew and matured, we were able to express our love for each other in two-way conversation and communication. The relationship I now have with my grown children was built upon the foundation of consistent, daily contact.

So it is with our heavenly Father. We must take time to build that relationship, for if it has not been properly secured, then clear communication with God will not be ours. Without such clarity, the following steps of confirmation will be difficult for us to use. If you are a person who has yet to establish a relationship with the Lord, I suggest that you do so before you proceed with this chapter. Only a truly committed believer will adhere to the following steps of confirmation because performing them will require a degree of self-motivation and patience that will be hard to sustain without the Lord's assistance.

## Seven Steps to Absolute Confirmation

**Once you discover your God-ordained purpose, you must hold it under the bright, revealing floodlamp of His confirmation.** (W.G.)

Hearing and following the voice of our Lord can simultaneously be the most exciting and the most nerve-frazzling exercise of our Christian lives. The fear of "missing" God on any given instruction can paralyze the strongest disciple. But Jesus did not come to bind those who desire to do His will; instead, He came to free the captives. God has a will and purpose specific to you, which He will reveal by His Spirit. By utilizing the following steps of confirmation, you will be capable of attaining freedom from the binding chains of fear. Rest assured, God will dispel all your doubts when He shows you your purpose and His plans for your destiny.

The following seven steps are to be employed for any or every item you desire to confirm as being from the Lord. These steps are scripturally based and time-tested. No longer will you need to wonder about your answers or leadings; just put these seven steps into practice and enjoy the freedom of being absolutely sure the Lord has spoken to you. I know it sounds too good to be true, but we *are* dealing with the Creator of the universe here. He *is* an expert at letting His children know His will beyond any and all doubt! I have created a Confirmation Checklist for you, which is located in the Appendix of your *Destiny Planner®*. If you do not have a planner, simply make your own by placing these seven headings on a clean piece of paper. Then write in the confirmations under the proper heading as they come to you.

### Step #1: Prayer

> *And when you pray, you are not to be as the hypocrites; for they love to stand and pray in the synagogues and on the street corners, in order to be seen by men. Truly I say to you, they have their reward in full. But you, when you pray, go into your inner room, and when you have shut your door, pray to your Father who is in secret, and your Father who sees in secret will repay you. And when you are praying, do not use meaningless repetition, as the Gentiles do, for they suppose that they will be heard for their many words* (Matthew 6:5-7).

Jesus was laying the foundation for personal prayer. He explained that *when* we pray (not if), we should walk into our prayer room and shut the door behind us. We are to be alone with God, without the distractions of TV, phone, or other people. We should speak to the Lord in secret. If we do this, He promises He will reward us outside the prayer room. One of the ways God rewards His children is through a greater ability to hear His voice and live out His instructions. My time in prayer is often my greatest time of inspiration and my most productive time of communication with the Holy Spirit. It was during such times of communion with God that I began to understand His language and to establish an unshakable relationship with my heavenly Father.

When the Lord reveals to you your purpose in life, He will confirm it during such times of prayer. By the thoughts in your spirit and mind, He will communicate to you whether or not you have received His vision for you. In John 10:27, Jesus made the statement that God's sheep will hear His voice and follow Him. We are His sheep and we will know His voice if we learn to listen for it. This means we must take time during our daily prayer sessions to listen for His words in our minds and spirits. We should not be rude and monopolize the conversation; instead we should sit quietly and listen so that He may speak His will. He is our Father. If we truly love Him as we say we do, then we must listen so we can obey. Prayer must become a two-way channel if we are to receive our confirmation clearly.

### Step #2: Inner Peace

> *But the fruit of the Spirit is love, joy, peace, patience, kindness, goodness, faithfulness, gentleness, self-control...* (Galatians 5:22).

We see here that peace is part of the fruit the Holy Spirit will develop in our lives. If God is giving you a vision or dream that reveals His purpose for your life, He will always confirm it with the feeling of peace within you. This is often referred to as the witness of the Holy Spirit. Here's a good way to test this issue of peace. When you think about your purpose—the vision set before you—when you dwell on it and daydream about it, do you have a peaceful feeling inside or an uneasy feeling? If your purpose is from the Lord, there will be peace and gentleness, without a hint of restlessness mixed in.

> *Be anxious for nothing, but in everything by prayer and supplication with thanksgiving let your requests be made known to God. And the peace of God, which surpasses all comprehension, shall guard your hearts and your minds in Christ Jesus* (Philippians 4:6-7).

Also, by praying from a stance of faith, trust, and reliance upon the power and goodness of God, you can secure peace beyond the normal limitations of human existence. This deliberate disregarding of fear and anxiety on your part, due to your total trust in the Lord, opens the door to His presence and peace. This peace will actually set a supernatural guard over your thoughts and over the emotions and beliefs of your heart, to keep out further fear and doubt. I can attest that this is quite true.

Many times fear and doubt plagued my soul over the things God had shown me concerning my purpose—only to be decisively chased off by an act of trusting prayer on my part. Then, in the face of circumstances that had not changed one bit, I had peace that the Lord would prevail and that all would be as He had said. My wife used to scold me that I never worried and that she had to worry for both of us. (I tried to tell her that worry is a sin, but my delivery must have been flawed, for it rarely produced the effect I hoped for. Is that a surprise?)

Try your own Peace Drills right now. The purpose of these drills is to give you firsthand experience with the feelings and thoughts that accompany the Lord's peace, as compared with those that are not found with His peace. For each of these drills, keep this question before your mind, "Is this Your will for me, Lord?" Be still and quiet for a moment, checking for the feeling of peace within you. Then, write down your impressions of the feelings and thoughts you have.

**Drill #1:** Think about something you know, without a doubt, to be God's will, such as going to church or reading your Bible.

**Drill #2:** Think about something you know is absolutely *not* God's will, such as stealing or lying.

The following questions will help you evaluate your feelings:

- What does God's peace (or the absence of it) feel like?
- How is your physical state effected by this peace (or the absence of it)—e.g., your muscles and facial expression?
- What do you experience in your heart, your inner man?
- Where do your thoughts take you during this time of peace (or the absence of it)?

I suggest that you perform this drill again and again until you have a strong understanding of what God's peace, or the lack of it, feels like. Get to know those feelings well, for they will serve you well as you pursue God's will throughout your life. Remember this point when you are confirming your purpose (or anything from the Lord): If there is no peace, do not move toward that goal!

### Step #3: The Word of God

*Thy word is a lamp to my feet, and a light to my path* (Psalm 119:105).

*All Scripture is inspired by God and profitable for teaching, for reproof, for correction, for training in righteousness* (2 Timothy 3:16).

These two verses explain that God's Word is both a light to assist in our search and the fulfillment of our direction, and a tool to train us in the areas needed to accomplish our goals. Our Father in Heaven desires not only to illuminate our path but also to equip us for the journey. His Word is more than able to handle both tasks. Please understand that the purpose God gives you will never contradict the Bible, but will always be in line with it. There are three methods the Father may use to confirm His will to you through His Word.

*Method #1: Illumination*

You may be reading the Bible one day when a verse seems to leap off the page at you. It will almost stand up on the page. You may not be able to leave that verse and may read it over and over again. This is one avenue God uses to confirm His purpose or a vision, thought, or idea to you. When a verse seems to jump out at you in this way, and it is in line with what you feel you have received from the Lord, it will be a point of positive confirmation for you.

*Method #2: Repetition*

This is a common means by which the Holy Spirit confirms certain items to believers through His Word. The exact same Bible verse pertaining to your purpose may come across your path several times in one day or over a period of time. It may be spoken by a friend, read in a book, heard on the radio, or found in the Bible itself during daily reading. Many times such constant occurrence of the same Scripture is the Lord confirming to you that you have actually heard from Him in a precise manner.

Here's an example. Meg and I were living in Fort Collins, Colorado, when the Lord told *me* to move to Tampa, Florida, and begin Circus Alleluia Ministries. I had no doubt that I had heard from the Lord, but I knew Meg would have a hard time with it. I had dragged her around the country before—chasing my dreams of stardom—and I refused to do it again. So, I told Meg what I believed the Lord had said to me and assured her that we would not go unless He confirmed it to her as well. She agreed to fast and pray with me for three days about the matter.

Part way through the first day she came to me and said that she had her answer. Three times that morning, from three separate sources—her daily devotional reading, a Christian radio program, and a ministry newsletter that came that day in the mail—the Lord had brought to her mind the Scripture concerning wives submitting to their husbands.

*Method #3: References*

Another way the Lord may use His Word to confirm a thought or idea is by dropping Scripture references into your mind through the Holy Spirit. Many times when I have prayed over certain ideas that I felt were from God, several references would enter my mind in rapid succession. Whenever this happened, I wrote them down and immediately looked them up. Quite often, these verses pointed toward or away from my idea, depending on whether or not God is the author of that idea. (He can also give Scriptures to confirm that your idea or vision is *not* His will.) One thing you can be sure of is that if a thought, idea, vision, or purpose is from the Lord, He will *always* confirm it by His Word.

**Step #4: Wise Counsel**

> *The way of a fool is right in his own eyes, but a wise man is he who listens to counsel* (Proverbs 12:15).

> *Through presumption comes nothing but strife, but with those who receive counsel is wisdom* (Proverbs 13:10).

> *Many are the plans in a man's heart, but the counsel of the Lord, it will stand* (Proverbs 19:21).

Success is guaranteed when you enlist wise counsel. The key word here is *wise*. A wise counselor is someone who is already experienced in the area you discuss with him. If you need wise counsel in the financial arena, you talk to someone with expertise in money matters. If you need wise counsel in automobiles, you should approach someone experienced in that area. But if you go to the plumber when you need your car fixed, you may not be receiving the wisest counsel available.

The finest counsel of all is the counsel of the Lord. In the verses above we see that only His counsel will stand long term. This being true, it is always best to seek wise counsel from godly people. Your first such counselors should be the pastors and elders of the local church body to which you are committed. These men and women are specifically anointed by God to help direct your Christian life. Their knowledge of your personal life will be a valuable resource during such seeking times. However, they may not always be the most experienced authorities in the specific areas for which you are seeking counsel. This would be cause to approach those people who are. I have been in Christian leadership for many years, but I would not consider myself a wise counsel in such areas as aeronautics or mathematics. I could pray for you and ask for some divine words of wisdom, but I would find few of my own in my memory banks.

Concerning a purpose or vision God has planted within your heart, always seek godly people who have experience in the area of *that* purpose or vision. You can be assured, based on these Scriptures, that the Lord will share much confirmation with you through wise, godly counsel. It is mandatory to get *wise counsel* to confirm what you receive from the Lord. Yes, it is time consuming, but it is worth it. Better to take the time now to be sure of yourself than to take the time later to correct yourself. Going slow, after all, is a great way to avoid later problems.

Another glory to the words of the wise is their ability to add substance to your ideas and plans. It is wondrous to me how in just a few seconds of being asked, an experienced, godly counselor can add something positive to my idea. I recently sat with a friend who has become a wise counselor to me in business matters. I shared with him my ideas for marketing some items. He took less than a minute to peruse the papers I handed him, then gave me several more items that have proved to be extremely beneficial. Never underestimate the deep well of additional plans and ideas that wise counsel can offer. And if you are not in the beneficial habit of seeking such counsel, begin immediately! You will earn a mountain of great advice that will save you much time and money.

**Step #5: Circumstances**

The Lord will manipulate and control natural circumstances to confirm His Word—His revelation to you. Through everyday happenings in your life, the Lord can give you crystal clear direction toward or away from your vision. Many Christians often refer to the cliché, "The Lord seemed to open the door," when referring to guidance on a certain item. This *is* a biblically based idiom, yet it can be a dangerous one if direction based on circumstances is given total obedience without the individual seeking and receiving any other forms of confirmation.

The reference to "opened" or "closed" doors comes from the apostle Paul's mention of it in First Corinthians 16:8-9: "But I shall remain in Ephesus until Pentecost; for a wide door for effective service has opened to me, and there are many adversaries." Obviously certain circumstances directed that evangelism was in season in Ephesus, and Paul meant to harvest some souls. But to think that Paul was acting solely on such circumstantial evidence would be ignorance on our part. The apostle had many years of missionary work under his belt and was well versed in the guidance of God's Spirit. In fact, in this same letter Paul teaches on the supernatural gifts of the Lord and the master plan God has for the Church—each member being specifically placed within His Body. Paul did not base his actions on open doors alone, and neither should we.

Let me share a personal example with you. My wife, Meg, and I were seeking confirmation whether or not to buy a certain house. During our time of seeking, several key circumstances fell into place that all pointed toward a direct confirmation of the word we felt God was giving us, which was to purchase the house. One such circumstance was that the owner of the house we were then renting wanted to move back into the house on a certain date. That date was directly in line with the time that we could move into the house we desired to purchase. Another circumstance was the amount the seller required as a down payment. It was almost the exact amount we had just received from an inheritance. We eventually bought the house.

### *Pinball Problems*

These circumstances, although quite convincing, were not the deciding factor in our purchase of that house. We considered these only as part of the confirmation we sought. Circumstances should never be employed as the only means of direction or confirmation. By applying circumstances as your sole means of confirming a word from the Lord, you may find yourself bouncing like a *pinball* from circumstance to circumstance, without ever really attaining the goal the Father has set before you. A pinball is directed by whatever it encounters. Led and guided completely by its circumstances, it actually has no direction at all and accomplishes nothing of lasting value. Many Christians operate in a similarly haphazard way, which is devoid of divine guidance. In order to avoid the pinball trap, you must trust circumstances only in conjunction with the other points of confirmation discussed here.

## Step #6: Supernatural Happenings

God uses the supernatural. He uses open visions and He uses dreams. He appears to people or has His angels appear to them. God can speak in an audible voice from the clouds or from a burning bush. He can speak through prophecies, animals, and storms. Our heavenly Father can cause oceans to part and trees to wither. He is a supernatural being.

As an assistant pastor and elder in two separate churches of several thousand members each, and as a traveling teacher/evangelist, I have been both thrilled by the use and shocked by the abuse of the gift of prophecy. Many wonderful words of direction have been given by God through anointed saints, and much good has been done. I have marveled at the utterances of young and old alike. But I have also sat heartbroken in many counseling sessions as I listened to the tears of those who had been destroyed by a "personal" prophecy. They followed the prophecy to the letter, only to be blown out of the water by an enemy torpedo in the spirit when it did not manifest the goods as promised. By receiving "a word" from a well-meaning brother or sister, they ran headlong into the snare of the devil. No prophecy should ever be lived out without the guidance and confirmation of a spiritually mature leadership and with additional confirmation steps also supporting it.

First Corinthians 14:29 admonishes us to judge prophecies. Receiving a "prophecy" unchecked can lead to disaster, but a prophecy tested and approved by godly leadership can prove very prosperous. Also be alert to the spiritual maturity of the one prophesying. Although any believer can be used of the Lord to share a word of prophecy, it is a good and safe rule to consider the source. Seek godly confirmation on every supernatural utterance and avoid costly missteps.

Again and again, throughout the Bible, God used supernatural happenings to lead, guide, and confirm His word and will to His people. He can and may do so with you. However, I caution you again: Do not use supernatural happenings as the sole means of confirming the purpose and ideas God may impart to you. First, the Bible states that satan himself can appear as an "angel of light" (see 2 Cor. 4:4). Many brethren have been deceived in this way. Second, such happenings are rare when compared to the total time span of biblical history. In thousands of years only hundreds of occurrences have been recorded among millions of believers. I believe we will see a dramatic increase in such events as the time of Christ's return draws closer, but even now, they are the exception and not the rule. Always make sure that supernatural manifestations are not your only means of confirming the word you feel God has spoken to you.

**Step #7: Timing**

> *There is an appointed time for everything. And there is a time for every event under heaven* (Ecclesiastes 3:1).

If ever there was a stumbling block of galactic proportions, this is it. Man, you get a vision from God, and He confirms it. And you know that you know that you know that you *know* it's right! Wild horses and a marching band couldn't move you from your position of knowing! So you naturally think now is the time for it all to take place. Wrong!

When the six Steps of Confirmation listed above are in agreement, you can be sure that God has spoken to you to confirm the word He has revealed to your heart. But if you launch out before His perfect time dictates, you can still fail miserably. You must see to it, when you confirm your purpose, that you continue to seek Him concerning the correct moment for stepping out and acting on that purpose.

Remember, it is the Holy Spirit's duty to lead you and guide you in all truth. All truth includes God's exact timing. He will reveal it to you, and it will again come through His language of visions, dreams, thoughts, and ideas. For many, including myself, this point of timing can be the most difficult to wait for the Lord to reveal. Our zeal often overpowers our patience. Too many plans have fallen short of God's intended mark due to either haste or tardiness. God has a perfect time for your purpose and destiny. Find it and follow it.

Let me illustrate the importance of this seventh step. When my wife and I bought the house I mentioned earlier, it still needed much work to be finished on it. After we moved in, the pressure to complete the work created a great deal of friction between us. It seemed as though we would never get it all done. My wife began to ask such questions as, "Do you think we heard from God on this house? Should we have done this?" Honest wondering can kill your faith.

However, when this occurred, we immediately thought back to the steps of confirmation and discussed each point. The confirmation for buying that home seemed crystal clear...until we got to the timing issue. We suddenly realized that we had never sought the Lord about *when* we should make the purchase. Over the next few days as we did seek Him on this point, He revealed that we had been premature. He had wanted us to give a portion of our inheritance money toward our pledge to some church-related work. By giving to the Lord's work first, we would not have had enough for our down payment on the house. The time needed for God to bring in the balance of the down payment would have allowed the builder to complete the house, and we would never have experienced the anxiety of doing the work ourselves.

It was a costly error, to be sure. We endured not only the pressure of finishing our home but also the distress of not paying off our commitment to the building fund on time. This was not the ideal method of learning the lesson of God's timing, but it was a lesson that we will never forget and hopefully will never repeat!

**A confirmed word from God is settled forever in the heart of the receiver.** (W.G.)

The seven Steps of Confirmation we have discussed in this chapter can deliver commanding peace in the midst of the storms that may rage against you. Knowing beyond a shadow of a doubt that the Lord has spoken His perfect will to you brings a bold confidence to the heart. I pray you will learn from the successes and failures mentioned here and utilize these points diligently in your quest to find and live your purpose.

### Fleeces and Lots

I wish to share two more steps with you concerning guidance and the confirmation of the purpose God puts in your heart. These ideas concern "putting out a fleece" and "drawing lots." I mention these two

Confirmation Steps with great caution, for even though both are biblical and can often be effective, they can be extremely dangerous if used alone.

In Judges chapters 6 and 7, we read about Gideon, who used a fleece—a sheepskin—to test God concerning a certain vision he had received. To make sure the Lord had spoken to him, Gideon laid the fleece on the ground one night and asked God to make the dew settle only on the fleece and not on the ground around it. The Lord did as Gideon requested. The next night Gideon tested the Lord again, asking Him to have the dew rest only on the ground and leave the fleece completely dry. God also granted this request. Gideon took these supernatural occurrences as a sign that he had received orders from the Lord, and acting upon that confirmation, he led Israel to victory in battle.

Drawing lots is found in Acts chapter 1, where this method was utilized to choose the apostle who would replace Judas Iscariot. The use of this method was probably based on Proverbs 16:33, which states, "The lot is cast into the lap, but its every decision is from the Lord." The apostles prayed and asked the Lord to direct the drawing of the lots. When the lots were drawn, Mathias received the apostleship.

As I mentioned, both Steps of Confirmation are biblically based and were effective when they were used. Both are dangerous, however, because they deal with supernatural happenings. By employing these types of confirmations, you are *asking* the Lord to intervene supernaturally into your circumstances. This is an inferior form of guidance. You must remember that satan can also manipulate natural circumstances.

As we study Gideon in Judges chapter 6, we see that he had a *weak* relationship with God when he put forth his fleece. In fact, in verse 13 he even questioned whether God had His hand on Israel at all, let alone on Gideon. This explains why the Lord honored the requests of Gideon as He did. Because there was little communication taking place between Gideon and the Lord, God had few other options open to Him. Gideon is not the model of daily communication with the Father that he has been made out to be, and we should *not* be following or teaching his example alone.

I don't ask my wife every morning to give me a sign that she is still my wife or that she will have supper ready when I come home from work. I know my wife. We communicate. We do not rely on signs and wonders to trust one another because we have developed our relationship beyond that point. When we first began dating, we used romantic niceties to impress upon each other the love we shared. Even though such signs and wonders are still in practice in our lives, they are no longer necessary for convincing each other of our feelings. Our relationship with the Father God should be just as good, and in fact, even better!

In the Book of Acts, we can also see the real reason the apostles picked the new apostle by drawing straws. They had been trained by the man Jesus who was no longer with them, and they had not yet established their spiritual relationship with the Holy Spirit as their guide. Therefore, they were forced to use the only other means of communication and confirmation that they knew. They required a natural means to confirm the Word of God—casting lots as was taught in the Old Testament, the only written Word of God available to them.

Years later, in Acts chapter 13, the story was quite different. By this time, the disciples had learned the new art of being led and guided by the Holy Spirit through thoughts, ideas, visions, and prophecies. They expected the Lord to speak to them in their inner man. When Paul and Barnabas were called out by the Holy Spirit—probably through a prophecy—during a gathering of prophets and teachers, there is no mention of lots being cast or of fleeces being laid on the ground overnight. Instead, the word of the Lord came through men yielded to His Spirit as they were ministering to Him. Their relationship with the Lord had grown to the point that they could hear Him from within. Even after they had received the word, they took more time to pray and to be sure that the word was confirmed to all. Only then were the two missionaries sent out. Our relationship with the Almighty should be ever marching toward that goal.

I caution you: Don't "get fleeced" or end up with the "short end of the stick" by using uncertain guidance systems. Never use these two steps as your sole means of confirmation. I advise you to grow in your relationship with the Lord to the extent that you do not need such natural means to confirm His word to you, but you can trust the conviction and guidance of the Holy Spirit within you.

## Final Thoughts

We have a Father who loves us dearly. He has a definite purpose and plan for each of our lives. To make sure that we discover His purpose and achieve His plan, without any element of doubt, He devised the steps of confirmation that we have discussed in this chapter. As we strive to utilize these steps, they will become a strength and bulwark in our daily lives, not only for our overall purpose in life but also for any instruction we feel the Holy Spirit is sharing with us. Once we have confirmed the will of God, we must then take the next step. We must take ownership.

# Section Two

## *Direct Your Destiny*

*And for this* [reason] *I was appointed…in faith and truth* (1 Timothy 2:7).

# Chapter 8

# Destiny Is

*For whom He foreknew, He also predestined to become conformed to the image of His Son, that He might be the first-born among many brethren; and whom He predestined, these He also called; and whom He called, these He also justified; and whom He justified, these He also glorified* (Romans 8:29-30).

*He predestined us to adoption as sons through Jesus Christ to Himself, according to the kind intention of His will, to the praise of the glory of His grace...also we have obtained an inheritance, having been predestined according to His purpose who works all things after the counsel of His will* (Ephesians 1:5,11).

## What Is Predestination?

I feel like I'm tackling a very large and very slippery octopus by trying to answer this question. I have no doubt about what *I* think it means. I know some will take issue with me, and that is their prerogative. But predestination is an issue I believe that all Christians need to come to grips with one way or the other. So here goes.

*Predestination* is from the Greek word *proorizo*. It implies that there is a specific reason for a believer's life. Its actual meaning is, "to limit in advance; to mark out; to set the boundary of; to appoint, decree, and specify." It comes from a root word that we use to speak of the horizon.

Now, if you put that all together, you see that predestination carries the idea of *a specific appointment that covers a specific area with boundaries already set.*

Personally, I do not believe we are puppets. I do not believe that the Lord calls the shots *for* us. However, I *do* believe He gives us the options to *choose* from. Among those options is our perfect purpose and calling in this life. We can say yes or no to it. Predestination is an option, not a sure thing. If it were already decided, we would have no control, and therefore, we would have no freedom of choice. Neither would we be the brethren for which Jesus is the firstborn.

But we *are* in control of our destinies. We *are* free willed. We *are* the brethren of our Lord and Savior. We *are* sons and daughters of God.

## A Closer Look

According to the verses previously quoted, this whole issue of predestination revolves around our relationship with God our Father, not God our controller. As a parent, the free choice of my children is something I will fight anyone to preserve. God is a far more loving parent than I am. Therefore, I have no reservations in stating the following: *I believe that no one on this earth has ever had the luxury of a predetermined new birth before he or she drew his or her first breath, in the sense that it was fixed and settled without need of his or her deliberate efforts.*

If such *was* true, every man, woman, and child who has ever lived would be born again and living eternally with God. We know this is not the case, so predestination *must* take the will of the person into account.

Predestination speaks of pre*known*, not pre*settled*. No man's salvation is a settled issue until he repents and makes Jesus the Lord of his life. But God knows who will and who won't make that choice, and therefore, He can inspire such Scriptures in a way as to *imply* the issue is presettled. Yes, God chose us, we who are believers in Jesus, from before the foundations of the earth to be holy and blameless (Eph. 1:4), but does this mean that He loves everyone else less? Of course not. God *desires* that all men are saved (see 1 Tim. 2:4); but not all will be. Does this mean that God's will can be ignored by godless men? In the instances where freedom of choice prevails, the answer is unequivocally YES! This is powerfully acknowledged in the following Scripture:

> *But the Pharisees and the lawyers rejected God's purpose for themselves, not having been baptized by John* (Luke 7:30).

God's will in the individual lives of people is in their hands, not His. If this were not so, there would be no need for the Scripture describing the eternal hell that some will know. Your will can supersede God's if you so desire. It is foolish to do so, but it is within your ability nonetheless. God's desire is to perform His will through us, and as He does, to give us the best possible purpose and destiny in the process. That is how predestination works in our lives. He pre-ordains our best case scenario, and then He gives us the option to live it or not. It's that simple.

## Final Thoughts

The verses above show the link between God's predetermined will, our sonship with Him, our calling, our justification, and our glorification. In the end it's all about becoming conformed into the image of Jesus. The destiny God has picked out for each of us will accomplish all these things with the utmost efficiency and totality. It will change us into new people and affect the world around us more than anything we could possibly come up with on our own.

I'll close here with more definitions from the dictionary. I believe you'll find them congruent with my ideas on predestination as far as our personal purpose and destiny is concerned.

- Destine: To set apart; appoint for a special purpose; predetermined. (*Webster's Dictionary*)
- Destination: A predetermined end of a journey; the purpose for which anything is intended. (*Webster's Dictionary*)
- Destiny: Your fortune; the inevitable. (*Webster's Dictionary*)
- Destiny: Your fortune; the inevitable, predetermined journey of your specific purpose, which is achieved by what you decide to make happen as God directs you. (Greenman's Dictionary)

# Chapter 9

## Your Destiny Team

*Two are better than one because they have a good return for their labor. For if either of them falls, the one will lift up his companion. But woe to the one who falls when there is not another to lift him up. Furthermore, if two lie down together they keep warm, but how can one be warm alone? And if one can overpower him who is alone, two can resist him. A cord of three strands is not quickly torn apart* (Ecclesiastes 4:9-12).

### Who Should Be on Your Team?

Wise counsel is mandatory, but building a Destiny Team is just as essential for success in your destiny plan. A Destiny Team is merely a group of people whom you gather to yourself for counsel and accountability as you live out your destiny. This can take the form of an advisory board, a corporate board of directors, or just a gathering of trusted friends. No matter what name you give it, the men and/or women on your Destiny Team should be people you know and trust. They should have some "mileage" in your life and really know you in all your good, bad, and ugly states.

Their greatest values to you are their wisdom and their unconditional love for you. Their wisdom will bring a multiplied storehouse of experience to your aid. Their love will allow them to speak into your life and destiny without fear. This means they can compliment you or reprimand you as needed. Their ages may vary, but your team members will usually be your age or older. I personally like to have some gray-haired heads on my Destiny Team for added experience. You will have your own choices. Rarely is there a successful man or woman who does not have such a group. Even rarer is the person who has such a group and is willing to do without it!

**Success is proportional to the quality of the people with whom you surround yourself.** (W.G.)

There is no set number of members for a Destiny Team. It may just be you and your spouse or best friend. It may be several people. Although there is no set number, the precedent for having a team is clearly given throughout the Bible. Jesus had the 70, the 12, the 3, and the 1. Moses had only Aaron at first, but eventually he received counsel from others and appointed 70 to help him keep order. The 12 apostles worked together in the building of the early Church. Paul and Barnabas, in Acts chapter 13, met with a group of teachers and prophets before they went off on a missionary journey. David and Jonathan formed a covenant team. Most of the Old Testament kings had seers, counselors, and prophets. At times, Paul and Peter answered to the elders in Jerusalem. Do yourself the favor of creating your own Destiny Team as soon as possible. You will *never* regret it.

Your Destiny Team should be people with the following abilities. First and foremost, they must be people of the Word of God and of prayer, people with a strong track record of hearing from the Lord in a clear and accurate manner. They should be confrontive, yet compassionate. They should be reprovers, yet listeners. They should be able to instruct, yet be teachable. In other words, they should be of such strong character and personality that they can contribute to your growth and destiny whenever called upon and in whatever capacity necessary. Obviously there won't be a lot of people in most of our lives who fit that description, so choose wisely.

Be open to the fact that everything ends. As the years go by, there will be times when some will leave your Destiny Team and others will join. I have found this to be true as the Lord has moved us across the country several times. Each move forced us to gather a new team for maximum wisdom. However, we maintain strong relationships with all who have been a part of our Destiny Team in the past, and at times we still go to them for counsel.

## Where to Look

I strongly recommend having several people on your Destiny Team who are older and more experienced than you are. Persons with gray hair are usually a boundless source of wisdom that few of us take the time to tap. Personally, I believe that the Lord will judge many of us for the way we have herded our elders into retirement homes, telling them it is youth we hold dear and ignoring the wisdom of the aged. I often ask young leaders who their heroes are, and few mention men and women older than themselves. That is unfortunate. We should be magnets who draw such elders to us on a regular basis. Who knows how much wisdom and knowledge lies dormant in retirement homes and communities, knowledge that could save time, money, and even lives. Go find out!

## Synergism

The power of this Destiny Team is the synergism that their collective experience and knowledge brings to the table for you. Synergism is the fact that the ability of the whole group is greater than the sum of each individual. Simply put, if I have three friends who can each lift 100 pounds, together they can lift 500 pounds. We can do more by working together, with each contributing what he or she can do. Members of your team will have skills in areas where you have few, which can be priceless in times of need. The number of ideas that can come from a group like this is multiplied far beyond the number of people in the group. Brainstorming sessions will yield the highest of dividends, and I advise you to have *many* such storms.

**We all live...by what others have given us in the significant hours of our lives.** (Albert Schweitzer)

The networks of friends and colleagues of those on your team will automatically double, triple, quadruple, and more that of your own contacts! I can tell you from experience that to have such a group to go to for major decisions is a most calming and confidence-building experience. And when a decision has turned to mud instead of gold, it is nice to have them stand by you, sharing the load of responsibility and the confusion of missing the mark you thought God had set for you. I tell you with regret that the times in my life when I operated *without* such a group, everyone involved with me or the projects I was working on *suffered* for it.

A sad case in point occurred when I tried to raise money for another ministry. I wanted to help them establish their new base in the town I was living in, so I asked them what they needed. The answer was $50,000. Although that was more than my entire annual budget at the time, I still *decided* to raise the money myself, and I emphasize the "myself." I *never* asked the Lord about it. Nor did I have a Destiny Team to consult with. I had people in my ministry with whom I consulted—which means I told them, "Here's what we're going to do"—and they complied, figuring that I had heard from the Lord. We spent hundreds of hours and over $12,000 and even raffled off a new car to raise a whopping $1,600 after expenses. Now, if I had been the only person with my head on the block, this would not have been so bad, but the entire ministry that we were raising the money for had banked on my emphatic promise of raising the money. It was irreversibly on its way to our town to establish a new base, with $48,400 less than they had figured on!

It was with none too little pain and embarrassment that I told the director of that ministry of my dismal failure. He was extremely gracious to me, but it was obvious that I had let him down in a very *big* way. He was forced to tell his people the news, and of course, they had a rather tough time of it for a while, although they eventually did succeed in their relocation efforts. This was the hardest lesson with money (and also with the consequences of acting on my own) that I have ever known.

A happier case took place a few years after the above-mentioned fiasco. It was an unpleasant circumstance to live through as well, but this time I had a team to share the load and to tell me that I was not losing my mind. In the summer of 1988, I had finally admitted that our circus ministry was coming to an end. Actually, it had been slowly fading for well over a year or more; I just had trouble accepting it. So, whether it was my own idea that the Lord agreed to let me pursue or whether it was His idea all along, I took my newest idea to my Destiny Team, which at that time I simply called my advisory board.

The idea was to create a high-tech extravaganza that would meld circus, dance, drama, and illusions, complete with light shows, smoke, and pyrotechnics. We would call the show MAXIMUS, but our organization would still be called Circus Alleluia. To the man, the entire board, after prayer, agreed that the show was of the Lord. I, of course, immediately took off after the vision.

My first task was to hold a fund-raising banquet for the new ministry venture. We had a small turn out, but we raised just enough money to put on our first performance. Although the show was not quite the blockbuster I had imagined, it did give us the impression that we were headed in a new, groundbreaking direction. Our peers from the Christian performance ministries who attended gave us great reviews, and the Lord moved on people to bring salvation and healing. It was a lot of fun, and I thought we were off and running. Wrong!

Two months later the Lord told me that I was to end Circus Alleluia Ministries (including MAXIMUS) and pursue the prophetic gifts and ministry full-time. To say the least, I was surprised. I went back to my advisory board and shared the news. Again, they all agreed that it was the Lord's will. Now the fireworks started. First, some of the people who had made donations to our MAXIMUS vision were crying foul. They could not understand the abrupt change, and I had no trouble seeing their point: Why would God change His mind so quickly? Some folks accused us outright of deliberate deception just to get the money. Others were simply disappointed. People told us that we missed God completely with the dissolution of the circus. It was heart-wrenching for me, for Meg, and for others in our ministry. But the glory of the tale is that my advisors stood beside me and defended the actions of those last six months because they had all agreed that we had heard from the Lord. It was a dark time for me to be sure, but it was not nearly as dark as it would have been *without* my Destiny Team.

## Building Your Team

There are several ways that you can begin to gather your Destiny Team. You can make a formal invitation with a specific time frame of service and with formal meetings set for several times each year, or for once each month, as you desire. Or, you may simply ask your prospective team members to informally agree to "be there" for you when called upon, be it a one-on-one meeting or as a group. The choice is up to you, but whatever you choose, be sure that you are committed to the team and they are committed to you. You can use the Destiny Team Worksheet in your *Destiny Planner®* to keep vital stats on your team members for quick access when you need to contact them.

Obviously the best way to tap the synergy of the group's collective knowledge and experience is to meet as a group. Much more energy and spirit is activated by such a gathering. Your meetings should be isolated from interruptions and have a clearly defined agenda that has been sent to everyone ahead of time. This allows maximum focus and, therefore, maximum input and results. Nothing is more frustrating than a meeting without an agenda that turns into merely a bull session. Don't waste your time or that of your team with such drivel. Be precise and effective, even if it's merely a phone conference call. Be respectful of everyone's time and efforts by being prepared.

Also, when you draw up the agenda for your Destiny Team meetings, please do not succumb to the ploy of merely giving your team members patronizing nods when listening to their thoughts and ideas, which you have solicited. If you are going to get true strength and power from your team, you must *take* their advice. Nothing is more deflating than giving people your best insights only to have them ignore them—while still giving the impression that they are in agreement. See your team as individuals sent of God to give you the essentials that you do not have without them. Take every bit of advice, insight, and ideas to the Lord, and as a group get the mind of God on them *all*. Then create your destiny plans according to your newfound, divinely confirmed information.

## Final Thoughts

A Destiny Team is invaluable. You cannot afford to pursue your life purpose without such a group. The safety, increased wisdom, and support are more than worth any inconvenience of time or effort. Allow your team members to be honest and open with you about everything that you share with them concerning your destiny plan. Ask them to "plus" your ideas. Ask them to confront your errors and applaud your achievements.

And when you have completed a valued goal, be sure to give your team the recognition they deserve. Let those who shower you with accolades be made aware of the others with whom you tapped and acquired the mind of Christ. Be sure to thank them, pray for them, and thank the Lord for their contributions. If you diligently build your Destiny Team, you will find yourself accomplishing more with less effort and fewer mistakes. You will stand among the greats!

# Chapter 10

# Owning Your Purpose

**Your destiny is the hash mark between the day you were born and the day you die. Its meaning is for you to decide.**
(Peter Daniels)

### The Two-Minute "Reason" Drill

Read no further until you complete the following task. Take exactly two minutes and list on paper every reason that your life is not what it could be or what you'd like it to be. Be very honest about what you want and what's keeping you from it. When you have completed this task, read over your list one time to make sure that you have not missed anything. You must not take any more than two minutes. GO!

I hope you did not cop out and just kept reading here. This task is monumental for helping you to gain control of your environment and for preparing you for achievement. Please, if you did not do the Two-Minute "Reason" Drill, stop right now and do it. You'll be glad you did!

Okay, let's see how you did. Look over the list right now. What is the number one reason why you have not achieved what you feel you are capable of or what God has ordained for you? Say it out loud. Now quickly answer the following questions:

- If I am not the number one reason on my list, shouldn't I be?
- What can I do to accept and better steward my personal responsibility for *me*?

- What excuses have kept me from being responsible for my life, and how can I avoid them in the future?
- How did I let myself believe that the issue at the top of my list has priority over my personal responsibility in the management and achievements of my life?
- How can I avoid this next time?

This exercise may have made your toes bleed a bit, but it's good for us all once in a while. My toes have similar scars. The point to this exercise is that you must become accountable for what you have or have not done where your personal purpose is concerned. That includes your success in every area of your life. You are the bottom line—no one else. Blame shifting has been elevated to an art form these days. Everyone is a victim, and no one is responsible. It's always someone else's fault. We even have "no fault" insurance policies! What a joke, and what an even bigger tragedy. Please do not misunderstand: I realize that we are all affected by the people and situations we encounter throughout our lives. My own life was saturated with insecurity because as I grew up, every male authority figure in my life constantly put me down. As far as I can remember, no one ever told me that I was good at anything.

However, one day I had to stop and say to myself, "Those people are not me. They do not live with me or for me. I will *not* be controlled by their thoughts about me. I will think about what *I* desire and become what *I* want and believe I *can* be." Eventually, I exchanged that last line for "thinking and becoming what *God* wanted for me."

**No matter what events have happened in your life, they are just that—events—and you cannot allow an event to dominate your entire life.** (W.G.)

Events are just one piece of life. Your past is your past, but it need not be or dictate your future! Excuses are cheap and useless. You have the right and the responsibility to sift through the events of your life and to hang on only to the events that you have learned from and want to use to shape you into the person you and God want you to be. You can do it!

Society is making it acceptable to *not* be responsible for our actions and our inaction. But the saints of God must not be counted among the irresponsible! We must exemplify responsibility. This is especially true concerning our *goal-setting* and achievements.

No one should be setting your goals or fulfilling them for you. Such would make you an impotent robot whose mind is going to waste. The world is worse off if you do not set and perform your own goals—and so are you! Your individual creativity is too unique to lose. You must stop making excuses and start discovering and setting the goals necessary for your God-ordained destiny!

Let me give you an example. In the early years of my Christian life, I spent a lot of time and money repairing the doors I "tattooed" with my knuckles during fits of anger. As I grew in the Lord, I was puzzled as to why I was still having this problem, and finally, my lightning-fast mind thought it would be a good idea to ask the Lord about it. He answered quickly, "Decide you want to change, then make yourself do it. I will help you as you study and meditate on what My Word says about the subject of anger." Now that wasn't what I wanted to hear. I wanted Him to zap me! Do it with a blast from Heaven. Send an angel. Give me a vision. But I did not want Him to make me get involved! That would mean I was responsible!

Well, after some soul-searching, I decided that I would follow the Lord's leading and get control over my anger. My goal was to get to the point that I would not hit anything, raise my voice, or recklessly (or otherwise) hurl obscenities. I began to study God's Word regarding anger. I meditated on it. I asked people to pray for me. I told myself what I wanted. I prayed for myself. I fasted. It was a long and tough struggle that took several years, but I won. As I write this, that was some 20 years ago and I have not slipped back into that behavior. I have had one or two incidents of anger since then, but I have never reverted to my old raging as a part of my lifestyle.

The interesting thing is that God helped me when, and not before, I finally set the goal and went after it. Is God into goal-setting? Emphatically, the answer is yes! Is it so He can watch us squirm and struggle? No, it's because He knows the journey to reach the goal will cause us to become a far better disciple than the goal itself could ever produce. Embrace the change. Set the goal. Do the stuff!

## Who's the Boss?

*So then, my beloved, just as you have always obeyed, not as in my presence only, but now much more in my absence, work out your salvation with fear and trembling; for it is God who is at work in you, both to will and to work for His good pleasure. Do all things without grumbling or disputing; that you may prove yourselves to be blameless and innocent, children of God above reproach in the midst of a crooked and perverse generation, among whom you appear as lights in the world, holding fast the word of life, so that in the day of Christ I may have cause to glory because I did not run in vain nor toil in vain* (Philippians 2:12-16).

If you are a born-again Christian, God is to control your life now. He will exercise His control through your permissive will. He expects you to make good on your pledge to live for Him, which you made when you asked Jesus to become your Lord, not just your Savior. There will be no one to point to when you stand before Him to answer His questions concerning what you did with the life and purpose He ordained for you. Your destiny is in *your* hands, and it will require effort in both the planning stage and the achievement stage. Let's take a look at the work side of our responsibility.

## Work Power

*There is one who scatters, yet increases all the more* (Proverbs 11:24a).

*He who tills his land will have plenty of bread* (Proverbs 12:11a).

*Wealth obtained by fraud dwindles, but the one who gathers by labor increases it* (Proverbs 13:11).

*In all labor there is profit, but mere talk leads only to poverty* (Proverbs 14:23).

*He who tills his land will have plenty of food* (Proverbs 28:19a).

*You yourselves know that these hands ministered to my own needs and to the men who were with me. In everything I showed you that by working hard in this manner you must help the weak*

> *and remember the words of the Lord Jesus, that He Himself said, "It is more blessed to give than to receive"* (Acts 20:34-35).

Human beings were created to perform and enjoy hard work. Work does not refer just to manual labor, but to anything that taxes the strength of our spirit, mind, and body. We must embrace that fact if we are to be the truly productive people whom we were destined to become when we were born again by the Spirit of God. You see, Christianity, and your particular part in the great scheme of this age, is to be anything but passive. I find nothing in the Bible to suggest that the Christian life is meant to be docile or boring. In fact, all I have ever found is the exact opposite, which is why those verses from Acts chapter 20 are so poignant. Why, even the Great Commission is just that, a commission, a call to a mission of action!

> *Go therefore and make disciples of all the nations, baptizing them in the name of the Father and the Son and the Holy Spirit, teaching them to observe all that I have commanded you; and lo, I am with you always, even to the end of the age* (Matthew 28:19-20).

These verses from the Gospel of Matthew are replete with action of the highest kind. There is the physical action of "*go*!" into *all the world*. What does that mean? It means get up and get out of the house! It means take action and take it now. This is followed by the no less urgent, "*make disciples of all the nations*." "Make" is a fairly strong action word, wouldn't you say? How about, "*baptizing them*"? Nothing laid back about that either. Next we have the ever active, "*teaching them*." The commission ends with the instruction to be sure that we teach these new disciples to "*observe*" all the commands of Christ, which of course includes the commission that He just gave. No matter how you cut it, this is one action-oriented commission! There is no room in it for laziness or passivity. It is work, and it is given no boundaries of time or space. I like that!

It's thrilling to realize that we each have purpose and destiny from God on high. It's exhilarating to think that the One who created the entire universe actually included our seemingly insignificant lives in the equation. But if you set up camp there and never get down to the business of mapping out the journey your life is to travel, you will never leave the parking lot! Nobody wants that. The only way to avoid that tragic scenario is to work. Myles Munroe in his book, *Releasing Your Potential,* presents the most eloquent and inspired treatise on the subject of work I have yet to read. I want to share here a portion of Myles' word on this subject:

> "Work is a gift from God. Every assignment God has ever given required work. Noah worked to build the ark (Genesis 6). Joseph worked to provide for the Egyptians during a seven-year famine (Genesis 41:41ff). Solomon worked to build the Temple (2 Chronicles 2–4). As each accomplished what God asked of him, he fulfilled God's purpose for his life. His willingness to do the work God gave him blessed himself and others. Through work these people and many others have met the various responsibilities of their lives…
>
> "Work is honorable. God designed you to meet the needs of your life through work. ***When you refuse to work, you deny yourself the opportunity to fulfill your purpose***, because God created you to act like He acts, and God worked. The release of your potential demands that you admit that you need to ***work***… Don't become a burden on others. Work to provide for yourself and your family. Settle down and get a job. Put your roots down and do not allow yourself to be easily deterred from your responsibilities. God gave you work to earn the bread you eat. … God also ordained that work would show you your potential…
>
> "A commitment to work will also permit you to develop a perspective that rejoices in achievement more than pay. Then you can find happiness in your work even when the pay is less than what you expect or deserve…
>
> "Finally, work profits you by enhancing your self-esteem. If you feel worthless, find some work. Get busy. When you have something to do, your ability to feel good about yourself can change overnight. As you take the opportunity to focus on the results of your labor instead of the losses in your life that tempt you to feel unlovable and incapable, your estimation of yourself will grow. Work keeps you healthy, physically and emotionally."*

*Myles Munroe, *Releasing Your Potential* (Shippensburg, PA: Destiny Image Publishers, Inc., 1992), 134-137.

Let me conclude this section on work with some insights from world renowned psychologist Abraham Maslow:

> "Even if all needs are satisfied, we may still often [if not always] expect that a discontent and restlessness will soon develop unless the individual is doing what he is fitted for. A musician must make music, an artist must paint, a poet must write if he is to be ultimately at peace with himself. What a man can be, he must be."*

Maslow's conclusions prompted the U.S. government to publish a report called, "Work in America." This report cited a 15-year study that found the strongest predicator of longevity was work satisfaction. Simply put, if you want to live longer, learn how to work, and work at what you were created for. Do you understand the power of that statement? Do you understand why people with seemingly everything commit suicide? Do you see why Christians should live longer than anyone?

Long life due to the fulfillment of your purpose and destiny makes absolute sense if you are a believer. The Bible tells us that God is life and love. It stands to reason, then, that if we are doing what we are ordained to do, God will be in our work. Therefore, we will love what we do, and we will live longer as He flows in us while we work. Tremendous!

## Final Thoughts

That is the entire premise for this book—to help you discover what your purpose is and to supply you with useful, easy-to-understand tools for planning and performing the work of fulfilling your purpose. I want you to have a destiny that fills you with life! I want you to love to work because you love your work! There is no other way to do that aside from finding and doing your God-given purpose. *But no one is responsible for that purpose, that destiny, and that work except y-o-u!*

Some people find that intimidating. You should find it exhilarating! When *you* are responsible for your own destiny, no one can stop you! It's completely your choice. Even if you're reading this in a prison

*As quoted in Richard J. Leider, *The Power of Purpose* (San Francisco: Berrett-Koehler Publishers, 1997).

cell, you can still find and fulfill your purpose because God is bigger than any prison and any judicial system on the planet! Don't make excuses; make a decision! Decide to make a difference by taking responsibility for all your actions—especially the fulfillment of your God-ordained destiny. Once you have made the commitment to own your purpose and its achievement, you can begin to formulate the plan, the mission, of your destiny.

# Chapter 11

# Create Your Mission Statement

*Write the vision plainly...so those who read it may run* (Habakkuk 2:2b, paraphrased).

## Write It Down

The command to the Old Testament prophet Habakkuk is a powerful one. God meant it for our long-term good and for the achievement of His and our dreams. The Lord knew that it is the written word that solidifies the thought, the idea, and the dream within the heart of an individual. It is the written treatise that finds root within the lives of those who read it. It is almost supernatural the way that the mere penning of an idea can transfer it from the invisible into the tangible reality of this world. You see, when we write down what we believe, what we desire to do, then we are already stepping *toward* that desire and belief. It activates us. It energizes us when we read it. God knew that would be the case, so He commanded the prophet to write, and He commands us to do the same.

When you have a dream in your heart, a vision, a purpose, there is a very real oppositional force immediately arrayed against it. Part of that evil army is within your own inadequacies and insecurities, while the other part is the actual lord of darkness who uses those same human frailties against you. Make no mistake, the devil and his demons are very real. If you are a Christian, he is your sworn enemy for life. Whatever and whenever he can take from you, he will, including your purpose, your mission. He will cloud your mind with doubt as he did with Eve in the Garden of Eden, saying, "Did God say...?" He will contradict the word of the Lord to you, twisting its meaning, and weakening its impact. His main goal is to get you to wonder. If you wonder about what you heard, you will waver. If you waver, you will not act. And if you do not act, satan wins by default!

Why is there a Lamb's Book of Life? Why were there scribes in Israel whose sole occupation was to copy the Scriptures so meticulously that not one dot or letter could be left out or the manuscript would be unusable? Is God forgetful? Does He need to read these things once in awhile to stay focused or to keep up to speed with the times? Of course not! The command and example of writing down the Word of God, including the word of God to us personally, is for *our* benefit. We are forgetful, just as Eve was. She had part of it right, but the smallest error cost her everything! God wants us to avoid as much speculation and poor memory as possible. Therefore, He instructs us to write down our visions, dreams, and purpose in a way that they are not only easy for *us* to pursue but also for those He will send to help us.

No man or woman of God is called to a vision of survival only. Our purpose in this life will meet the needs as well as require the assistance of other believers. Ours is the life of shared dreams and family interaction. However, to provide others with the opportunity to share in our visions, we must see to it that they are informed—hence Habakkuk's plea. There are also three personal reasons why you should write down your purpose or mission statement.

1. It will solidify for you that your purpose is from the Lord.
2. It will help you focus the details of that purpose.
3. It will cause you to commit yourself to the purpose.

With a written plan ever before you, the Lord can sink it deep into your soul.

## Runners Are Standing By

Through Habakkuk the Lord instructs us to inscribe the vision on "tablets of stone." A message hammered into stone is permanent. A written vision will set its permanence within our hearts. You may attempt to cover it over or even run away from it, as many have tried throughout history. But once that vision has been written down, God will see to it that your deepest desire is to run with it! God takes no pleasure in the single-handed visionary. He delights in shoulder-to-shoulder workmanship. Habakkuk alludes to others who will read the vision that is written down and will then take up the race with the writer. These verses in the Bible imply that the runner who reads the vision should be able to do so quickly, with ease of understanding.

Participants in a race must know in advance the course that they are to run along. Without such information, they would not know where to start the race, where to finish it, or which route to take in between. If the race director simply explained to the runners, "This race will go from Los Angeles to New York City and back," their first question would be, "What route do you want us to take?" He might describe the route in full detail, but after a few miles those details would be forgotten by most. The person who envisions the race must also envision the plan for the course and put it on paper for the racers. Without the plan—without written directions—the runners could travel far off course and perhaps never finish the race at all—hopelessly lost! Consequently, every race *does* have a plan. A course *is* set. The vision of the race course *is* clearly written—with arrows, flags, and people along the way to keep the runner pointed in the right direction.

Your purpose in this life, as ordained by God, is very similar. The Lord has believers who will desire to run alongside you and assist with the accomplishment of your dream. If there is no written course, direction, or plan for them to observe, then it will be difficult for them to run with or proclaim your purpose, no matter how enthusiastic you may be. You *must* write down your purpose on paper. Multitudes of people are anxiously waiting for a dream—any dream—to run with! Although God has given His people many visions of their purpose and destiny, only those who have written them down can expect to fully enjoy the rewards that come as others run with them.

## Fire Trucks!

As I meditated on the Scripture in Habakkuk chapter 2, the Holy Spirit revealed to me just how this principle operates. Speaking to me in His language, I saw a vision, a picture in my mind. In the picture, I saw a bright red fire truck adorned with chrome handles and huge aluminum ladders sitting motionless by the curbside of a busy city street. There were no firemen anywhere around it. Many types of people walked by the truck and casually glanced at its gleaming exterior, but no one stopped or seemed very interested in it at all.

Then I saw a second fire truck. Suddenly this truck, which was an exact duplicate of the one sitting by the curb, came screaming down the narrow street with lights flashing, horn blowing, sirens blaring, and firemen dangling off the sides! It was heart-stopping! Everyone on the sidewalks turned their heads to see what was going on. Then an amazing thing began to occur. The very people who were all but ignoring the idle fire truck started leaping into their cars and chasing the speeding truck to its destination! The Lord spoke to me in my spirit and said through my thoughts, "People don't follow parked fire trucks. They follow the truck that makes noise and is obviously heading somewhere important. When you write down your purpose and begin to proclaim it with conviction, that it *will* be done, people will follow you too." That word changed my life when I put it into practice and found it to be true. I hope it changes yours in the same manner.

**We Need People**

When I launched Circus Alleluia Ministries, all I had to go on was one thought: Start a circus that gives glory to Jesus Christ. That was my total vision. It was not my purpose, although I thought so at the time. (I'll share my purpose with you in a moment.) If I had been content to allow that vision to remain a mere idea in my mind, Circus Alleluia would never have become a reality, hundreds of thousands of people may never have heard the gospel of Christ, and tens of thousands of people would not have been saved, healed, or delivered from demonic activity. But I took that thought and wrote it down. I began to write down every idea that could enlarge and advance that thought. Then I began to share those ideas with others.

An entire year passed before the first runner joined me in the race. That runner was my wife and she did not come quietly! It took a wounded cat and the world's shortest three-day fast to convince her that I was *not* insane and that God *was* leading me. Soon after Meg began the journey, my mother caught the vision. She was followed a few months later by my pastor, Dale Brooks. About three months after Dale began to run with us, the majority of his congregation was in hot pursuit. Over the ten years of its existence, literally thousands of people from across the U.S. and Canada came to believe in our vision and ran alongside us. Why? Because we did not let the fire engine sit quietly by the curb. We hit the sirens, flashed the lights, and took off! We produced. We worked hard. We did what we said we were going to do.

You must do the same with your purpose and destiny. People will run with you when you write down what you're going to do and get started on it. If you haven't yet written anything about your purpose, take out a pen and paper and jot down just the main points of it before you read on. This will be the beginning of your mission statement, which you will modify and work from for the remainder of your life.

## The Foundation Stones of Your Statement

There are six specific foundation stones to every mission statement. If any one is left out, you will have an uneven platform upon which to build the rest of your plan. Be sure that you understand each of these stones before you go on to create your destiny plan for the achievement of your purpose.

### Foundation Stone #1: Why

You must have a clear understanding of exactly why you are going to pursue the mission you are undertaking. Why do you have this purpose? Why do you want to see it done? Why will you refuse to quit along the way? Be careful not to answer these or any of the following questions too quickly. Pat answers have little power in them and will not withstand the objections and roadblocks you will encounter along the way. You must understand that long-term motivation also requires more than a simple "because God told me." You must have an unshakable confidence in your "why." You must be immovable, unstoppable, and irresistible! I cannot set forth the details of why you have the purpose that you do or why you will pursue it, but I can tell you that it is the most important stone of all. It is the cornerstone.

When you have an unshakable "why" engraved in your spirit and mind, others will be drawn to it because so few people ever attain a *passion* for anything. The world-trekking explorers, the great inventors, the champion athletes, the undaunted and often martyred missionaries know of this "why." They have experienced the rewards and the help rendered by those who see the "why" within them and wish to see them fulfill it! You can know the same rewards. You can help others reap their rewards as well, for you will inspire many with your "why." You will be a beacon to those who are groping in the darkness of their unsatisfied lives. You will take them with you, some in mind and others in body. Know and embrace your "why"; then write it plainly for all to know and understand as well.

### Foundation Stone #2: Who

**Try not to become a man of success, but rather to become a man of value.** (Albert Einstein)

Who are you? This is a question each person must answer for himself and for those going with him. This question must be answered in three distinct ways, though. First, you must know who you are personally and articulate who you are on paper. What have you accomplished to date? What is your personal history to the extent that it is relevant to your cause? Few of us take the time to think on such questions, but they are paramount to our purpose. They are a quick study on whether we presently have the ability to accomplish the purpose. If you have always been a plumber, but your purpose is to be a teacher, then you need to know that so you can change accordingly. You must know who you are.

Second, you need to know who you are philosophically. What is it that you believe? What do you stand for? What is the code you live by and will operate your purpose by? This is perhaps the most important of the three "who's" and is second only to your "why" in your mission statement. Your philosophy, your code of ethics, will color everything you think, say, and do—including the sum of your purpose and destiny.

Our philosophy is the code we live by. It is what our personality and character are founded upon. We have a perfect example of a godly philosophy in the Ten Commandments. Those commands are a written agenda for the people who would follow after God wholeheartedly. They address every area of life: spirit, soul, and body. They explain how we are to act toward God, toward our families, and toward our fellowman. They are a master list of living and have never been improved upon in over five thousand years of human existence. Entire civilizations have risen and fallen based upon their adherence to or neglect of those commands. My nation, the United States of America, still has the commandments posted in government offices and judicial buildings, even though our quickening decline from following them has been steadily rotting our society at the core.

I realize that Jesus said that if we love the Lord with all our heart, mind, and strength, and our neighbor as ourselves, then we will fulfill all the commandments. But I believe it is good for us to check the "Top 10" now and then to see how we're doing with the "All-Encompassing Two"! Also, there are many other teachings in the New Testament that apply to the Ten Commandments, but are not specifically mentioned in these two. For several years, as I contemplated these commandments, I longed for a simple way to remember and encompass them all in one short phrase or word. I finally found it. I call it the H.I.S. Way Code.

*H = Humility*

Humility is not often taught as a character trait, but it should be a basic one. Most people think of humiliation when they think of humility. They equate "doormat behavior" with humbling themselves. Nothing could be farther from the truth. Jesus was the most humble man who ever walked this earth, but no serious student of His life would consider Him a doormat. It was His humility that caused Him to say that He was "the Bread of Life" and "the Light of the World." He called Himself a prophet and equated Himself with God. To understand the humility Jesus exemplified, we need only turn to the Epistle to the Philippians. Here is what the Word of God has to say about the subject.

> *Do nothing from selfishness or empty conceit, but with humility of mind let each of you regard one another as more important than himself; do not merely look out for your own personal interests, but also for the interests of others. Have this attitude in yourselves which was also in Christ Jesus, who, although He existed in the form of God, did not regard equality with God a thing to be grasped, but emptied Himself, taking the form of a bond-servant, and being made in the likeness of men. And being found in appearance as a man, He humbled Himself by becoming obedient to the point of death, even death on a cross* (Philippians 2:3-8).

As we can see in this passage, humility is about giving your life away for others. It's about looking at others' lives and actually saying to yourself, with sincerity, that their needs are more important than your own. Christ's humility led Him to see His Deity as nothing to strive for, but as something to give up for the salvation of people, even though it called for His horrific death. That is powerful! That is humility.

To live a life of humility requires deciding to go against the grain of your pride and usually of society's view of you. But think of the rewards Jesus received. He not only got His life back in a glorified way, but His name became the greatest name in the universe and He opened the way for millions, and perhaps billions, to follow Him and even to do the miracles that He did! We will never surpass Jesus' work at the cross and tomb, but we can know His rewards. The law of the universe, sowing and reaping, is applicable in the life of humility. God does not forget. The law that states it is more blessed to give than receive is also played out for the humble person, because when you give your life to others and see their faces shining with gratitude, it is better than any material reward could ever be!

Right now, kneel before the Lord and ask Him to teach you about real humility and the tremendous rewards that it brings. Giving your life away for the lifting up of others is the best investment you can make. Why not start today?

*I = Integrity*

*He who walks in integrity walks securely* (Proverbs 10:9a).

*Better is a poor man who walks in his integrity than he who is perverse in speech and is a fool* (Proverbs 19:1).

*A righteous man who walks in his integrity—how blessed are his sons after him* (Proverbs 20:7).

*Vindicate me, O Lord, for I have walked in my integrity; and I have trusted in the Lord without wavering* (Psalm 26:1).

*O Lord, who may abide in Thy tent? Who may dwell on Thy holy hill? He who walks with integrity, and works righteousness, and speaks truth in his heart. He does not slander with his tongue, nor does evil to his neighbor, nor takes up a reproach against his friend; in whose eyes a reprobate is despised, but who honors those who fear the Lord; he swears to his own hurt, and does not change; he does not put out his money at interest, nor does he take a bribe against the innocent. He who does these things will never be shaken* (Psalm 15).

Integrity is such a powerful force. As you can see by these verses from Psalm 15, integrity entails so much of the Christian life. It is the way we walk out our life. More than a singular event in our lives, it is to be our lifestyle. It affects not only us but also those around us, especially our children. Because we have no darkness in our hearts, it allows us to ask boldly for vindication when we're in trouble. It has to do with honesty, kindness, and keeping our word.

Psalm 15 tells us that a man of integrity will *never* stumble. Do you understand what the word *never* means? It means not ever. Never stumble? I could enjoy that kind of life, couldn't you? Am I enjoying it? Are you? For the most part I believe that I am, but I want all of me to be that way. I want my integrity to be obviously evident in my life every day, every place, in every situation. But that will require more work on my part, for integrity is a decision and not a gift. God does not give you integrity; rather you develop it, cultivate it, seek it out, and chisel it out from the granite of your being.

As a child I became a pathological liar. That means it was sort of like a disease within me. I didn't even think about telling the truth if I thought a lie would do me better. This problem lasted long into my college years and I did not address it fully until I was in ministry. Yes, I had stopped most of my lying by then. I was honest about most everything. But if I was telling a story and thought a good embellishment would get a better laugh or more sympathy, I added the lie. Sad, isn't it?

After a session of storytelling one night with friends, Meg pointedly asked me why I felt it was necessary to lie about such things. I denied lying, of course, and a heated argument ensued. After the smoke cleared, the Lord convicted me through Meg's words, and I apologized and even asked for help. We decided that if she ever caught me lying, she had the right to stop me in mid-sentence and correct me. Sounds simple to the ladies reading this, but I can hear the men curling their toes up in their shoes! Let your wife correct you in public? Are you nuts? No, I was desperate! I was desperate to be clean before God and my wife. I will tell you that it was most unpleasant and quite embarrassing at times, and many times I lashed out at Meg afterward (only to apologize later). But I can also tell you that together we were able to kill that unclean habit. There are still times when I catch myself telling someone a "little white lie" (as if the color makes a difference), but I stop myself and say, "That is not true; it was like this."

My example may sound unnecessary to some, but honesty is paramount to a Christian's integrity and anointing. A philosophy void of integrity is void of God's power and strength. Keeping your word is a must for a life of integrity, yet many find it acceptable not to do so, even in Christian circles. Psalm 15 emphatically states that a righteous man will swear to or keep his word, even if it does him harm. That is powerful in a world where signed contracts are not worth the paper they are written on. Can we ever be right when we do not keep our word? Will our excuses stand before the presence of God and be counted worthy? If we are not ashamed to break our promises, are we truly disciples of Christ?

Give yourself this little test to see what your integrity quotient is.

1. Do you embellish stories for effect?
2. Do you intentionally drive over the speed limit, even though you signed a driver's license vowing that you would obey the speed laws?
3. Do you read, watch, or listen to things you would not if your spouse was with you or if Jesus was with you?
4. Do you cheat on your taxes?
5. Do you add items to your expense account that are not job related?
6. Is your word all that anyone ever needs in an agreement or commitment?
7. Do you hold any anger or unforgiveness toward a person whom you say you have forgiven?
8. Do you tithe ten percent on the gross instead of the net?
9. Do you give false or lame excuses to cover yourself when you do not keep your word, instead of admitting the truth?

10. Do your children feel confident that you will always keep your promises to them?

These are tough questions. But if you are to be a person whose philosophy is the guiding force of his existence, then that philosophy must be based upon the same integrity that Jesus walked in. It must be stumble-proof. The best question ever raised by which to judge our thoughts, words, and actions is this: What would Jesus do? Please don't walk away from this issue of integrity without being completely honest with yourself and taking your every thought, word, and deed into the convicting light of Christ's love. Your gain from nurturing integrity will be far greater than any you could possibly enjoy through neglecting it.

*S = Servant*

Becoming a servant allows you to be in control in every situation—in the right way. Think about the most serving people you know. Don't they seem to enjoy what they do for you and others? It's almost impossible for them not to serve people. My wife, again, is my greatest example in this area to me. When we go to someone else's home for a meal, she will always, 100 percent of the time, begin to clear the table and will usually wash the dishes unless the hostess aggressively insists that she not! While I'm sure we receive many more dinner engagements due to this phenomenon, it is simply a great example of someone whose heart is totally given to serving others.

I did not have this kind of heart. Mine was content to *be* served continually. I would have strolled through life, pleasantly allowing others to take care of me and rarely giving thought to serving them. But, of course, that is why the Lord arranged that Meg should be my wife. I needed to change and she was my example. When the Lord illuminated these verses in Philippians to me—that Jesus had become as a bondservant, a willing *slave* to the people around Him—I asked for such a heart as well. He gave it to me as I earnestly began to seek Him and it.

I began to study other Scriptures on serving and servanthood. Jesus taught His 12 disciples continuously that to be the one in charge meant you became the one who served. Being the "head honcho" was not the issue; being the willing servant was. As before, the Lord changed my heart when I began to seek the change. I began to follow my wife's lead and began clearing plates and offering help all over the neighborhood.

One summer I became the main furniture mover for some dozen or so families in our church congregation who were moving to new homes, often loading truck and trailer long into the night to get them on their way. I looked for every opportunity to serve someone else. It did not take long for my heart to relish this kind of life. It is, after all, the life of Jesus.

As our ministry grew, I began to teach our members to take on this servant's attitude. When we were on a tour with the circus, I instructed our troupe to wash the host's dishes, clean the house, and help in any way possible. It became a great blessing to us all. We also were showered with accolades of what servants we were. A servant's heart is one that wants to bless others, that looks for ways to help and care for them. That is what we became. Serving is our lifestyle now. It is who we are and who we want to be. I cannot think of one time when we served someone else that we did not learn and grow stronger from the experience. I'm sure that was the Master's plan all along.

Your philosophy, whatever you choose it to be, is what your purpose will reflect throughout your life. But be sure to stand every goal and dream of your destiny next to your philosophy and see if they complement each other. If they don't, change the inappropriate one. To be sure, no philosophy and no purpose will last long together when they are in disharmony with each other. The only way to ensure harmony is to ensure that your philosophy and purpose are God's.

**Foundation Stone #3: What**

What will you do? What are the main objectives of your mission? What do you plan to accomplish in your destiny? The "whats" of your mission statement are the nuts and bolts that you will build with. They are the goals you will strive for and attain over the years. These must be fully developed and laid out in a Master Destiny Plan. You must ask yourself and answer these "what" questions before you can create a mission statement or have a destiny. In subsequent chapters we will discuss exactly how to formulate goals and create your Master Destiny Plan. For your mission statement, however, you need only know the major goals of your purpose. Each major goal will be supported by multiple minor goals, and there will be too many of those to place inside a mission statement clearly. If you have truly discovered the purpose for which you were created by the Lord, you will obviously have some idea of what it will take to accomplish it. Simply take what you believe to be the main points and write them down. (The next chapter takes an extensive look at goals and goal-setting, so I will spend no more time here on the subject.) I suggest that you read Chapter 12 before you attempt to formulate your main objectives for your mission statement.

### Foundation Stone #4: When

Time lines are mandatory for every goal of your destiny. Without time lines you have no set point of departure or attainment that is measurable. Yes, you will have minor points to each goal, but if you never set the time to begin or have no idea of when you will end, then you cannot honestly judge your progress. A builder who takes ten years to complete one house will not be in business long, if at all. Time frames are a must. The world, like it or not, revolves around the timely completion of things.

Your mission statement must have clearly defined time lines for every goal. You must have a definite date by which you will accomplish your life purpose, as well as the major and minor goals that will get you there. Even though your purpose and destiny may expand as you discover new goals to achieve along the way, you must still enlist the use of target dates and deadlines to reach each of those steps. (This subject of time is addressed at length in another chapter where I will cover the many facets of how time affects our destiny.)

### Foundation Stone #5: How

This is the strategy you will employ to achieve your goals. It's the details in a summarized form, in a manner of speaking. When you work on your Master Destiny Plan for the fulfillment of your destiny and purpose, you will be quite detailed in the "how" of things. For your mission statement, though, you will give only the overview. Of course, it will still require you to *know* the details. That means you must understand your main and minor goals; the applicable, workable time frames; and other resources that we will discuss later.

### Foundation Stone #6: Where

No surprises here; it's just exactly where will you live and perform your destiny. Of course, this can be tricky if your destiny requires travel, but people will normally have a base of operations for whatever the Lord has for them. Simply include the physical location of your work by city, state, and nation. If you will be traveling to accomplish your goals, be sure to have a list of the general and/or specific places you will be going. This can be especially beneficial for those whom the Lord is preparing to bring your way to assist you. If someone has a purpose in England and you do too, when he or she reads it on your mission statement, the Lord can use it as a confirmation for that individual to join with you for a time, or maybe even permanently.

After you have completely secured these six foundation stones, you must again ask yourself these questions:

- Is this really what I believe the Lord has planned for me?
- Am I passionate about this?
- Can I give my life to this?

If you cannot answer yes to these questions, then you need to go back to the Lord and ask Him to show you what the problem is. If changes are to be made, have no fear. Even though the major and minor goals may change across the map of your lifetime, your purpose will remain the same: It is your life goal, that one thing you were created to go for and accomplish.

**Your mission is not what you aim for; it is your very reason for being. It is your destiny.** (W.G.)

When I first discovered that my purpose was to preach the Word of God and train others to do the same around the world, I had already started Circus Alleluia Ministries. I naturally thought, in my youthful lack of knowledge, that I would accomplish my life's work through the circus and the different facets of the ministry we felt that we were to create. I was wrong. The Lord directed me differently.

When we ended the circus in 1988, it was with the understanding that I was to pursue the prophetic ministry full-time until further notice. Did my purpose change? No. My plans changed on how to walk it out. My major and minor goals were adjusted. My location was changed. My sphere of influence was suddenly radically different. But I never received a word from the Lord that my *purpose* was any different. That is very freeing in the midst of radical changes. (We will discuss the power and necessity of change in the chapter entitled, "Powered by Change.") Here's how the Lord changed my plan, but not my purpose.

During the four years after laying down the circus, Meg and I were moved by the Lord to Kansas City, where we became involved in the leadership of the church that is now Metro Christian Fellowship, pastored by Mike Bickle. I was groomed in the prophetic ministry for six years by some very seasoned ministers and still take their counsel in many matters. Four years into that apprenticeship time, the Lord powerfully led me out of full-time ministry and into the business world. Did my purpose change then? Not at all. I was still teaching the Word in home group settings and at Grace Training Center, an affiliate Bible school with Metro Christian Fellowship. I was still taking people through intense counseling. I was still helping fledgling prophetically gifted believers to learn their gifts. All the while, I was full-time in business. My plans changed, but *not* my purpose.

This is the dichotomy of creating a Master Destiny Plan and writing a mission statement. We must prepare as if they will never change, yet always hold them with an open hand, ready to change at any moment. But that is not a cause for confusion. God is not interested in keeping us on edge, wondering if we will get to finish one thing before He changes His mind. If and when He redirects our path, our purpose will not change and we will continue to fulfill the destiny He has set before us. He will usually let us know in advance and will give us plenty of time to adjust to the change. After all, He loves us.

> *For I am confident of this very thing, that He who began a good work in you will perfect it until the day of Christ Jesus* (Philippians 1:6).

## Life Areas

An easy way to gather the information needed to write out your general mission statement is to make a mission statement for each life area and then transfer the main issues to your overall mission statement. Using the form in the Appendix of your *Destiny Planner®* makes this an easier task.

For example, one of the major goals on my overall mission statement is to have a lifelong, loving marriage to my wife, Meg. (This would come under the "Social" heading of the Life Areas section in my *Destiny Planner®*.) When Meg and I were married, we agreed on several objectives. These became our minor goals. For instance, we wanted to 1) remain married our entire lives; 2) raise godly children to serve the Lord; and 3) open our home to let others who needed help live with us.

All these goals required education and skill that we did not possess in our early 20's. But we made plans to get the know-how we needed and so followed the plan. We have accomplished almost every one of our goals after more than 20 years of marriage, save the ones that will be walked out until the day we go to Heaven. It has not always been easy, but our agreed-upon goals made us more willing to persevere during the rough times.

We did not have a form to fill out a mission statement, nor had we even the thought of such a statement. But we did write down our goals as they came to us and we agreed to do them. We did so by *choice* because we wanted to please God and help people. It has proven to be extremely beneficial and has allowed others to observe our lives and follow our example as we lined up with God's Word and will—which is my overall life vision, to "be an example of one who believes." None of this would have happened if Meg and I had not sat down and discussed what we wanted and what the Lord was leading us to do. It was up to us. It was those humble beginnings that led to our development of more skills in goal-setting and the daily accomplishment of the will of God for our lives.

We have applied these skills to every area of life and have found them to be just as effective. We have developed plans for finances, health, spiritual growth, and so on. Most of those plans have developed into strong daily habits that demand little or no maintenance. It has required discipline and will power in many of these areas, but the cost has been balanced well into the benefit side of the equation.

## Final Thoughts

I urge you to look over the list of Life Areas in Chapters 4 and 5. Then begin to write out goals in each of them, which will flesh out your overall mission statement. Take all the time necessary to formulate these goals under the correct headings. This will be invaluable in formulating a clear and concise statement of your destiny within your mission statement.

The clearer your goals in your mission statement are, the easier it will be for you and those running with you to stay focused and on track to successful accomplishment. In our next chapter, we'll discuss just what goals are and how to make them release their innate power to your benefit and to the benefit of those you'll encounter along the journey of fulfilling your purpose. We'll also discuss how to avoid the traps that goals can present.

# Chapter 12

## Releasing the Power of Goals

*I press on toward the goal for the prize of the upward call of God in Christ Jesus* (Philippians 3:14).

I have listened to dozens upon dozens of tapes on success, planning, motivation, and time management and have read scores of books, including biographies of many great men and women. The one factor that is constant above all else in every message and in every biography is that of creating within yourself the invaluable skill of goal-setting. Each successful person whom I have studied, interviewed, read, listened to, or sought counsel from agreed: *Goal-setting is not an option*; it is mandatory for high achievement. Yet it is a skill that anyone can develop through diligent practice. Don't wait until you are proficient to actually begin creating goals; just get started and the skill will come. As your proficiency increases, it will mean that you spend less time actually formulating the goals, and your goals will be more measurable and attainable. So with this in mind, let's begin our course in goal-setting.

**You only get the goals you set!** (W.G.)

Like it or not, that is the truth. But to set a goal you must know what you want. If you never decide what you want, then you won't have much more than what others give you—and that may not make you very happy. It certainly won't fulfill you. Goals are the stuff of life. They give us course. They are our destiny, our future, our source of doing. The need to have goals is built into the fabric of every person's being—we can't escape it. Our individual purpose, destiny, and achievements are all subject to and fulfilled by the doing of the goals that make them up. That truth should be enough to make all of us expert goal-setters.

**To get what you want, you must know what you want and passionately want what you want!** (Anon.)

When Jesus said, "All things are possible to him who believes" (Mk. 9:23b), He was stating the two facts that make mankind different from any other being in creation.

**Fact #1:** You have the ability to believe in something before it happens.

**Fact #2:** You can accomplish whatever you believe will happen.

That is the stuff of goals! Goals fire us with hope. They kindle the flames of belief. They are not merely stepping stones to a greater good; they are the very heart and soul of that greater good. Most of the time it is the *journey* along the "goals path" that is more important than the *destination.*

Earlier in this book we mentioned the soul-stirring truth that an individual without a personal purpose is doomed to perish, being unguided and unrestrained, without a cause higher than his or her own existence. What is a purpose? A vision? A revelation? Are they not goals? It is the destination of our purpose that captivates us and draws us through our lives with hope, curiosity, and excitement, and it is the goals within the vision that make up the days, weeks, years, and decades upon decades of life. If you have a fear or disdain for goals or for setting them, please discard it now. You cannot go on in this book, or with any power in your life for that matter, without a healthy love for goal-setting and goal-achieving. So, from this point on I will assume that you have such a love and are eager to tap the power inherent in goals.

*The primary key to setting goals is to have a clearly defined desire.* Ask yourself again, "What exactly do *I* want?" If you cannot answer that question, then you cannot set your goals. We have already discovered the groundwork of desire: It is your God-ordained purpose in this life. Once that is established, your goal-setting can begin. At the same time, do not be afraid to have desires that seem to stem from your own heart, but are not directly ordained as part of your purpose. I firmly believe that if you are seeking the will of God with all your heart, you will not have, or at least give in to, desires that are out of line with the will of God for you. If you *do* have such good desires, don't be afraid to plan their achievement in the same way we will outline next.

I have found, over the past 25 years of setting and achieving goals, that there are six basic phases many people tend to go through in this process. I believe that if you have a proper understanding of the process and of the possible hindrances that you may encounter, you will have a greater confidence to begin or complete the goals you need to fulfill your destiny. The following is not an exhaustive list, but it has served me well over the years, and I have found similar lists among the volumes of books I have studied. As you read through these phases, you may be inspired by new possibilities in this realm of goal-achievement. (If you do discover new areas, would you please write to me and allow me to incorporate them into our training materials? The one thing I know for certain is that I certainly do not know everything!)

## Phase #1: Goal Failure

Failing to complete a goal can be devastating and discouraging. But I believe that not even attempting to set goals is far more dangerous. It's my contention that if you are made aware of the pitfalls that cause the failure to achieve goals, *before* you fall into them, then you can easily avoid them. Hopefully such snares will *never* overtake you. As with everything shared in this book, the choice is yours.

### Cause of Failure to Set and Achieve Goals #1: Fear

Many people fear setting goals for two main reasons. First, they are afraid that they will never reach them! The fear of not accomplishing something you really want to get done is what the writer of Proverbs meant when he stated, "Hope deferred makes the heart sick" (Prov. 13:12a). Fear saps us of strength and divests us of joy. We've all experienced such setbacks, and the thought that we might inflict another such wound through dreamy goal-setting can be unpleasant to say the least. Pain, our mind will tell us, is to be avoided at all costs. But it is precisely when such thoughts pop up that we must take them "captive to the obedience of Christ" (see 2 Cor. 10:5) and say, " I *will* do this thing! I will *not* be stopped! I *will* succeed!" We must believe God's

Word when He said, "For God hath not given us the spirit of fear; but of power, and of love, and of a sound mind" (2 Tim. 1:7 KJV). (We'll talk more about controlling our mind in a later chapter.)

The second fear of failure is we're afraid we *will* reach our goals. I believe that this second fear is the more insidious of the two. Fear of success is actually *fear of change.* Change, as we will see in a later chapter, is what being a Christian is all about. It's about becoming a new creature, a new person in Christ. However, stepping outside our comfort zones or the status quo, which is the daily actions/results of our lives, requires that we be vulnerable. Being vulnerable to becoming something different from what we presently are can be paralyzing. But if we allow the paralysis to take root, we deny ourselves the as yet unknown glories of change. For instance, it's hard for a baby who's been crawling for several months to one day just stand upright and begin to walk. The child falls continually, and sometimes painfully. But when the goal of walking is achieved, it opens up many new avenues of opportunity to the little one, usually to the chagrin of the parents! Suddenly more things are in reach and the time it takes to get to where that little one wants to go is cut in half. So it is with many changes in life.

*Be anxious for nothing...* (Philippians 4:6).

To be afraid of successfully achieving a goal is sin, pure and simple. Why? What we are really saying through our immobility is that we do not trust God to take care of us through the changes that accomplishing these goals will render. If we cannot trust God to change us, we have a very shaky relationship with our Creator/Father. But we *are* to become something we never were before, and that will require a lot of change! When we make Jesus Christ our Savior and Lord, we change our speech, our attitudes, our temperament, our thoughts, our friends, and many other things. Believe it or not, very little of that happens without our agreeing and setting the goal to make those changes.

Refuse to let any kind of fear paralyze or discourage you. I realize that is easier said than done at times, and you may need help in resisting fear, but do it! Remember, "perfect love casts out fear" (1 Jn. 4:18). Don't let satan steal your dream at the goal level. Remember how much God loves you. Just like the parents whose baby is learning to take his first step, God's arms are outstretched to catch you should you fall. God's love compels Him to watch over you. He's more than able to take care of you.

### Cause of Failure to Set and Achieve Goals #2: Irresponsibility

We covered this subject sufficiently in a previous chapter, so I will not repeat myself here. Suffice it to say, you are ultimately responsible for setting your own goals and seeing them through. Fingerpointing is for the immature. Achieving your goals is up to you.

### Cause of Failure to Set and Achieve Goals #3: Lack of Knowledge

Knowing the "need-to" or "how-to" of goals is pivotal to achievement. The Bible clearly states that God's "people are destroyed for lack of knowledge" (Hos. 4:6). Just follow the logic and you will see that if you do not know how to set and perform goals, you will never do so, and therefore you will achieve multiple times less than if you had the needed knowledge. How many inventions have been postponed or lost because someone lacked the knowledge of how to set goals along the way to his or her discovery? What time has been lost as would-be artists, builders, leaders, and business people were forced to learn their crafts without the aid of solid goal-setting and their achievement techniques? Why, even though every successful venture in life requires it, is goal-setting not yet a subject taught in our grade schools or in the majority of our universities (though one of *my* personal goals is to change that!)?

Don't let a lack of knowledge in setting and accomplishing goals steal from you. Learn by taking advantage of every seminar, book, and tape you can find. Get it in you! Be tenacious about gathering knowledge, and you will never be disappointed—ever. Learning to learn has been the best lesson I have learned to date!

### Cause of Failure to Set and Achieve Goals #4: Not Believing in Yourself

This is another paralyzing state of mind. The moment we believe we cannot, we will not! Whether our lack of confidence is based in fact or fiction, the results will be the same: zero! We cannot afford to fall into the trap of "self unbelief." We must believe the Scriptures that say, "I can do all things through Him [Christ] who strengthens me" (Phil. 4:13), and "all things are possible" (Mt. 19:26) because we believe in Jesus! We cannot allow ourselves any other options if we are to live out our God-given purpose.

Of all the failure traps, this one has snared me the most. I was not a self-confident child, youth, or young man. I still struggle with thoughts of insecurity. For whatever reason, I just never felt confident in myself. This insecurity, however, actually forced me to confront it. I realized that no one was going to help me through the dark nights of my soul until I did. If I didn't do something about it, I knew that I would wind up a statistic in some boring magazine story on teen dysfunctionalism. (That possibility was scarier than my insecurity!) Before I learned of the Scriptures just quoted and gave my life completely to Christ, I had to push myself out of the shadow of my insecurity totally by myself. It was not an easy task!

It was the pain of not being accepted by my peers that first gave me the impetus to move out from under the cloud of self-doubt. I did this in sports—surfing—and in school. Surfing was great; there was no competition. Progress was easy to see, and in a short while compliments were many from my fellow surfers. Scholastic sports were a different story, as I mentioned in Chapter 3 in our discussion of gifts. It was plain and simple: When it came to most sports, I had no gifts! But just attempting those sports brought some recognition, even if it was mostly sympathy. Anything was better than nothing at that point. Those bits of recognition were enough of a boost to my confidence to propel me into college, where I chalked up more peer recognition in martial arts and circus, which spurred me on to enter the ministry.

I read an article years ago that summarized my feelings on this subject of insecurity. Its basic conclusion was, if you are afraid to do something, then do it scared! I thought that was so profound. It is okay to be afraid of your own inadequacy; just go do anyway whatever it is you want to do. I realize that this may sound simplistic to you, but it was freeing to me. When I read in the Florida State University newspaper in April 1973 that men were needed in the Flying High Circus, my first thought was that I'd be afraid to be embarrassed learning new things in front of my peers. But my second thought, *Go give it a try anyway!*, actually set the course of my life for the next 17 years. So I give you the same mandate: Don't be paralyzed by your personal lack of confidence; just go do it scared!

## Phase #2: Goal Measurability

Without the ability to measure our progress, we will never know if we are near to completing a goal. No athlete competes without daily practice sessions to see how much closer he is to his best time, longest jump, or farthest throw. It would also be foolhardy to run a business without some sort of record keeping to see if we are gaining or losing money, clients, and assets. Therefore, it is imperative to set goals in such a manner that we can easily track our progress toward achievement. We must know that we have advanced; it is our fuel for greater confidence and greater achievement.

## Goal Types

There are two types of goals, measurable or tangible and immeasurable or intangible. The measurable goals are those you can actually see taking place, such as building bigger muscles, earning more money, or getting a new job. You can touch, taste, see, hear, or smell a tangible goal. It has actual substance. Intangible goals are things like becoming stronger in your Christian faith or increasing your ability to make decisions. You can't actually feel or see these types of changes or goals being accomplished, even though they are just as real as the ones you can see and touch. The goal to build a circus to preach the gospel of Jesus Christ was a tangible goal. The goal to gain control of my anger was an intangible goal. Regardless of the type, your goals can still be tracked by setting smaller, minor goals along the way to achieving your main goals.

## Minor Goals

Each goal you have must be broken down into small, measurable, bite-sized goals for easier accomplishment. This will allow you to project many years into the future (your destiny) with goals, and yet begin working on them today. Simply put, you need only to decide on the goal and immediately begin to plan for its fruition, taking the first step as soon as possible. Of course some of your goals will not allow you to begin on them until others have been completed or at least have gotten under way. But if you have planned out the needed resources and have plotted your personnel and finances, then your long-range goals can be kept in front of you until the opportune time arrives to start their engines. I have set goals for business and ministry decades ahead but have the plans prepared for them now. I have no idea as to when some are to begin, but when that time comes, I am already prepared and cannot be caught off guard. That is a confidence builder! You can do it too, with any goal of your destiny.

## Phase #3: Goal Force

**The stronger the "why," the easier the "how."**
(Anon.)

### Motivation

Motivation is a funny concept. It is amazing what can motivate people. Some are motivated by money; others by things. Still others are motivated by love or hate. Some people are motivated by sheer will, while others are motivated by fear. But there is only one motivating factor that can stand the test of time and the trials of life. This motivating force is not subject to the whimsy of the mind or the fickleness of emotions. It is not directed by our needs, wants, or fears in the long term. It is the one factor that no one can stop and that has spurred men to conquer the unconquerable and win the unwinnable. It is the very thing that we began this study with. The number one motivating factor in life is belief in something higher than one's self—it's *believing*.

A person energized by his belief in something, be it a quest, an assignment, a person, or a pipe dream, is unstoppable.

- When Goliath taunted the entire army of Israel into fearful immobility, it was the unobstructed belief of a teenage shepherd boy that took the giant's head from his shoulders and defeated an entire army in a single day!
- When a century and a half of racial segregation loomed seemingly impenetrable on the landscape of America, Martin Luther King, Jr.'s belief in a dream of equality led the African-American community to defy the dangers of protest and changed the face of a nation in a generation.
- Belief caused Thomas Edison to endure over 10,000 experiments on one idea before he successfully created the incandescent lightbulb and illuminated the world.
- Belief pushed Columbus to the limits of the known world and brought him back again with a new land on the maps for all to explore after him.

- Belief led Abraham Lincoln to endure years of political defeat and a presidency ravaged by civil war, and to unify a nation and end slavery as it was then known.
- Belief was the motivator behind the greatest act of love ever displayed, when Christ Jesus gave up His life for the lives of all who went before Him and would come after Him. Thousands of martyrs have followed His path by choosing to lose their lives rather than deny their belief in Him as Lord. There is no stronger motivator than belief.

**Motivation is a fire from within.**
**If someone else tries to light that fire under you,**
**chances are it will burn very briefly.**
(Stephen Covey)

Temporary thrills or perishable crowns can rarely sustain someone for a lifetime. Mere goals in themselves are shoddy motivation. It is the greater whole of which the goals are a part that urges us on. It is "the prize of the high calling of God in Christ Jesus" (Phil. 3:14 KJV) that is to be our motivation, however He ordains that we are to live it out. It is the only motivation that can keep us fulfilled for a lifetime. It is the only source reliable enough, the only source worthy enough.

There is tremendous power in believing. Scientific studies have shown that human beings can actually change their physiology through believing. Researchers have given volunteers strong depressant drugs and told them that the drugs were powerful stimulants. The "human guinea pigs" believed the scientists and their bodies actually began to create the drugs they thought they were receiving! Their physical systems began to bring into reality what the person believed and actually overrode the drugs they had ingested. This was not "mind over matter." This was mind *manipulating* matter! Their bodies merely did what the people believed. "For as he [a man] thinketh in his heart, so is he" (Prov. 23:7a KJV).

This type of belief-initiated change, which is a Neuro Physical Response (NPR), is well documented. It has even been seen in classroom studies with differing ages of students. Teachers are told that certain students entering their classes are exceptionally bright, but can get distracted, so the teacher must be sure to keep them concentrating. The truth is that the students are actually poor learners. But the belief of the teacher that the students are smarter than average is related to the underachieving kids in such a way that in a few weeks they have become some of the top students in their classes!

This life-changing power of NPR is somehow linked directly to the physical and mental abilities of a person. It is not inspired by devil worship or hypnotism. It is a real mechanism placed in your being by your Creator. Neuro Linguistic Programing (NLP), which is based on these same principles, was introduced as a way to deliberately *program* your brain and life to become exactly what you want it to be. I am not going to address NLP or any other similar sciences as good or evil in this book, but I do give this caution: As a Christian, your beliefs must be in line with the Word of God and must be rooted and grounded in a relationship with Him. Dabbling in such things as NLP without focusing your desired end on the will of God is dangerous, and I would not advise you do so without being accountable to a group of spiritual leaders or peers.

Humanism, a recognized religion that places the will of *man* at its center, thrives on such mind-based science because it so easily elevates the person to equality with deity. Because NRP, NLP, and other such sciences *do* work and *have* changed countless lives, it can be tantalizing for a Christian to think that all his or her troubles may be solved with this miraculous technique. Although that may be true, you must be completely honest with yourself about to whom you are giving control of yourself. Is *God* leading you in such activity? Will it bring Him glory? Will it benefit others? If you can answer yes to these questions, and I make no judgments here about that possibility, then you could proceed as you feel confident enough to do so. But if you cannot answer yes, put it on the shelf until such time as you feel the Lord releases you. Be sure, as I said, to stay accountable to wise, spiritual leaders and peers along the way.

## The Source of Our Motivation

Each of the previous examples—the belief-motivated achievements of some of history's greatest—are rooted in a "why" strong enough to make the person face fierce and often deadly odds to achieve his goals. The "whys" of your life must be greater than you. They must be stronger than you. They must be more valuable than you. They must be more worthy than you. And as I noted at the beginning of this book, they must glorify God and help people. You see, those are the strongest "whys" there are. Those two "whys" will make any "how" easier to endure. If your purpose is centered on the good of others and on the glorification of the Lord Jesus, the "how" will be merely steps along the way. Yes, those steps may be perilous in many ways, but the source of your motivation, your belief in the goal, will make them pale in comparison.

You are motivated more by what you believe than by any other aspect of your being. A man filled with the desire to serve God is aware that the source of his belief is at the same time the object of his quest: namely, the will of God for him personally. Know what you believe. Guard your heart and mind from beliefs that are not firmly grounded in the will and Word of God. It is only in God's will and Word that you can stand in perfect confidence. It is there your belief is coupled with the supernatural power of your Lord Jesus. It is there you will find the strength to give in to nothing but what you believe. No matter what your goal, as a Christian, the Lord Jesus is the final destination. It is fulfilling His life through you that must be your ultimate belief and therefore your ultimate motivation. Such a source, such a power, is unstoppable.

**Benefits**

There is no need to apologize for being rewarded for accomplishing your goals. Many times the completion of the goal is all the reward you need to spur you to victory. But God is not against rewarding those who achieve. David was angered that Goliath defied the armies of Israel, the nation who had a covenant with God, but the bounty of the rewards was also of enough interest to him that he asked about it more than once before he went to battle. David received several rewards upon completing the goal of ensuring Goliath's demise.

1. Israel was liberated in spirit and body, and the enemy's army was destroyed.
2. David was heralded as a hero mightier than the king himself.
3. David received the king's daughter in marriage.
4. David's family was relieved of all taxes for the rest of their lives.

Not a bad haul for acting on what you believe!

Again though, be sure that your benefits list is not filled solely with what rewards you. People and God are the bottom line. Although God is definitely interested in our pleasure, He also wants us to share the wealth with our fellowman. Benefits need not be merely temporal, either. Our goals should point to a purpose and destiny that extends beyond the limits of our personal life. We should look for the benefits we generate to reach at least two generations beyond our own.

Proverbs exhorts us to leave an inheritance for our children and our children's children (see Prov. 13:22), but I have no intention of stopping there. My purpose dictates the production of materials that will be timeless in nature and just as relevant in 200 years as they are the day I publish them. I want to leave behind far more than a nice tombstone and some faded photos. Go past your own time and space and see history holding a long-term place for your accomplishments. No matter what your purpose is, you can and should expand its limits far beyond your finite time here on earth.

When you begin to think in that realm, you will begin to believe that you can do much more than you ever dreamed of. I personally believe that Christians should be the grandest thinkers and dreamers on the planet, only to be outdone by their accomplishments! I believe that Romans 11:36 is true: "For from Him and through Him and to Him are all things..." That means everything of value on this planet is for God, is from God, and should be given back to God by His people. We must take off the limits and go farther! The benefits of our goals, the stepping stones of our destiny, are to be extraordinary! Could we do any less for our God, especially when He has pledged His help to us?

## Phase #4: Goal Fields

**Goals give you the specific direction to take to make your dreams come true.** (Bob Conklin)

### Your Life Areas

I have mentioned the six major Life Areas in other chapters, so let's spend a little more time on them here. These are the same areas you used as categories when you made your dream list in Chapter 2 and included as part of your mission statement (or made a mission statement for each). Now you must commit to setting definite goals in these areas if you wish to see your dreams and desires come true. I have found over the years that few people think about these areas as actual segments of their lives that *require* goals and plans. Consequently, most people suffer in the areas they do not esteem. I do not want you to fall short of the benefits that your goals in any area of your life will produce. But before we talk about goal-setting for these areas, let's talk some more about *benefits*.

Everything we accomplish has benefits or rewards beyond the actual achievement itself. We see that David reached his goal of killing Goliath and then reaped multiple benefits beyond the goal. Such benefits will, when in the realm of your God-ordained purpose and destiny, accomplish three distinct things:

1. Bring God glory.
2. Help people.
3. Bring positive change to you.

These benefits spread out as you achieve more and more, creating a sort of ripple effect. Drop a pebble into a pond and before long the ripples will touch every drop of the water surface and every inch of the shoreline. So it is with reaching goals in our Life Areas. There is little you will achieve in one Life Area that does not ripple into other Life Areas, bringing more glory to Him and helping more people, while changing you more for the better. That is the economy of God. When He ordains our purpose, He makes sure that as many blessings are given out as possible. Everyone wins!

To this end, I have placed three columns pertaining to the rewards and benefits just discussed on the Destiny Goals Worksheet in your *Destiny Planner®*. This worksheet allows you to keep not only your goals but also their benefits before you for added motivation.

*The Half-Dozen Rule*

Although there can be multiple goals under each Life Area, I find it easier to keep the number small for better control and accomplishment. This is more consistent with what is called "success by the Half-Dozen Rule," which states that everything you want to learn or master has only about a half dozen points to it. These are the basics. I have listed below each Life Area and the half dozen or so points of mastery for each. These are the *prerequisites* that I have found to be most beneficial to concentrate on over the past 25 years in attaining my goals, though you may place emphasis on others.

These basics are the daily disciplines you should master first, before you set specific goals in a Life Area. For example, if your goal is to be a worship leader, then you must first master a life of private worship. If your goal is to own assets of one million dollars, then you must first master the basics of budgeting, saving, and investing. If your goal is to be an Olympic champion, then you must first master the basics of good nutrition, exercise, and rest. Your goals will fail or succeed by the quality of your diligence in the basics of the Half-Dozen Rule. Again, this is a partial list, but by doing these you will find yourself discovering others.

1. Spirit
   - Bible study
   - prayer
   - worship
   - fellowship with other believers
   - giving
   - witnessing to unbelievers about Christ
2. Intellect
   - being decisive
   - taking time to think
   - taking your thoughts captive to the obedience of Christ (2 Cor. 10:5)
   - meditating on the Word of God (Ps. 1; Josh. 1:8)
   - promoting self-education (books, tapes, seminars)
   - gaining wisdom (study Proverbs)
3. Personality
   - be passionate about life
   - be humble
   - have integrity
   - be a kind and compassionate servant
   - be confident, yet vulnerable
   - have a positive attitude

4. Physical
   - nutritious food
   - daily exercise
   - rest/sleep
   - good hygiene
   - stress reduction
   - nutritional supplements

5. People
   - extended family
   - spouse
   - children
   - friends
   - fellow workers
   - neighbors
   - community and church groups

6. Money
   - budget (income greater than expenses)
   - tithe (at least ten percent of gross)
   - give generously
   - save (at least ten percent)
   - obtain adequate insurance
   - make wise investments

If you have not yet established specific goals for these six areas of your life, you can concentrate on just the half dozen items under each heading above. Many people never get started because they think that there is too much to change or do. Just pick one item in one heading at a time to keep from feeling overwhelmed. Then set your goals and go after them. If you will *diligently* perform these simple half dozen skills, your life will take a dramatic turn for the better in every way. Once you begin to master these basics, you will be well on your way to attaining any goals you may set in these categories!

**Inch by inch, anything's a cinch!** (Robert Schuller)

### Phase #5: Goal Flow

Your purpose will affect all the areas mentioned above. Every goal of each area should form a complementary chain with one another. Would it make sense for the Lord to give you a purpose and destiny that required goals not flowing in the same current? Of course not. It is a simple matter to check your personal goals and see if they all point in the same direction—your destiny's direction. If you find any that do not, then you will need to take them before the Lord and discuss them. You cannot afford to be sidetracked or misguided by incongruent goals.

This does not mean that you cannot have goals that are not directly in line with your purpose. For instance, I have goals that entail some rather adventurous endeavors, like rafting the Snake River or flying in a jet fighter. They also happen to be a lot of fun, and my heavenly Father loves it when I have fun. If you've ever seen the movie *Chariots of Fire*, you might remember Eric Lidell's famous line, "When I run, I can feel God's pleasure!" That's how I feel when I do those types of things.

Goals out of sync with your purpose might be something like this. Say your purpose in life is to be a grade school teacher. To join the Marines and become a drill sergeant would take you from the classroom and is obviously not be in line with your purpose. Or if your purpose is to be a professional athlete, but you sign up to be an astronaut, then you are probably off the mark. You must make sure that you don't waste time on goals that take you away from your purpose instead of leading you toward it. Ask yourself this question when you doubt that a goal is congruent: *Is this what my destiny is about?* As you contemplate this question, trust the Holy Spirit to confirm its truth to you using the confirmation steps outlined in Chapter 7.

## Phase #6: Goal Follow Through

*But we are not of those who shrink back to destruction, but of those who have faith to the preserving of the soul* (Hebrews 10:39).

Following through on a goal or a series of goals is by far the most important, and often the most difficult, effort in your entire destiny. It requires the flow of so many different aspects of your being into one continuous stream of action. That may sound a bit dramatic, but it is true just the same. You cannot simply divide up your life and then concentrate only on a singular action. Everything you do will affect everything else in your destiny to some extent. You are not a series of finite actions, but an infinite flow, like a river flowing to the sea, the destination.

There are twists and turns and boulders and waterfalls and dams along the way, but *persistence* keeps the flow going strong.

Water is a persistent and usually unstoppable entity. (Just ask a plumber!) If the source is never sealed off or dried up, a river will flow forever. You must see your life as similar to the river. Every area of your life is a tributary adding strength and power, mass and ability to the whole. The Amazon River is only as powerful as the sum of its thousands of rills. I've seen the mighty Mississippi all but dried up due to the lack of rain in its contributing streams. But I've also seen it overflowing with the surging forces of its supply lines. Our goals, our lives, will act similarly, ebbing and flowing with the supply of each Life Area as we work toward their completion.

There are specific actions to take as you perform each goal. The idea is not to check these off as your perform them, as on a list, but instead to make them a part of your daily lifestyle. These items are to be woven into the fabric of your being through repetition and continual meditation on them. It won't take very long, because as you do them, they will pay rich dividends, which will act to solidify them to your spirit. I will give these points here in an overview fashion, since each of them is discussed in detail in other sections of this book.

1. **Passionately believe** in your goals, destiny, and purpose; it is mandatory to sustain motivation for the long term.
2. **Decide not to quit** no matter what gets in your way as you work toward achieving your goals.
3. **Write out your goals** in detail so you can be sure not to miss any part of your destiny.
4. **Plan proactively**, looking at the details of your goals and covering every resource.
5. **Set time frames**, or deadlines, for each point of each goal and do your best to stick to them.
6. **Anticipate possible problems** that you may encounter and have ready a proper and expedient solution.

7. **Learn any needed skills** or gather to yourself those who have such skills.

8. **Seek mentors or coaches** who can give you their wisdom and help guide you toward your goals.

## Final Thoughts

We've said a lot about goals in this chapter and I do not want you to be overwhelmed by the prospect of having to know or do all these specifics immediately. We will cover the how-to's of turning your goals into proactive and productive plans in the next chapter. What I do want you to consider, though, is the fact that you will *not* fulfill your purpose, you will *not* live the destiny you were meant to live, you will *not* achieve your proper destination in life, without a clear *commitment* to formulating and performing the goals necessary to get you there. Do not be fooled into thinking that life just "happens" to you and that you will simply "happen" to achieve the heights of accomplishment ordained for you by your Creator. That will *not* "happen"!

You must take the bull of your future by the horns, look it squarely in the eyes, and tell it where you want to go and how you are going to get there. If you can hold on to that picture, that commitment, then you will go farther than you ever dreamed possible! You will accomplish more than the majority of your peers. You will be in demand by those wanting to do the same. As always, the choice is yours.

**Winners make goals; losers make excuses.** (Anon.)

# Chapter 13

# Proactive Planning

**I will study, I will prepare, and my day will come.**
(Abraham Lincoln)

If there is any one place where people fall down in the pursuit of their purpose, it is in the area of planning. Planning sounds mundane, boring, tedious, and just plain not fun. Well, all that can be true, but it need not be. If you can grasp the big picture of just what productive planning can do for every area of your life—how it can motivate, stimulate, and inspire your daily endeavors—you will change your mind about the negatives and embrace the positives of planning. I'll show you how in this chapter. Let me begin with a very interesting example of the power of planning. I read about the following story years ago, and I believe you will find it as fascinating as I did.

## The Power of Planning

In 1953, the entire graduating class of Yale University was interviewed. The results of that interview revealed that only three percent of the graduates of this prestigious institution of higher learning had formulated any plans for accomplishing their life goals. (That shocked me when I read it—this is Yale we're talking about; it's Ivy League!) Two decades later the interviewer searched for and found the graduates strewn across the world in various endeavors of accomplishment. His questions were the same, but his findings this time were even more staggering than the first!

In 1973, a full 20 years after having been confronted with questions about their destiny and how they would accomplish it, the same 3 percent were light years ahead of the pack—just as they had been in proactively planning their goals in 1953. The other 97 percent were pathetically lacking in comparison. The 3 percent were now worth more financially than the entire 97 percent combined! They had more self-esteem and felt more fulfilled (what a surprise!) than their counterparts. All this because they chose to take the time to plan what they desired to accomplish and then went to work doing just that. My question to you is, "What group would you want to be in?"

Another example of planned success begins with a teenager. At the ripe old age of 15, a young man looked around himself and decided not to stay in the same town and become the same as those who lived there. He had big dreams—I mean, really *big*! The boy sat down and wrote a list of everything he desired to do in his life—over 125 personal goals. These goals were not mere financial and social dreams, as most would pen; his were teeming with adventure, travel, excitement, and daredeviltry. This young man was John Goddard, now an icon of adventure and accomplishment to all who know of him. He has spent his entire life, over half a century, living out those dreams and goals he set as a 15-year-old. As of this writing, he has accomplished over 115 of them. He has become a world-renowned speaker, sharing his adventures with millions in live, audio, and television presentations. He is a consistent part of many National Geographic specials and expeditions. He has nearly lost his life several times in the pursuit of his goals in such settings as African jungles and Himalayan mountains. He is one of my all-time heroes of accomplishment. But John Goddard would have been just another "wannabe" if he had never made a plan to see the goals done.

Then there's the example of the football coach who "dines with kings." Notre Dame's football teams have produced many legends of the game, and one of its esteemed coaches, Lou Holtz, has been both legend and legend-maker. Lou set over 100 goals for his life at an early age and has seen almost all come to fruition. My favorite story is how he accomplished two goals at one time—both of them being quite spectacular in their own right.

Lou had a dream of having dinner with the President of the United States at the White House. He formulated a plan to get there. He knew that the collegiate national champion football team always had dinner at the White House. So Lou figured that if he could take the Notre Dame team to the championship winner's circle, he'd get his dinner date. You guessed it—he did it!

## My Own Pilgrimage

As a child of six, I began to set goals for my own life (sort of). The first was when I was in kindergarten and had been appointed Master of Ceremonies for the Christmas pageant. My entire job description consisted of leading a very short parade of classmates around the small cafetorium stage and then bowing before the enthralled audience of assembled parents and siblings. As I bowed that night in December 1959, something wonderful took place. As the thunderous round of applause resounded in the echoing room, I knew in my little kindergarten heart that this was what I wanted to do with my life: make people smile and clap when I did something on a stage. I realize that may seem impossible for a six-year-old to understand, but it is the truth.

From that moment on, I began to pursue what has become my life's work: performing for others. Of course, it has taken many different paths and multiple avenues, but the gist of my work has always been to make people smile. Through the years, this desire manifested itself on grade school stages and high school athletic fields, at Boy Scout events and surfing spots up and down the East Coast of the U.S. (and even Hawaii), in literally thousands of circus performances under canvas tents and steel-beamed arenas over a 17-year span, and now when teaching seminars and preaching the gospel on the continents of the world.

Actually, it was when I finally left the circus world behind that I understood what is my most foundational gift, desire, and purpose: to impart to others everything I know. I looked back over my life at the age of 40 and said, "Everything I've ever done of real value [which to me does not necessarily include my performances, but rather what I said to others during or after those performances] consisted of imparting something to someone that I felt could help him or her in some way." I love it!

**Even the best team, without a plan, can't score.** (John Wooden)

## Jesus' Example

I have been asked if I thought Jesus and the disciples had such grandiose planning systems in place as I will share with you here, as they wandered about the countryside preaching the good news. I cannot state all the facts, but I can surmise that they absolutely did plan ahead. The facts we do know are these: Jesus was responsible for a home in Capernaum; traveled with 12 men He had to train and feed; covered a lot of terrain in three years of ministry excursions; kept His treasurer busy giving to the poor and paying for His expenses; fed 5,000 and later 4,000 people in two different settings with very specific and orderly instructions; and held to a prayer time every morning before the sun rose. You don't accomplish those kind of scheduling nightmares without some very good plans in place! Did He have it written down? Absolutely—before time and till the end of time! His entire life was planned by the Father to culminate in the cross and His resurrection. Also, the names of all who have made and will make Jesus Christ the Lord of their lives are already written in the Lamb's Book of Life. Nothing was or is a surprise. Everything happened and is happening as prophesied hundreds of years before. *That* is first-rate planning!

Goal-setting can be wonder-filled stuff, all coated in the sweet taste of creativity. But if you really mean business with the goals you set in your Life Areas, as related in the previous chapter, then you will have to put on your planner's hat and rise to the next level of success. No goal, no dream, and no desire will be fulfilled in any expedient, lasting way without a *proactive, productive plan* to make it so. What do I mean by "proactive"? Simply put, being proactive means you are on the *aggressive* side of planning. You are not waiting for someone to come along with a plan that you can use. You yourself are taking the offensive mode and doing it. *Proactive* means being up before the sun in the morning and having the day planned before dawn breaks the horizon! It means that your future is no surprise; you already have the events on paper. It means being ready and waiting instead of surprised and wailing. Like the man said, "Fail to plan and you plan to fail."

What good would it do you to have plans that are impossible to fulfill? You can't just splatter a piece of paper with mere ideas on how you'd like something to be done. You must be sure that your plans will produce what you want. That requires a proven, workable *planning system*, one that works *every time* for *everything* and for *everybody* involved. I've cultivated planning over the past 30 years, beginning in junior high school when I realized that I wanted to be a great athlete in some sport (which never actually happened, unless you call trapeze and acrobatics a sport). I certainly didn't realize that I was formulating such a fail-safe planning system; I just started to do things that worked for me and that seemed successful for others. Eventually I was working this system for everything. As I grew up, I modified it, learned more, and achieved greater goals.

## Creating Plans

> *The plans of the diligent lead surely to advantage, but everyone who is hasty comes surely to poverty* (Proverbs 21:5).

When I read this verse many years ago, I decided there and then to become a great planner. I learned how to do it, and it works just like the divinely inspired King Solomon said it would. Remember the top 3 percent of the Yale class of 1953? They definitely had not only the financial advantage but also every other advantage over the 97 percent! Planning is too highly beneficial for you to stay ignorant of its nuances. Take a moment and let your finances be the measuring rod of your planning; then see if you could be counted among the Yale 3 percent. It's sobering isn't it?

**A goal without the plan is like a glove without the hand—lifeless and fruitless.** (W.G.)

## Choices

Your destiny is in *your* hands, not God's or anyone else's. I know there are those who will take great issue with that statement, but it doesn't keep it from being true! *You* are the master of your destiny, not God, not your father, not your mother, not your pastor, not your government, and not me! Can you see that? Have I piqued your interest or ignited your indignation? I hope so, because if you are in either of those states, you are alive and feeling, and both are paramount to getting on with your destiny and fulfilling your purpose. Throw off false assumptions and grab hold of the truth.

> *...I have set before you life and death, the blessing and the curse. So choose life...* (Deuteronomy 30:19).

The reason I can say that you control your own destiny is because you are a self-willed being. You can choose to do or not do whatever you wish—even with a gun held to your head, if death is of no consequence to you. God protects your right to say no to His Son's redemptive work and to live your eternity in the agony of hell if you so desire. Is that His will? No! But your choice supercedes His will—and He will not override your choice unless you give Him leave to do so. Therefore, when it comes to designing your destiny by planning your goals into the future, you are in control! Of course, as Christians we should be seeking the will of God for every step of every plan for every goal. Yes, our destiny is ours to choose and our choice should be His will, not ours. We choose to obey, and by so doing direct our destinies by our own hands as willing servants of our Lord because we want to—not because we have to. If we had no choice, we would not be in control of our destiny or any part of our existence. God would take no pleasure in such lives.

From this point on I will assume that you agree that your destiny is dictated by the choices you alone make. Obviously every detail of your daily life cannot be planned precisely because you do not live in a vacuum; you can be affected by the choices of others at any given time. But for the most part your life and its achievements will be yours to design and live out.

## Food for Thought

So, we believe that we need to plan, and we agree to make that choice. Now what? Simple: *Think*. The productive side of planning requires you to put deep thought into your plans. Thinking is perhaps the most underrated pastime of the greatest achievers. Some call it "meditation." Others call it "imaging." Some call it "daydreaming," while others call it "visualizing." Whatever you call it, it's essential to planning and you need to become an expert at it! Don't buy into the fear peddlers who say such meditation is "only Eastern religion and mind games wrapped in a sheepskin." Anything found in those dead religions is a counterfeit of what the Lord created. Here's what God has to say about it.

> *But his delight is in the law of the Lord, and in His law he meditates day and night. And he will be like a tree firmly planted by streams of water, which yields its fruit in its season, and its*

*leaf does not wither; and in whatever he does, he prospers* (Psalm 1:2-3).

Planning begins with our own minds and imaginations coming into contact with the divine thoughts of God. It is there in the union of spirit and mind that God can paint the picture of His will upon the canvas of our hearts. It's a supernatural exchange that often doesn't feel like it is supernatural. In fact, we're all so used to such imagining that we can miss much Holy-Spirit-inspired information if we aren't listening. (This is where knowing the language of the Holy Spirit really comes into play!) I want to share a dynamic technique of tapping into the thoughts of God.

## Prime the Pump!

*A plan in the heart of a man is like deep water, but a man of understanding draws it out* (Proverbs 20:5).

*Watch over your heart with all diligence, for from it flow the springs of life* (Proverbs 4:23).

Your plans for whatever you desire to achieve are in you at this very moment. It only makes sense that if your purpose is within you, then your *plans* to make it happen are in you as well. Why would you think they would be otherwise? Why would someone else have them to give to you? Why would a book, a tape, a seminar, or a sermon contain your plans? Your plans are in you *now*. If anyone does have plans for you, those plans are not yours but theirs, and those plans may not be very good for you! Never seek your plans from the hands of someone else. Go get them for yourself from the deep well of your heart. It is there that the Holy Spirit of God will meet you and give you the plans you want and need to design your destiny.

Your heart is the wellspring of your life. Your life will find its zenith in the purpose that God has ordained for you. Therefore, your destiny plans should be held in your heart for you to discover. But if your plans are in your heart and your heart is like deep water, just how are you to go in and get them out? It was when I asked the Lord this question that the most profound changes were able to take place in every area of my life. I learned how to draw out those plans and gained a wealth of knowledge I never knew existed. I want you to do the same. Here's how I learned the secret.

While praying one day, I recalled a memory of when I was a young boy at our house on Song Lake in upstate New York. I was with some other children in the backyard and we were trying feverishly to make the old, dusty, red hand crank water pump give up its cooling waters—to no avail. Each of us tried valiantly, but all we got for our efforts was the raspy cry of the rusted crank handle.

Then my father appeared and performed what seemed like magic. He took a large glass jar filled with water and emptied its contents into the old red pump. While he poured, he firmly and rhythmically worked the handle up and down. Suddenly, to our wide-eyed amazement, the old pump began to pour forth cool water in a steady flow from its underground source somewhere deep below our feet. We cupped our hands and drank and splashed each other for a few minutes as my father smilingly pumped away our sweat and thirst. Then, just as we were settling down again and were about to ask him how he had gotten the water to come out, he answered our questions. "Son, if you want water from the well, you've gotta prime the pump first."

As the memory faded, I understood what the Lord was trying to tell me! It was the seed/harvest principle again. If I wanted to draw the plans from within my heart for the goals I was setting, I first had to *prime the pump*! The law of seed and harvest states that to get oranges you must plant orange seeds. To get apples you plant apple seeds. So to get plans, which are nothing more than ideas and thoughts, I must plant thoughts and ideas. How simple! All I had to do to get the plans for anything I needed was to take the time to meditate, daydream, and think about the very goals I needed plans for, and the plans would come up from the depth of my heart. You know what? It worked!

Of course, this is great news for all you dreaming, meditating, thinking types out there, because you can now justify your mental taxi trips! But for those of you who have been stuck fast in the mire of not knowing how to find the missing plans or parts of the purpose puzzle, this should be truly liberating. It's not hard to do; it's easy. All you need to do is give yourself some time, space, quiet, and relaxation. Let your mind and body relax and ask the Holy Spirit to help you concentrate on the goal you wish to plan. Begin to picture the goal from the beginning to the end and all the points in between.

## Then Ask Yourself a Question!

Why ask a question? Questions are the cleanest water with which to prime the pump of your soul. They are the ultimate thoughts of ignition. When you ask yourself a question, your mind instantly goes to work to answer it. That makes your subconscious mind go to work too. Your subconscious will automatically begin to access every memory and every bit of information in your brain in order to answer the question put before it. At the same time, you will open your spirit to receive input from the Lord. Remember, "The spirit of man is the lamp of the Lord, searching all the innermost parts of his being" (Prov. 20:27). God will touch your spirit with illuminating ideas and plans. It is astounding how voluminous a spring of answers bubbles up from within when you let your mind receive without judging those answers first. Attempting to qualify each thought, picture, or idea will stifle the stream. Just let the flow begin and write down the answers. Save the judgment for a later time of confirmation.

## The "Magic" Question

There is one question that rises above the rest in its ability to draw forth information from within. It is the cleanest water of all with which to prime the pump of your imagination and tap the wellspring of your plans. I call it the "Magic" Question, for obvious reasons. (Please, don't let a connotation of sorcery distract you from the power of this question; it has nothing to do with wizardry.) Learn to use this one great question to turn your thinking in the right direction and so begin to siphon the plans you seek to the surface of your mind.

I learned the "magic question" in 1978. I won the lead role of Master Magician in an illusion show that was to begin at Busch Gardens in Tampa, Florida. I was to share the weekly load of shows with another young man, and we began rehearsals after the park closed each evening. Our teacher was an experienced illusionist and actor. One night our cast was discussing a certain illusion, one we were not using in our show. As our magic mentor spoke of the times he had wowed the crowds with that particular ruse, someone asked him, "How do you do that trick?" To which he answered in a most magical and experienced way, "Never ask how did *they* do it; always ask, 'How would *I* do it?'" The answer usually comes and sometimes with an even better way than the one currently being used." I never forgot that moment. In fact, I have used that very question countless times when seeking the plans for my goals and dreams. "How would I do it?" This creates a potent flow of ideas!

A final thought on priming the pump. The more often a pump is used, the less water is needed to prime it. Therefore, once you get into the habit of priming the pump of your imagination with thoughts and questions, your needed information will flow out with less and less priming as you progress. Get into the habit of priming your pump on a daily basis—on purpose. Take time each day, several times a day, to daydream and get the flow started. You will discover that the flow of ideas and information you need will pop up even when you are not actually trying to acquire it! It may simply pour forth unhindered when someone asks a question or speaks of something pertaining to your goals, dreams, or plans. I've found this to be the case for many years now and it still fascinates me. Of course, it is the simple yet universal law of seed and harvest: The more you plant, the more you reap!

### Write It Down!

If there is one thing you must learn while pursuing the purpose and destiny of your life, it is to become a consistent writer of what you think about. I cannot tell you how many ideas, answers, and profound thoughts have been washed away by my forgetful mind because I failed to write them down. Never, never, never believe yourself when you say in the midst of some inspired, mind-tingling thought that you will remember it later! Write it down right then! Have paper and pencil or pen, or a hand-held recorder, obviously ready and near you at all times. After all, who goes to a pump without a bucket? Obviously someone who is not seeking much water, for what does come forth will be lost forever to the spongy soil at his feet. Do not allow such to be the fate of your dreams. Don't be lazy and lose your plans. Buy a journal at your local drug or grocery store, or use the appropriate worksheets from the Appendix of your *Destiny Planner*®, and write down your thoughts. (We will discuss the other valuable benefits of journaling in more detail in a later chapter.)

### Confirm the Source!

Now don't be so naive as to think that your goals and plans may not be infiltrated by things not necessarily appointed by God. Even the best of believers have trouble with the flesh now and again. There are some things I have dredged up from the depth of my heart that were not necessarily divinely inspired. Our humanness can rise up in a way that seems like God. If our desire is truly to follow the Lord, such thoughts may not seem to be wrong, since a goal or plan that is way off the mark will be easily detected and rejected. These goals and plans may not be inherently evil but could still be wrong for us as far as God's purpose for our lives is concerned. This must be discovered before adverse consequences arise. There *is* a way to know the difference. Simply take the confirmation steps used to find your purpose and utilize them for the goals and plans in question. Usually it won't take much to expose the erroneous.

## Reverse Planning

Details, details, details! How do you keep track of all the details while planning the accomplishment of your many destiny goals? The answer is simple. Utilize a Reverse Planning Worksheet like the one at the end of this chapter and learn the Six Universal Resources. We will discuss these Six Universal Resources later in this chapter, but because they must be included as details in reverse planning, I urge you to study them before using a Reverse Planning Worksheet for any of your goals.

Although there are six resource categories to be recognized, there are two that must be known before any others: "Item" and "Time." "Item" details encompass every specific step along the way to the completed goal. "Time" simply refers to the dates by which each item must be accomplished. These details are revealed by starting with the completed goal and working back to where you are now. They are given separate columns on the Reverse Planning Worksheet. I learned this technique early in my planning career, and it has served me well ever since.

Why start at the end and work back to the beginning? It's easier to "see" the details and the time needed for each. You see, what I discovered in my planning journey was that I could set goals and plan their achievement with little problem. But I was tripped up many times by missed details and insufficient time. I simply did not see them until they were upon me. But I found that by sitting still, seeing the end result, and then methodically picturing every step along the way, from the end to the beginning, I missed far less.

Let me illustrate. Within every major goal is a large group of minor goals that must be accomplished. Take a major goal like having a traveling circus troupe. To reach that goal, we must recruit new performers, build or purchase new equipment, acquire vehicles, and so on. These minor goals consist of even smaller, subminor goals. In order to recruit performers, I must research the possible sources of potential acrobats and set up meetings with those whom I wish to interview. And if I wish to hold a performance by a specific date, I must know how long it will take me to find, interview, and train my acrobats. Minor and subminor goals are like stepping stones to achieving major goals, making it possible for you to fulfill your overall purpose.

The key is in properly prioritizing the minor and subminor goals. What comes first—the show or the performers? Obviously the performers. But before I can put my troupe on the road, I must have the proper training facilities and equipment. And it does me no good to put the performers on a bus if I don't have the trapeze bars, juggling clubs, or trampolines to practice and perform on. Priorities *must* be seen and set. Once they are set, we must know the time needed to accomplish each.

Once I have completed a Reverse Planning Worksheet, I review it several times until I am sure that I have every detail written in. I usually like to give the list to someone else to check for anything I may have missed. When the list is done, I simply put it onto a Goal Planning Worksheet (which we will discuss next) to be sure that personnel and costs have been included within the proper time frames. This Goal Planning Worksheet gives me a detailed, step-by-step checklist for the achievement of the goal.

By starting at your target date and working backward, you are able to figure what your starting date must be in order to accomplish the goal. This is a valuable tool when you are figuring out whether you can or cannot do a certain thing within the time you have available. You may find that once you figure in the time line for every detail, you just *cannot* make the deadline work from the date from which you must begin. You must also learn to pad your target dates, since you will be relying on people most of the time, which means a loss of control on your part. I usually pad every target date by several days, and up to a week or more for some.

## The Six Universal Resources

Now that we have discussed (and hopefully you have embraced) the glories of meditating and daydreaming to bring forth the plans of your goals, and have understood the principles of reverse planning, let's get even *more* specific. As I mentioned in the previous chapter on goals, there are usually only half a dozen basics to cover in any area of our experience. This is true in the resources as well. *Every goal you will ever attempt to achieve will require items from one or more of the Six Universal Resources.* There is nothing mystical about these resources. They are basic, practical, and easily understood. So, for those of you whose heads may be reeling after our somewhat mystical-sounding essay on "pump priming," this will be a welcome respite. (Please direct your thanks to Myron Rush, author of *Biblical Management*, from whom I gleaned this list many years ago.)

In the appendix of the *Destiny Planner*® you will find a Goal Planning Worksheet to get you started on formulating your needed resources. This worksheet can be modified to fit the varying number of items under each resource for any particular goal, but the basics remain the same. You will notice that while the first column, labeled "Resource Item," has three separate sections, each section may fluctuate in the number of items below it, according to the goal. Some will have more of one and less of others. The other columns will remain static. You will simply fill them in after you have listed all the needed resources under the specific "Resource Item" heading. Each of the three "Resource Item" headings will need people, money, and time associated with them, so just fill in the blanks.

Before I go into the attributes of each resource heading, let me state that they are just that: headings. By that I mean that there may be literally hundreds of items under any one of these headings pertaining to a single goal. For instance, when I would prepare to plan a large convention or concert, I would have a wide variety of equipment to rent and scores of people to place, but very few soft supplies. In other words, do not be misled by the small number of headings or think for a moment that each will have the same number of items for each goal. It simply won't happen that way. I present this list to give you an outline to fill in for every step in your proactively planned destiny. By using this list, you can assure yourself of very few surprises along the way. You can also know exactly what to expect.

## Resource #1: People

There is no doubt that your most valuable resource is the people you will need for the fulfillment of each and every goal. Forget the idea that you are a "lone ranger," an "island unto yourself," or the "only pea in the pod." *It ain't so!* You need people to help you do whatever your purpose is, and every step along the path of your destiny will require interaction with others in some manner. This is not a maybe; it is a guarantee! You can't know everything or have every skill needed. Why would you want to try and learn so many things you may use only once, when there are people who have spent their entire lives honing the very skills you need? I have a phone book so that I don't have to remember everyone's number. Likewise, I don't need to remember every bit of available knowledge. I simply find the people who know what I need.

People are your most valuable resource, but they must never be *just* your resource; they must be people you have compassion for. The slowest delivery boy and the most punctual businessman must both be held with esteem in your eyes. They are not cattle to plow your field with. They are made in the likeness and image of the God who created you and them. You honor God by honoring your fellow human beings—especially if you work side by side with them. Ask yourself constantly, "Do I esteem these people? Are they here to serve my cause or to work together with me as equals in God's eyes, and therefore mine too?" I found out the hard way that I was not living in such a manner.

I had been in ministry full-time for almost seven years before I understood this principle. I was listening to a fellow minister. I don't remember his message title, but the point the Lord wanted *me* to get came through loud and clear. This minister made a statement similar to this: "You are in the ministry *for* people, not to *use* people to do ministry." Now as obvious as that may sound, it was a profound revelation to me. I thought ministry was to kick the devil in the behind as much as possible and to give God the glory for every hit! It had not occurred to me that the people were the reason for it all. Can you believe that!

I actually had a disdain for most Christians, let alone sinners, because I felt that most Christians were in my way by not doing what they were called to do. The sinners at least had an excuse. The Holy Spirit, however, radically changed my thinking, and I have not been the same since. I asked the Lord to change my heart, to forgive me, and to show me His heart for people. He led me to Philippians 2:1-8 and to Ephesians chapter 3. I spent the next 18 months studying and meditating on these Scriptures, praying daily for God to break my heart and to teach me humility and to count everything as loss compared to knowing Him. He did that and it was wonderful.

Where once I had been known for a lack of compassion for people, since my heart change I have had several people prophesy to me that *the Lord* calls me compassionate! And if someone asks me now what ministry is about, my answer is swift: "It's the people!" God gave His Son for people. He wrote the Bible for people. He set up the Church by and for people. He gave gifts of His Spirit to people for people. And He is coming again for His people. Now my heart beats for people too, and I am consumed with helping as many of them as I possibly can!

*Get Specific*

For every goal you will need specific people who have specific skills and who can be responsible for specific details and tasks. As you meditate on each goal of each aspect of your destiny, begin asking yourself, "Who will I need to help me accomplish this?" As you prime the pump with that question, the answers will come. Sometimes you will see specific people or have their names come to mind. Other times you will see the skill you need. Remember to write down as you go every type of person you need. Through meditating on the rest of these resources, you will discover more people whom you will need as well. Simply fill in their names or skills next to the appropriate item on the chart.

For example, when I was promoting concerts in the mid 1980's, I needed a large staff to accomplish the event correctly. I would begin my chart by first filling in the *equipment* I needed, such as a sound system. Next to that item in the "People" column, I would write the company to rent it from, the persons to pick it up, the persons to unload it, the persons to operate it, and so on. If I desired specific personnel, I would put their names in the space.

I would follow this track for every item on my Goal Planning Worksheet. When it was completed, I knew exactly who I needed to handle every task. This allowed me to contact the people well in advance and to know when to send reminders. It virtually eliminated mistakes on everyone's part.

*Networking*

To expedite your efforts in future endeavors (or to expedite the efforts of those whom you work with or for), I strongly suggest that you become a good networker. By that I mean you don't just hire or contract with people, but you *befriend* people. Become an expert at making friends with the people you enlist to help you achieve your various goals throughout life. Once you have worked with someone, you will meet others who could benefit from their services. Simply help them to connect with each other—just like a net is woven together of many different cords.

As you network more and more, you will be amazed at how you will need some of these people again and again—and they you. By keeping the networking attitude in mind when you seek people to help you, your future needs can be ensured for this most valuable resource. Of course, this is a two-way street and you must be ready to reciprocate with them if called upon. This is the beauty of having a planning system. By having everyone's name, phone number, and skill in your planning charts, you have a quick reference as to who the people are and how they have worked with you in the past. Simply transfer the info to an index system, and should they call on your assistance at any time, you merely access their name in your system. Of course, the most valuable part of all this is that you will have many new and widely varied friends!

**Resource #2: Facility**

When talking of facilities, you simply recognize every possible building, acreage, or arena you may need to accomplish your goal. For our circus we used a wide variety of facilities, depending on the town, the sponsor, and the event we were a part of. Our preference was a civic auditorium or large gymnasium, but we saw less of those than we would have liked. Here is a short list of some of the facilities we used over the ten years Circus Alleluia existed:

1. **Church buildings** with low ceilings and high ceilings; ceilings with steel beams and ceilings with wooden beams; dropped ceilings and plastered ceilings; churches with pews and some with chairs; church parking lots and grassy areas.

2. **School** gymnasiums, cafetoriums, classrooms, and playgrounds.

3. **Prison** gymnasiums, ballfields, chapels (see church buildings), and open areas next to electrified fences with gun turrets behind them.

4. **Civic auditoriums** with cement floors and wooden floors; steel-beamed ceilings and plastered ceilings.

5. **Horse track** infields with grass; the dirt tracks themselves.

6. **Stock car race tracks** of dirt and asphalt; the grassy infields.

7. **City parks** under large trees; baseball fields, football fields, and running tracks.

8. **People's backyards** of many sizes and shapes.

9. **Downtown squares** of asphalt, concrete, brick, and stone.

10. **Tents** of many sizes and shapes; some with several main poles, others with one main pole; some high, some low; some with stages, others without stages; some on hills, others on flat ground.

11. **Television studios**, With big sound stages; others with almost no sound stage at all.

As you can see by this partial list, we had to be quite flexible—and totally planned ahead. We could not afford to arrive at the show site unaware of the facility and without the proper rigging to put on our show. Each venue afforded its own problems and challenges—ones we had to know of in advance. Because it was on our Goal Planning Worksheet, we were prepared. But we needed more than just a place to set up rigging. We also needed a sound booth, dressing rooms, a product sales area, a concessions sales area, a ticketing area, loading docks, audience entrances and exits, and so on. "Facility" means facility for every aspect of your goal. But we knew these details in advance because we had completed the planning chart.

Of course, the places for our shows were not the only facilities we needed as a ministry. We also needed practice facilities, offices, storage areas, printing shops, t-shirt manufacturers, and many other things. Every aspect had its own specific needs, and yours will also. Again, simply prime the pump of your imagination with the right questions on facility, and as you walk through your goal in your mind, you will see every detail that you need to attend to.

Try it right now with one of your goals. Close your eyes and ask, "What facilities do I need to accomplish this goal?" Then look at the movie screen of your mind and pay attention to the details. Write down what you see. Don't be too quick to shut down the process either. The longer you look, the more you may see. That's how easy it is. Pay attention to the details, and the details will take care of you.

**Resource #3: Equipment**

Nothing fancy is meant here; it's just the precise hardware you will need for the goals to be accomplished. Of course, every tool and machine will need a person to handle its proper operation, but the basics of what equipment you will need are usually not hard to come by. The best way to figure out exactly what tools you will need is to again employ the pump priming method. Actually, as you get better at visualizing your goals being accomplished, you will be able to see all the resources at once and save some valuable time by not having to prime the pump for each individual resource. It just takes a bit of practice. Ask the question, "What equipment do I need to achieve this particular goal?" Then simply let your mind go to work. Typewriters, computers, copiers, backhoes, trucks, sound systems, volleyballs—whatever fits the goal.

When we ran our circus, we found ourselves in need of some very unique equipment, and most were items you could not find at the local rent-a-tool place. For instance, when we were to perform inside a building and there were steel I-beams accessible in the ceiling, we would use specially designed clamps to secure our equipment directly to the beams (such as the trapeze items). Different clamps fit different beam widths. However, there was only one place in the U.S. we could get them, and they didn't have a store. Instead, we ordered from the factory. So, as usual, we had to know ahead of time the width of the beams so we could have the right clamp ready.

## Resource #4: Supplies

These are the soft items that you will need. "Supplies" refer to anything consumable, things that you will use up and/or eventually discard. Again, this is fairly basic deduction. Simply think of all the needed items that will be replaced after you are done reaching your goal and write them in the "Supplies" column. Be sure that you become a detail-oriented person, or at least procure the services of one, to help you with making your equipment and supplies lists. You cannot afford to be caught unawares on the highway of your destiny without the proper supplies or tools. Take it from an expert at doing just that!

For the circus we had a fairly constant flow of supplies. Items such as adhesive tape for wrapping wrists and ankles, rosin for keeping our hands dry while catching someone in mid-air flight, paper for copies and letters, envelopes, stamps, food and drink for the troupe, gas for the trucks, lightbulbs, and such were all consumable supplies. Probably the hardest thing about figuring supplies is knowing the quantity of each. Of course, you will also need to list on your Goal Planning Worksheet the specific people who supply, purchase, deliver, and/or pick up those supplies.

## Resource #5: Cost

Nothing is free. Jesus taught that anyone who desires to build a barn or go to war had better count the cost first. This being true, why are most people so reluctant to preplan their spending? Why do so many new businesses in America fail? Why are so many Christians hopelessly in debt with credit cards and bank loans? I'm not sure I know all the answers, but one of the main reasons is this: Due to either ignorance or laziness, we do not plan how we will spend our money.

Nearly every goal you will ever set will require money at some point along the way. Why not know ahead of time exactly what amount you will need? Using the Goal Planning Worksheet, you can know exactly how much each item of each resource will cost, including the personnel, and have it right in front of you at all times. The bottom line is that you cannot spend more than you earn. When I began to put together the seminar based on this book, it was very easy to discover the costs and prepare for them. Once we knew the entire list of resources we needed, we simply investigated the costs and found the totals. In most instances it required merely a phone call to a vendor and his return call with the estimate. It was neither hard nor mysterious, just extremely worth the effort. We were then able to figure out how many items we would need to sell or how many registrations we would need to collect to cover our costs with enough profit left over for further growth.

Don't let the lack of knowledge stop you from becoming a financial pro when it comes to planning and budgeting. Count the cost and then stick to it! And let me add this one very good word of advice: If you can *avoid* going into debt, please do so! I have never found even one instance in the Bible when God told His people to borrow money for things in order to fulfill His commission to them. Either they worked their way through or He supplied supernaturally—and sometimes both. Please don't take that as a license to sit around and waste your time doing nothing while you piously wait for God to show up with a bag of money! Go to work! Get a job! Be a productive member of your family and your community during your waiting times. The only thing God says about lazy people is that they are to be shunned and left hungry. Don't be counted among them. Be patient, but not lazy.

**Resource #6: Time**

The key components of the Goal Planning Worksheet are the target and actual completion dates for each item. Projecting these dates requires accurate knowledge of what is needed to achieve each specific item. This is also where most mistakes are made.

If you don't control how you spend your time, someone or something else will fill that void for you—and not necessarily in a positive way. The truth is, if you know what your goals are and you have figured out your resources, their costs, and who you need to help you, you are light years ahead of the pack and ready for time management. The key is to simply set realistic time frames for each aspect of each goal—be it the acquisition of a piece of equipment or the networking of a new person to help you. How long do you need to contact the people? To learn the skill? To raise the money? To get the job done? Once you know these facts, you can place them on a calendar in the proper order and get to work. But if you have not yet become a skilled manager of your personal and daily routines, it's *time* you started.

Just think for a moment. If you were going to take the 8 a.m. train to work and you showed up at 7 a.m., several things would probably happen. If you think you're on time, you'd be frustrated because the train is late. Or if you realized that you were early, you'd kick yourself for missing that last hour of sleep and making your spouse rush you to the station. But if the opposite happened—you arrived at 8 a.m. but the train left at 7 a.m.—you could waste a lot of time waiting for a train that had already departed without you. In the destiny of your life, there are many trains to catch, metaphorically speaking. If you arrive too late or too early, you could have a very unpleasant day, year, decade, or even the rest of your life! Time management is important.

You also must be careful to avoid what I call "time jams." By that I mean you shouldn't overbook yourself. There is only so much time in a day. For example, years ago when I was running full throttle with the circus ministry, I was trying to accomplish as much ministry as possible on every road trip. On one tour I had booked a TV show at 9 a.m. in Pittsburgh, Pennsylvania, and an 8 p.m. outdoor show in Baltimore, Maryland, on the same day. I had figured the mileage and the hours of driving to give us about 30 minutes to spare. What I didn't figure in was the extra time the TV show went over and the traffic we encountered. We arrived at 8 p.m., 1 hour and 30 minutes late. The sponsor was distraught. The spectators were only a little less agitated than the sponsor. My troupe was not very impressed with my booking arrangements. My wife was not speaking to me. And I was in anything but the mood to minister!

Tough lesson? You bet. Did I learn from it? Definitely. I have reminded myself of that incident many times over the years as I've sought to plan time frames. It is applicable in every situation. Please make sure that you do not have to learn your lessons of proper time limits in such a way. Give yourself a break, and be sure to get plenty of counsel to avoid "time jams" such as I experienced. It is always better to be methodical and steady paced.

Your planning must have the proper time tables built in to avoid mistakes and to take advantage of opportunities. Obviously there is nothing we can do about the yesterdays of our lives; they are history. But if we wasted some yesterdays, then we can learn from them and not let history repeat itself. *Time is the only resource you can never replace.*

It is not a supply to be bought or a piece of equipment to be rented, but it is very expensive when not used wisely.

It's been said that if someone were given $88,000, they would surely save some, invest some, and spend some. Well, if you expect to live ten more years, you will have been given 88,000 hours. How will you manage them? Will you *waste* them because you have not planned with specific time frames? *Invest* some? Spend it *wisely*? No one, I repeat, *no one* will give account to the Lord about those hours but *you*. Think about it carefully. As the days of this age grow closer to their end, wasting time becomes more serious.

Formulating plans for your purpose goals saturates your destiny with only those things that are needful for living out your purpose; therefore, there is no wasted time. You are actually directing your every achievement by having them planned out in clear time slots beforehand. Your directed achievements become your life. Isn't that what everyone really wants—control of his or her life? For those of us who have laid our lives at the cross of Christ, we are actually living the life He has given back to us.

*Daily Planners*

I recommend that you visit your local library and check out a book or two on time management, if you are not presently skilled at it. I will not take space here to further develop this topic, since I could not do a better or more thorough job than most of the books that are already available. To be sure, there is a plethora of information on how to manage your time. You will discover that all books on the subject, and I concur, will instruct you to take advantage of a daily planner of some sort. There are many to choose from and most all are good if used correctly.

Whichever planner you choose, be sure to study the tools of the planner in full so you get the full benefit of its facets. Also be sure to choose one that emphasizes the *values* of your life as being more important than the *events* of your life. We will study more about values in a later chapter, but to summarize the principle here: Be sure you put *relationships* and people before things and schedules. Value the valuable, not the manageable. Manage time and things, but value people and your relationships with them.

Finally, I caution you to not let time management become time imprisonment. It is very easy to become so good at managing your time that you become a slave to it. Your spontaneity becomes a burden. Your impulsiveness dies. And when that happens, a certain aspect of your creativity may go with it. I strongly urge you to factor into every day a time to daydream and to do something out of the ordinary. Take a different way home from work or get dressed differently. Eat a different lunch in a different place with different people. Give yourself the gift of time alone to think or simply *not* to think.

Our freedom to choose how we spend our time can be our bane or our bounty. Make your schedules and plan your days, weeks, years, decades, and lifetime—but let yourself live freely while you walk it out. Besides, if you get too bound to your planner, you will go nuts when something out of your control makes you miss something you've planned. Be at peace about such possibilities and trust God with everything.

Having completed the Goal Planning Worksheet, you now have your goal planned in detail and in written form—no missed items, no wondering about costs, no hassles with racing about at the last minute to find someone to fill a forgotten responsibility. I also suggest that, when applicable, you give everyone involved in the goal a copy of the Goal Planning Worksheet. This allows everyone to see the big picture, what he or she is a part of, and how important that role is to everyone else. It makes for more cohesiveness and loyalty. Also, you will find that those working with you will have ideas that will "plus" your goal, adding valuable insight. There is always another idea waiting to be birthed, if given the chance. Be sure that you are a good, creative, mental midwife for your helpers! You will not be disappointed.

## The Final Step in Planning Your Destiny

*Commit your works to the Lord, and your plans will be established. ... The mind of man plans his way, but the Lord directs his steps* (Proverbs 16:3,9).

All the planning in the world is futile if it is not submitted to the Lordship of Christ. Yes, we must plan. Yes, we must set and work toward our goals. Yes, we must commit ourselves to the task unflinchingly. But that commitment, that work, must never block out the One for whom is meant all the glory of our achievements. How sad it will be for those who stand before the King of kings as He remorsefully states, "Depart from Me, I never knew you." It won't be the atheists who hear those words; it will be people who thought they were doing the will of God in the name of Jesus. Unfortunately, they never actually knew Him in a personal way. He was not Lord of their lives.

Lordship obviously sounds easy enough to agree to, but it can be quite frustrating to comply with. How easily we hang on to *our* dreams and plans. Our motives may be the purest in nature—we may desire to work hard and long for the glory of God—but should the King require our hand to be applied elsewhere for a time, our hold upon our dreams, our very God-given purpose and destiny, can become a white-knuckled death grip.

In the verses from Proverbs chapter 16 quoted previously, you see the word *commit*. To *commit* means "to roll upon, to place in the hands of God." Rolling our works upon Him for His perfect timing can prove agonizing, especially after everything has been meticulously planned. His directions can, at times, seem ridiculously wrong for our vision. But this promise from Proverbs is our security in such times. Plans are written by us, but their establishments is *His* responsibility. Actually, that releases us from the fear of relying on our own finite understanding to make our destiny plans take place. The word *works* spoken of in verse 3 denotes the action taken to perform your plans. You must be willing to let God's timing for the sequence of events take precedence over your own. When you commit your works to the Lord in such a manner, He will see to it that your plans are fulfilled.

**The will to prepare must exceed the will to win.** (W.G.)

## Final Thoughts

If I was going to build a house, I'd want the most detailed plans I could get my hands on. The last thing I'd want would be lining up a wall through the kitchen sink drain or having my chimney on one side of the house and the fireplace on another! We'd call that "big league" ignorance! But how many of us have been guilty of doing just that with our destiny? We fail to plan and then we just plain fail! Or we plan without the proper tools and end up taking years longer than we should have to accomplish our goals, if we accomplish them at all.

No carpenter worth his hire would even *think* about going to his job without everything he needed to do the job right—plans, tools, helpers. Shouldn't we be just as professional with our lives? Our lives cost God the life of His only Son. He ordained us to live specifically in *this* time, in *our* culture, and in *His* family. We owe it to Him, and to our Lord and Savior Jesus Christ, to become experts with the tools we've read of in this chapter, and with any other tools that will serve us along the road to fulfilling our destiny. As always, the choice is ours.

# Goal Planning
## PDA Seminar
## Goal

| Resource | Personnel | Due Date | Projected Cost | Actual Cost |
|---|---|---|---|---|
| **Facility** | | | | |
| Contract signed | Bill | 9/1/97 | | |
| Convention center | Bill | 1/7/98 | $2000 | $2100 |
| Hotel rooms | Sue | 9/5/97 | $ 200 | $ 150 |
| Restaurants | Sue | 12/15/97 | $1000 | $ 750 |
| Print shop | Sue | 9/15/97 | $1000 | $ 800 |
| **Equipment** | | | | |
| Sound system | Ken | 9/15/97 | $3500 | $2500 |
| Lights | Ken | 9/15/97 | $2000 | $1500 |
| TV cameras, etc. | Ken | 9/15/97 | $5000 | $5000 |
| Podium | Ken | | | |
| Chairs | Ken | | | |
| Transportation | Ken | 10/15/97 | $ 500 | $ 550 |
| Shipping | Mike | 12/15/97 | $ 250 | $ 225 |
| Computer | Sue | 10/15/97 | $ 500 | $ 300 |
| Printers | Joe | 9/15/97 | $ 100 | N/C |
| **Supplies** | | | | |
| Flyers | Mike | 11/15/97 | $ 500 | $ 400 |
| Name tags | Sue | 1/15/98 | $ 10 | $ 5 |
| Break food | Sue | 1/7/98 | $ 350 | $ 275 |
| Water for speakers | Ken | | | |
| Audios/videos | Ken | 11/15/97 | $ 450 | $ 450 |
| Mailing | Mike | 11/15/97 | $ 600 | $ 575 |
| | | **Total Cost** | **$17,960** | **$15,580** |

## Reverse Planning

### Vacation to the Grand Canyon—June 25

**Create your action steps starting from completion to the present.**

| **Step** | | **Due Date** |
|---|---|---|
| 20. | Arrive at Grand Canyon. | June 25 |
| 19. | Depart Flagstaff, Arizona. | June 25 |
| 18. | Arrive at Flagstaff, Arizona. | June 24 |
| 17. | Depart Roswell, New Mexico. | June 24 |
| 16. | Arrive at Roswell, New Mexico. | June 23 |
| 15. | Depart Dallas, Texas. | June 23 |
| 14. | Pack the car. | June 22 |
| 13. | Pack the suitcases. | June 21 |
| 12. | Wash all our clothes. | June 20 |
| 11. | Decide what clothes are needed. | June 18 |
| 10. | Pick up cash and traveler's checks. | June 18 |
| 9. | Give key to next-door neighbor. | June 18 |
| 8. | Write instructions about pets for neighbor. | June 15 |
| 7. | Contact post office and newspaper office to hold mail. | June 15 |
| 6. | Ask next-door neighbor to care for pets. | June 1 |
| 5. | Plan travel route and make hotel reservations. | March 25 |
| 4. | Call Grand Canyon for reservations for donkey ride into canyon. | February 15 |
| 3. | Study books from library on Grand Canyon. | February 1 |
| 2. | Ask boss for that specific time for vacation. | January 7 |
| 1. | Decide on departure, arrival, and return dates. | January 1 |

# Section Three
# Achievement

*I can do all things through Him who strengthens me* (Philippians 4:13).

# Chapter 14

# Powered by Change

### Constant Change Is Here to Stay!

If there is any word that strikes fear into the heart of adults, it is *change*. We long for the status quo to continue and the boat not to rock. We long for routines and consistency. But that is not the way of God for His people. *He* may not change, but He certainly takes delight in ours. We must learn to delight in it also if we are to see the fruits of our purpose and destiny take form. God will not give us purpose or direction that will leave us the same or let us on one plateau for very long.

If, as Romans 1:20 explains, we can truly see God in His creations, then we can see that all creation is either growing or dying. We, above the rest of His works, have a choice in the matter. We can move across the country or around the world. We can speak a new language. We can learn a new vocation. Change is our prerogative.

**The only constant is change. God never changes, but He expects us to daily.** (W.G.)

I believe that constant change should be our banner as Christians. We should be the most creative and innovative force on the planet. I base that belief on God's Word. Let me share some Scriptures with you that have turned around my thinking where change is concerned, and then let's see how they apply to our ordained purpose and destiny. As I have been saying throughout this book, everything we do affects each of our Life Areas. You will see through Scriptures that every Life Area is to be changing continually. It is part of our growth and maturing process. I believe that it is God's preparation plan for our eternal life.

## Renewing Ourselves

### Spiritually Renewed

> *Therefore we do not lose heart, but though our outer man is decaying, yet our inner man is being renewed day by day* (2 Corinthians 4:16).

This truth refers to the spirit part of man. To *renew* means "to renovate, refurbish, and refurnish." It means "to change the structure of something." In this case, God explains that our very spirit will be changed on a daily basis if we follow Him as we should. (That is the *key* to all change by the way—obedience to His will and ways.) If we seek His will for us in the way He desires us to live it out, we will be growing in our spirit. New things will be added to us daily! What a thought! I have certainly found that to be true. When I am seeking Him daily, I am growing daily. When I slack off, so does my growth. Second Corinthians tells us that all things become new when we become a Christian. However, the renewing should never stop, not even for the remainder of eternity.

Spiritual growth is aggressive, as is the case with just about everything in God's Kingdom. There are a number of things you can do to facilitate such renewing, such as prayer, worship, Bible study, fellowship with other believers, speaking what you believe, and sharing Christ with unbelievers. All these have a part in the daily renewal, refurnishing, and refurbishing of our spirits. Spiritual change is God's will and way, and it is to be constant, daily change.

### Physically Renewed

> *Bless the Lord, O my soul; and all that is within me, bless His holy name. Bless the Lord, O my soul, and forget none of His benefits... Who satisfies your years with good things, so that your youth is renewed like the eagle* (Psalm 103:1-2,5).

The word *youth* is the root word for "juvenile" or "adolescent." We usually refer to this age as when we had the most energy and the least sense. In context the Lord is saying that we have certain benefits to enjoy, and youthfulness is one of them. The inference here is that even our physical bodies can be renewed to some extent. An eagle has the ability to go into the highest crags and rejuvenate itself. To be sure, it is not a pleasant experience. The majestic bird will find a safe ledge, after which it pulls out all its feathers and talons and scrapes off its beak on the rocks. It will be vulnerable for a time, but the new body will be stronger than the former. It will be renovated and refurbished. Obviously I am not insinuating that the Lord is expecting us to go through such an ordeal to renew ourselves. Nor am I saying that we can expect our physical bodies to live forever by such renewal. What I am saying is that one of the benefits of having a strong relationship with God is a renewed, youthful life. That must include the physical aspect.

But we also have some responsibility in this equation. We would be in error if we expected God to renew our youth while we flail against Him through abusive lifestyles of drugs, sexual sin, gluttony, and poor hygiene. We must care for our bodies. They are the very temples of His Holy Spirit! If you've done any study on the tabernacle and the temples of Israel, they were nothing short of the finest in all areas. Proper diet, exercise, adequate sleep, rest, and recreation are mandatory for physical health and longevity. The renewing of our physical selves, which is our benefit as believers, should be a significant goal for us. After all, the Son of God paid for our bodies as well with His very life.

**Personality Renewed**

> *But now you also, put them all aside: anger, wrath, malice, slander, and abusive speech from your mouth. Do not lie to one another, since you laid aside the old self with its evil practices, and have put on the new self who is being renewed to a true knowledge according to the image of the One who created him—a renewal in which there is no distinction between Greek and Jew, circumcised and uncircumcised, barbarian, Scythian, slave and freeman, but Christ is all, and in all. And so, as those who have been chosen of God, holy and beloved, put on a heart of compassion, kindness, humility, gentleness and patience* (Colossians 3:8-12).

> *That, in reference to your former manner of life, you lay aside the old self, which is being corrupted in accordance with the lusts of*

*deceit, and that you be renewed in the* ***spirit*** *of your* ***mind****, and put on the new self, which in the likeness of God has been created in righteousness and holiness of the truth. Therefore, laying aside falsehood, speak truth...be angry, and yet do not sin; do not let the sun go down on your anger... Let him who steals steal no longer... Let no unwholesome word proceed from your mouth, but only such a word as is good for edification according to the need of the moment... And do not grieve the Holy Spirit of God... Let bitterness and wrath and anger and clamor and slander be put away from you, along with malice. And be kind to one another, tender-hearted, forgiving each other...* (Ephesians 4:22-26,28-32).

These verses refer to the *soul* of man—the *self*, the *heart* of man—which is comprised of the emotions and personality of man. Our personality and our emotions should be affected positively by the presence of God in our lives. When we discover our purpose and begin to design and achieve our destiny, then our hearts, minds, emotions, and personality will all be renewed and renovated. Who we are will take on new meaning and perspective for us because we will see ourselves as God intended us to be. We will finally be stepping into the very reason we were created. Such revelation cannot help but change the way a person feels about himself or herself. Confidence grows! Esteem rises! Courage and fortitude increase within us!

Notice the verse that says we are to "put on a heart" of compassion, humility, gentleness, kindness, and patience (Col. 3:12), as well as the one that states we are to "put on the new self" by eradicating from our lives that which is ungodly (Eph. 4:24). These are social and emotional concepts. They have to do with our perceptions and choices in the realm of relationship.

But one of the most profound realizations I discovered in researching these verses was in Ephesians 4:23: "the spirit of your mind." I realized that the word *spirit* and the word *mind* both have the meaning of "purpose"! It could be read, "be renewed in the purpose of your purpose." Application would dictate that we renovate and refurbish our overall purpose by focusing on a new reason *for* our purpose. That reason would be the will of God for our lives. Our renewed *spirit* (purpose) for living is for God and His will, instead of for ourselves and our will. This new reason for living would then give rise to the very *way* (purpose) we live out His will and ways. This will dictate who you are—your personality and emotions—as shown in the verses from Colassians chapter 3 and Ephesians chapter 4.

That is the very nature of renewal! It is to focus on something totally different and to walk away from the old. You look, sound, feel, and act differently. That is what being a Christian is supposed to be about: becoming a new creature in Christ! Renew your *reason* for living and then renew your *living* to match the reason!

Again, as is always the case with the things of God, we are the ones who choose to be renewed in these areas. Our renewed, renovated, refurbished personality is directly proportional to the strength of our decision to make it so. God will supply the power to change, but we decide if and when.

### The Master Key of Change

> *I urge you therefore, brethren, by the mercies of God, to present your bodies a living and holy sacrifice, acceptable to God, which is your spiritual service of worship. And do not be conformed to this world, but* ***be transformed*** *by the renewing of your mind, that you may prove what the will of God is, that which is good and acceptable and perfect. For through the grace given to me I say to every man among you not to think more highly of himself than he ought to think; but to think so as to have sound judgment, as God has allotted to each a measure of faith* (Romans 12:1-3).

Transformation is what renewing is all about. It's a big concept. It means metamorphosis, like a caterpillar changing into a butterfly. It means to become something totally different. The laboratory of that change is the human mind. To be born again you had to change your thinking and renew your mind to a spiritual awareness. You had to recognize Jesus Christ as being the only Son of God who sacrificed His life for you. To continue in the *process* of salvation, though, you must sustain that same renovating of your thoughts. God is not interested in a *painted* house; He wants to *build* a new one! That process begins in your thoughts, your reasoning, your intellect. You must change the way you process thoughts and learn to think as He does. You must think and understand by the knowledge of His Kingdom.

The promise here is that as you begin this renewing of your mind, you *will* be transformed. The context is not just mental, however. As we have mentioned repeatedly, and as you can see in the Scriptures previously referred to in this chapter, God wants total change in all Life Areas. Notice the specific changes He speaks of in these verses from Romans. Present your *bodies* (physical) as a living and holy sacrifice, which is your *spiritual* service of worship. Avoid *conforming* (in all areas, is the implication), but *transform* yourself with a new way of *thinking* (intellectual). But stay in control of your *pride* (emotional/personality) and remember it is God's *gift* to be able to change like this in the first place. Thinking is the catalyst and energy of the entire transformation process.

### As a Man Thinks

> *Do not eat the bread of a selfish man, or desire his delicacies; for as he thinks within himself, so he is...* [*"as he thinketh in his heart, so is he"* KJV] (Proverbs 23:6-7).

You are today what you thought yesterday, and tomorrow you will become what you think today. If you are not satisfied with who you are and you want to change, then change your thinking. Transformation is forever linked with changed thinking. It's a spiritual law that always works, so why not put it to work for you? I have no doubt that if you have read through the previous chapters before reading this one, you have already begun to renew your thinking.

But as this Scripture tells us, be careful *what* you think about. Be sure that you are filling your thought life with worthy subjects—subjects you wish to take part in and have become a part of you. Be careful whom you associate with, for their thinking may not be what you desire. You must constantly ask yourself whether the people you are associating with are thinking in line with your purpose and destiny, and whether the thoughts you entertain while in their presence are in line as well.

Our thinking is the key to purpose, destiny, and achievement. We must set a much higher standard than what is set by those around us. We must *think* in the realm of *infinite possibilities*. We must think in the realm of God Himself. This is no small task, and it is guaranteed that you will undergo vast change when you do so. We are to be going "from glory to glory" and "from faith to faith" (see 2 Cor. 3:18;

Rom. 1:17). That means positive, creative change. Embrace it! Seek it! Love it! It will always serve you for the better.

## Thinking in the Realm of Infinite Possibilities

> *"For My thoughts are not your thoughts, neither are your ways My ways," declares the Lord. "For as the heavens are higher than the earth, so are My ways higher than your ways, and My thoughts than your thoughts. For as the rain and the snow come down from heaven, and do not return there without watering the earth, and making it bear and sprout, and furnishing seed to the sower and bread to the eater; so shall My word be which goes forth from My mouth; it shall not return to Me empty, without accomplishing what I desire, and without succeeding in the matter for which I sent it"* (Isaiah 55:8-11).

Notice in these verses that God never said we *can't* think at His level, but that we *don't* think at His level. A man's ways are dictated by how he thinks. Henry Ford's immortal words ring true for every man, "If a man thinks he can or thinks he can't, he's right." This is a paraphrase of Proverbs 23:7 above. There is no denying it! There is, however, a way to enjoy the honey of this truth, yet avoid the sting. Think as God thinks. Allow yourself to go beyond the limits of your past and the limits by which others say you must be bound. Step into the realm of infinite possibilities.

In First Corinthians 2:16 we are told that "we have the mind of Christ." What does that mean? Does it mean we are allowed only to say it? Or does it mean we have the ability to live it? Can you allow yourself to believe that you have the inherent ability as a Christian to tap into the mind of God Himself? Does that "short circuit" your brain? Or does it exhilarate you as it does me? The mind of Christ—what a power source! These are not the whimsical platitudes of some ancient philosopher; this is the Word of Almighty God! His thoughts, His words, His ways *can* become ours. As we let the mind of Christ operate within us, His results will follow. This is not mere hyperbole; this is actual fact! Do not buy the lie that we cannot live in such a way.

We, you and I, as believers in the Lord Jesus Christ, have *His* mind. If you can grasp that truth, if you can get your brain to wrap around that concept, then you will begin to walk in the realm of infinite possibilities.

All we have to do to enter this realm is believe His Word. When we let our minds dwell on His Word, His ways, and His thoughts, they will become a part of our words, our ways, and our thoughts. When that happens, the impossible becomes possible! Of course, there will be opposition, but even then we have the ability to tap the power of God's ways and thoughts and attain victory!

> *For though we walk in the flesh, we do not war according to the flesh, for the weapons of our warfare are not of the flesh, but divinely powerful for the destructions of fortresses. We are destroying speculations and every lofty thing raised up against the knowledge of God, and we are taking every thought captive to the obedience of Christ* (2 Corinthians 10:3-5).

By taking control of our thoughts and subjecting them to the radiant light of God's Word (which contains His thoughts and ways), we protect ourselves from wandering into errors in our purpose and destiny. As we become more and more adept at hearing His voice and following Him, and as we learn more of the Bible, our thoughts begin to flow in His realm. God has no limits. God has no fears. God has no lack. That is why He can speak and it comes to pass. That is why His Word never returns without accomplishing what He sent it to do. You and I can live in like manner by totally relying upon His guidance and by protecting our minds. This is not as ethereal as it sounds. It's like any other skill; it merely takes focused, repetitious practice.

### Focus Is Job One

**Focus your thinking and learning on whatever your personal purpose demands that you know, and you will be transformed into another and more valuable person.** (W.G.)

You must focus your thoughts on the purpose that God has given you. Don't be a floodlight in this respect; be a laser beam! Concentrate your thoughts along the singular line of your destiny until they burn right through it into achievement! Take every thought captive to the obedience of Christ's purpose for your life. Don't let anything distract you as you pursue your life's mission. This is the secret of the great people in every area I have researched. No matter the occupation or calling, every great leader and highly successful person has been keenly focused on his or her end result. I also have found it to be true for every goal to which I have applied it.

- Jesus kept "the joy set before Him [and] endured the cross" (Heb. 12:2)
- The apostle Paul was continually pressing "on toward the goal for the prize of the upward call" (Phil. 3:14).

We have spoken much about finding your purpose and planning its fulfillment. We have discussed the importance of writing down your ideas and goals. But to truly excel in your purpose, to truly direct your achievements in maximum form and power, you must be solely focused upon your destination, your completed destiny. By keeping your eyes so locked in laser-like commitment, you will be virtually unstoppable!

**Improve Your Skills**

You cannot afford to be fragmented in your direction. You must develop skills primarily in the area of your purpose. It is the skilled person, the masterful individual, who dominates an industry or accomplishes the unbelievable deed. As believers in Christ, how can we expect anything less of ourselves than skilled effort toward our purpose? When God planned the building of the tabernacle in the wilderness after freeing Israel from slavery, He called for the *skilled* craftsmen to do the work, not just anyone who wanted to volunteer. Then, after they came forward for the task, He *blessed* their skilled hands even more by His Holy Spirit. (Read Exodus 31:1-6.) A Christian who is constantly improving his or her destiny skills will feel the presence of the Lord more strongly, I believe. It's part of our stewardship to continually develop our gifts and skills in the areas that God calls our lives to embrace.

> *Do you see a man skilled in his work? He will stand before kings; he will not stand before obscure men* (Proverbs 22:29).

It is the skilled person who will stand before the kings of this world. It goes without saying that no king would summon a common, unlearned man into his chambers for counsel or service. So why be common when you can excel before kings! I plan to be one who fulfills that verse by developing skills both appreciated and needed by the leaders and rulers of the earth. Not in a prideful way, not for my exaltation, but for the opportunity to share the truth of Christ with them!

I urge you not to waste precious time, energy, and money with anything that does not pertain to your God-ordained purpose and destiny. Could a lifetime of work be counted as precious stones, gold, and silver if it is not part of what the Lord intended your life to produce? (Read First Corinthians 3:12-15.) I think not, and I do not want you or anyone else to discover that truth the hard way. As we seek to acquire more knowledge and skill, we must constantly ask ourselves the following questions:

- Is this necessary for me to learn to become skilled in performing my purpose?
- Is this information that is good for me to know or that I need to know?
- What skills *do* I need?
- Where can I learn more?
- Who can teach me?

Then we must set our face like flint toward those answers.

Please don't get me wrong, I am not advocating that we shun recreation and hobbies. Jesus clearly told His disciples to take a break now and then (see Mk. 6:30-32). Rather, I am advocating a continual growth in the things you will *most* need to achieve your God-ordained purpose, and to focus *more* on them than on anything else. For me that means continued research in the areas affecting purpose, destiny, and achievement, that I might become more expert at teaching others how to accomplish those things to which they are called. It means improving my speaking and writing techniques. It means more skill in consulting and management to help churches develop their visions. It requires me to be trained in finances and health, so that I can continue to travel and produce more educational and discipling materials. I have actually set my sights on peaking my skills in these areas when I reach my 90's!

**More knowledge is little help to him who has yet to act on what he already knows.** (W.G.)

**Condensing the Power of Knowledge**

*...the prudent are crowned with knowledge* (Proverbs 14:18).

*The mind of the intelligent seeks knowledge...* (Proverbs 15:14).

*The mind of the prudent acquires knowledge, and the ear of the wise seeks knowledge* (Proverbs 18:15).

There are over 200 references in the Book of Proverbs to knowledge, understanding, and wisdom. God obviously wants us to believe in their importance. Skill comes from knowledge. The knowledge of the world doubles every 24 months, as of this writing, and is doubling exponentially at a rapid rate. That means if you are not at least increasing your own knowledge in that time span, you are falling incredibly behind in skill areas. You may be a truly gifted person and, for a time, you may be able to get by without much practice of your gift and even stay in the forefront of your vocation.

However, rest assured that there are those with as much or less gifting as yourself who are honing their gifts into highly productive skills through constantly increasing their knowledge. They will pass you by like you are standing still if you do not join them in the acquisition of more knowledge for increased skill levels. If you believe in your personal purpose and are designing your destiny, you cannot afford to let yourself slip into the trap of complacency and lesser productivity merely because you have a gifting or even an anointing from the Lord.

**Skill also comes from repetition of knowledge acquired.** (W.G.)

When I was learning my slackwire act, I spent hundreds of hours in private practice sessions repeating the same tricks over and over and over. I would steal down to the circus tent during breakfast, lunch, and dinner, and even after dark to walk and balance uninterrupted. I wanted to be the best I could possibly be, and I knew that it wouldn't happen without *extra* effort at developing those skills through physical knowledge of the art. I knew that the difference between "ordinary" and "extraordinary" was the "extra" work, sweat, and repetitions.

I put my wire act together and had it show ready in about four or five weeks. That was record time if you go by the normal practice sessions of an hour or so per day. The other performers were marveling at the speed at which I learned. They called me gifted. I believe I had natural talent, but that wasn't all. I spent the same hours of repetitious practice as most did on the wire—only I condensed the weeks into days by *multiplying* the hours per day practiced. It appeared that I developed skills faster than anyone, but the hours and number of repetitions were probably the same.

What I'm getting at here is the fact that "you've gotta pay your dues." There is no free ride with skill. You can pay your dues slowly or you can condense the time, but you must pay them. I like to condense the time. When my first book, the original of the one you are now reading, was accepted for publication in 1986, people said it was miraculous to get contracted by the first publisher you send a book to—when you've never written anything before. But they did not know of the hundreds of songs, poems, newsletter articles, Christian follow-up materials, and Bible training curriculums I had already written. The dues don't change. I want to get more done in less days, even though the hours may be the same. Let me share with you how I've done this continually in many different areas of my life. I call it…

*Tapping the Power of Role Models*

**Mentors:** When I want to learn something new or enhance a skill, I first seek out someone who already has such skills. I watch this person for awhile and learn all I can from a spectator's point of view. Then I go to that person and ask him if he will allow me the privilege of learning from him directly. I am up front and honest about it. I cannot remember anyone turning me down, and I have been very sure not to turn down anyone who asks the same of me. Next I spend as much time with that person as I possibly can. I try to live in his hip pocket, so to speak. I ask questions continually. I take notes when necessary. I become a dutiful student.

The strategy here is to condense the time it would normally take me to learn the skills that my role model has spent years learning. I realize that I will still need to put in the hours with particular skills, but I can avoid many of the trials and errors my mentor endured by learning from his experiences. A mentor become a sort of educational "mine sweeper" for me—removing the unseen and unknown "time damaging mistakes" for me. I believe that this is what Jesus did for His 12 disciples. He poured three intense years of training into them by living with them *day and night*. Those men obviously had a perfect role model to see exactly how to do things right! When *they* made errors, Jesus was quick to teach and correct. That is great mentoring.

I used this role modeling technique in the wire act I mentioned. I sought out the best wire walker at FSU and he consented to give me his valuable time in private sessions and to help me learn his secrets. I later did the same for those who came to me. When I stepped into the ministry, I did the same with my pastor. I went everywhere with him, even in the middle of the night to pray for the sick on emergency calls. I stood at his side when he ministered to people in the church services and listened to teaching tapes with him in his office. He taught me more in a few months than most preachers learn in years of seminary. Now, I'm not knocking seminary; I just learned differently and faster.

The point is, whatever you want, go find the role model who's already an expert at it and copy that person as much as possible. Discover every secret found and every mistake made; then act accordingly with the information. Refuse to associate with anyone who does *not* think in terms of tremendous achievement. Surround yourself with the top achievers. Why? You reap what you sow—it's the law of the universe. Do you want to achieve great things and fulfill your destiny? Then sow that kind of seed into your spirit, soul, and body through associating with those who have cut the path!

When I wanted to write a book, I called writers. When I wanted to sing, I spent time with singers. When I wanted to learn to surf, I paddled out and hung around with the best! It was *always* worth my effort and time. But there were times when I couldn't find any mentors to spend time with me. The people I wanted to learn from were hundreds or thousands of miles away. I had no way to establish a relationship. So I did the next best thing! I studied their materials.

**Study:** Find every book written by the mentor you want to learn from. Let experts you may never meet teach you everything they know for free! Do you have a library card? Did you know that only about three percent of Americans have a library card? (That's probably the same three percent found in the Yale class of 1953 who made plans for their goals!) The knowledge of the world is waiting for us in the library at "no charge," and the majority of us never even darken the doors! Pathetic. But you and I are not so foolish. I have spent wonderful hours studying the works of those before me who, by writing their knowledge for me to read, have let the sweat of their brow save mine. Books are literal storehouses of skill. Tap into the source of *any* skill you need and change your life: Just drop into your local library. You'll feel smarter just walking around in it!

But don't stop with books. Libraries have audiotapes and videotapes, Internet access, periodicals, newspapers of the day, and even micro-shrunk catalogues of the works of yester-years. Think of libraries as free universities open six days a week just for you! Become someone of consequence! Every person of great repute whom I have studied has proven the adage that "leaders are readers." Whatever your purpose, your destiny should be filled with time in the books that pertain to it. Create your own library and begin to stock it with a legacy of insight and educational wonder that your inheritors will love you for.

Invest in your mind! Be sure that you don't spend more on movies than you do on books and teaching materials. "Pass" on going out for dinner; purchase a book and stay in! Enroll for seminars in your area of purpose. Buy teaching tapes and videos that will enhance you. What you can't find in the library, buy in a bookstore. If you're frugal like me, find a half-price used bookstore—the best stuff at the best prices! I have found some goldmines of information for mere pennies in those stores. Just believe the fact that you are worth the investment. I do not believe there is a better dollar for dollar purchase than a book or a teaching tape.

Be a reader! Be a perpetual learner! Be a student *for* life and *of* life! See your purpose and destiny as an ongoing college or graduate level course and never cease to seek more knowledge and wisdom for it. It's been said that if you want to be a local expert on something, read about 100 books on the subject. If you want to be a national expert, read about 700 books on the subject. I average about two books, tapes, and/or periodicals per week in the areas of my purpose. Why not go for the gold and hit the books!

Here are two projects to spark your thinking concerning using role models on your way to achievement. You may need to visit a library to complete this task. If so, go do it and know that you are stepping into the three percent range of top achievers!

**Project #1:** Make a list of the top 20 people with skills pertaining to your purpose, whom you would like to learn from (in person or otherwise).

**Project #2:** Make a list of the specific books or other learning materials produced by the people on your Top 20 list that you will need to create the knowledge and skills necessary to fulfill your purpose.

Mentors and their teaching products are mandatory for ensuring success. But there will come a time when you must take the next step up, which is to go beyond your mentors. It is a step toward even greater skills through what I call…

*The Expansion Process*

*The expansion process is simply taking all the knowledge and skills you have accumulated and asking yourself what you can do to go beyond it all.* With my wire act I created new tricks, some not done before or since, to my knowledge. In ministry I asked, "What more is there beyond the books, the teachings, and the skills I see in my mentors?" (I'm still working on those!) In marriage I asked, "How can I be a more effective husband and father?" ( I'm really working on those!) I sought new ways to serve people and to teach what I learned. And with this message of purpose, destiny, and achievement, when I asked, "How can I go beyond my first edition of the book?" a vision large enough to last my lifetime was created! The more I think this way and pursue those thoughts to fruition, the more I realize how small I actually think. I also realize how *big* my God is!

## Constant Improvement

Continuous improvement is the name of the game. Knowledge brings improvement when coupled with our actions. I've made it a goal to continually study people who have achieved great things. I have constantly been inspired by the stories of ordinary people who became extraordinary producers. I wish to be such a person. My motivation is to glorify God and to help as many people in the process as possible. I have found this to be the case with most who have achieved greatness in the majority of their Life Areas. In this section I will share with you what I believe to be one of the best examples of creating a system of constant improvement for the betterment of individuals and those they touch.

**Our personal purpose should be so large that it forces positive change upon us.** (W.G.)

The miracle that took Japan from the ashes of World War II to the pinnacle of industrial success is accredited not to a *Japanese* philosopher or marketing personality, but to an *American* quality control expert named Dr. Edwards Demming. Demming is heralded by the Japanese as the father of their business triumph. He is the nation's hero! Each year a special and very prestigious award is bestowed upon the company that best exemplifies the principles of Demming's philosophy. When I read Demming's biography, I was struck by the sheer simplicity of this man's philosophy. It is only 14 points long and is easily condensed into one phrase: *commitment to constant improvement*. That phrase and those 14 points systematically turned "atomic ashes" into "global gold" for a depressed and defeated nation.

Demming's creed states that everyone involved in the end product of something should be knowledgable of its function and be able to make suggestions for changes in its quality. Every member of an assembly line should have the right to share positive ideas that will enhance the product. Management should encourage such ideas and implement them. Everyone involved should have the tools and authority to do their task with the utmost quality and efficiency. It is a *commitment* to increasing the quality of the product on a daily basis, be it a hard item or a service.

There is no reason in the world that you and I cannot enjoy this same type of continually improving growth, is there? The answer is an obvious *no*! As I studied these principles, I surmised that if a nation could benefit in such a way, I could also. I was right! In fact, I have been applying these principles for years now and have yet to see them fail. Here's the system I created for myself to employ this "constant improvement" ideology.

**Good S.I.E.D.**

The acronym S.I.E.D. stands for "Steady Improvement Every Day." I coined this phrase to help me tie Demming's philosophy with the universal law of sowing and reaping. By daily asking myself how I can improve the quality of my Life Areas and then acting on the answers, I am assured of constant growth in skills and knowledge. Sow the S.I.E.D. and reap the rewards!

- In *spiritual* matters I sow more time into prayer or reading the Word of God.
- In the *social* areas I sow more time with my children or wife—perhaps going to breakfast with one of the kids or to a marriage seminar with Meg.
- For the *physical,* I increase my repetitions of certain exercises by one each day, switching around weekly.
- *Intellectually*, I read every day and increase my application of what I have learned in a practical way.
- *Financially,* I study and seek new ways to earn, save, and invest.
- For my *personality,* I use my journals to track my daily progress in changing more into the personality of Christ.

Whatever the Life Area, I find some way to make an improvement each day. No, I don't always cover each area each day, but I do get at least one or two in without fail. How? I simply plan my improvements into my schedule ahead of time, as I do the other goals of my destiny. Once decided upon, they go into my daily planner. I have a code that helps me remember which ones I'm concentrating on that day or week, and before I go to bed I check that day's progress. Progress that cannot be measured is frustrating to track. Be sure to use a measurable tracking technique as you pursue your own S.I.E.D., and you will undoubtedly reap the harvest of personal growth and achievement!

## Change Agent Journaling

> *For whatever was written in earlier times was written for our instruction, that through perseverance and the encouragement of the Scriptures we might have hope. ... But I have written very boldly to you on some points, so as to remind you again...* (Romans 15:4,15).

I mentioned in the chapter on mission statements the importance of the written word in keeping your vision before you and before those who will join your efforts. Now I wish to share with you a valuable tool that will serve as a powerful catalyst of change in your life, should you choose to employ it. I discovered this idea in the book by Kenneth Wydro, *Think on Your Feet*. I call it Change Agent Journaling. Simply put, it means to use a daily writing journal to create in yourself the positive changes necessary to fulfill your purpose and destiny. I will give you an easy and simple method to track those changes as well. I believe that you will love Change Agent Journaling and will want to share the idea with others.

The first item you must acquire is a writing journal. Most drugstores and office supplies stores carry a broad array of journal-type books. Diaries are acceptable, but I find them too small and thick for my taste. I usually purchase a composition book designed for school term papers. These can last me about a year or more as I write extremely small and use every square inch of every page to conserve space. Whatever fits your preference will be fine, but the key is to get something immediately if you have not yet begun a journal.

The Change Agent Journaling process hinges on the premise that each of us has things in our lives that we desire to either change or develop in some manner. Few actually enjoy either because they lack a plan to do so. This one works quite well. Each evening, just before you go to bed, make an entry in your journal for the next day. This entry will require some thought beforehand, since what you write each night will be what you seek to change in your life the next day. By thinking of and committing to that particular item of change, you are doing two things at once: 1) activating your spirit to create ways to effect the change, even while you sleep; and 2) establishing a strong desire to actually *do* something about the issue on the morrow. You will find this process to be quite fascinating.

Let me give you an example of how this can be done. My life goal is to be an example of one who believes in Christ in speech, love, faith, purity, and conduct. I have formed a daily plan for developing these five traits by the use of my Change Agent Journal.

1. In my journal I write the specific item I wish to work on the next day to help change myself into that kind of person.
2. Then, in code form, I enter this same item in my daily planner for that day. For instance, in the area of speech I have penned

"no unwholesome words, but words that edify and encourage today" in my journal and "spch" in my planner.

3. I take time to imagine myself saying good things to people, especially those I will see the next day, such as my wife and children.

4. The next morning I awake and check my journal first thing to activate my mind to the item of change.

5. I again picture myself saying good and encouraging things to specific people I will most likely encounter that day.

6. As I go through the day, I check my daily planner to remind myself of the day's change agent.

7. At the end of the day, I enter my progress in my journal and decide what to work on the next day. If I feel that extra work is needed on the subject I worked on that day, I simply carry it over as many times as necessary until the change is solidly in place. I have found this to be a most successful way to change my habits and personality traits, to enhance skills and establish new ones, and to accomplish more than before in less time.

The key to Change Agent Journaling is to concentrate on the items in your life that pertain most to your personal purpose and destiny. Focusing on specifics will propel you farther and faster toward your goals, while simultaneously developing your optimal personality for what you are called to do. It is a very painless way to change because you are proactive. You are not having to learn and change through uncomfortable circumstances, but from the ones that you dictate for yourself. By asking the Holy Spirit to help you decide which items to pursue first, you will have an even bigger edge in the change process.

This kind of journaling can be used to overcome fears, depressions, failure thinking, and any other item you wish. There is no limit to the way you can use this method of written self-training. It's up to you, and the great thing is that no one can really hinder you in any way. By deliberately attacking a problem area, you remain in control of the change. Your only "must have" assistant is the Holy Spirit.

## Other Journaling

Change Agent Journaling is not to be a substitute for your regular journaling. You should keep a daily journal to record how the day's affairs have gone, what you have learned, and what part of your destiny you may have fulfilled. Such writing is a legacy you will leave to your children and friends should the Lord tarry. Your journal should be private; it should be a place you can go to pour out anything and everything you wish.

Journals can even be specialized. I have volumes of journals solely dedicated to the visions, dreams, and prophetic encounters I have had since becoming a Christian. That is some very interesting reading! But I have penned few journals just on my mundane daily life, for which I have deep regret. I thought only the things given me by God would be of any value, so for many years I concentrated only on these records. Now I realize that my experiences in everyday life were just as valuable in my learning and growing experience, and I've made this journaling a priority.

Please do not be condemned or intimidated by your lack of journaling or the suggestion to journal. There is no scriptural mandate for it, which will take from your eternity if you don't journal. It is more for your reflection and referral and for those who will read it after you. Besides, there is something about writing things down that just plain solidifies them in our spirits and minds. God twice wrote the Ten Commandments with His own finger in the stone. He instructed Moses to write and read the covenant laws before the people. Jesus referred to the Scriptures continually. Paul wrote letters saturated with eternal power. Our names are written in the Lamb's Book of Life. Writing things down is important to God. It needs to become more important to us. If you have not yet begun a life of journaling, do so today. You will never regret it.

## Final Thoughts

The bottom line for change, especially for a Christian, is to *always be content, but never satisfied*. It has been called a "dissatisfied satisfaction." However you say it, it means that you will have a contentment through your relationship with and trust in God, but you will be ever striving to increase His life in you, as well as the gifts and skills He has entrusted to you to achieve your destiny. If you are fully convinced that you have found your purpose and have designed the destiny He has for you, then you can never know full satisfaction because God's plan is to keep His people growing eternally.

We must proactively assess and change ourselves. We must ask ourselves, "What am I satisfied with in my life and why? Is it okay to be satisfied? Can I learn and grow more?" Those kinds of questions will spark your creativity, and creativity will elicit change.

Transformation is God's ultimate desire for us. He wants us to become like Jesus. That demands the renewing of our spirits, our souls, and our bodies. To deny ourselves that transformation—either deliberately or through neglect—is wrong. The price of Christ's death was too high for such denial.

When you become dedicated to the increase of your spirituality, your physical skills, your health, your knowledge and understanding, your finances, and whatever else you need to complete your goals, then your personal worth, your value to those around you, will increase accordingly and steadily. Embrace the changes. Enjoy the unsatisfied life!

**In any great endeavor, who we become is more important than what we accomplish.** (Anon.)

# Chapter 15

# The Master Keys of Achievement

## Living in the Realm of Infinite Possibilities

> *Then God said, "Let Us make man in Our image, according to Our likeness; and let them rule over the fish of the sea and over the birds of the sky and over the cattle and over all the earth, and over every creeping thing that creeps on the earth"* (Genesis 1:26).

> *But God, being rich in mercy, because of His great love with which He loved us, even when we were dead in our transgressions, made us alive together with Christ (by grace you have been saved), and raised us up with Him, and seated us with Him in the heavenly places, in Christ Jesus* (Ephesians 2:4-6).

> *But just as it is written, "THINGS WHICH EYE HAS NOT SEEN AND EAR HAS NOT HEARD, AND which HAVE NOT ENTERED THE HEART OF MAN, ALL THAT GOD HAS PREPARED FOR THOSE WHO LOVE HIM." For to us God revealed them through the Spirit; for the Spirit searches all things, even the depths of God* (1 Corinthians 2:9-10).

I want to take you from merely *thinking* about the possibilities to actually *experiencing* them. I am going to lay out in this chapter a master system for achieving virtually anything you wish. This system is comprised of spiritual laws that have been proven for thousands of years by both the godly and the ungodly. That's the way of laws; they work for everyone. But my focus here will be to tap the unlimited power of God and secure this system for use within His will.

Through His Holy Spirit, believers have the ability to live in the same realm as Him. It has been taught by some that mortal man cannot possibly understand the things of God. Ridiculous! The Scriptures quoted at the beginning of this chapter disclose the very reason the Holy Spirit was sent to us: It was so we *could* understand the things of God, even the *deep* things of God! This is the power of the Christian life: We have the power of God within us! We have the mind of God within us, which produces the ability of God to flow from us. These are the same abilities that were utilized to create every item in the entire universe.

**There is no "Dreams of the Apostles" or "Desires of the Apostles" or even "Ideas of the Apostles"— there is only the book of "The ACTS of the Apostles."** (Anon.)

I want you to begin to *see*, *say*, and *do* things in the realm of Heaven. I want you to open your spirit to the unlimited possibilities of achievement that God has in store for you. He longs to give you dreams and visions of your future, the magnitude of which will leave your jaw on the pavement in amazement! Do you really believe that the One who created the stars, the earth, and the creatures on it, would create something exactly like Himself (namely us) and then not allow those creatures to even know His realm of living? He died for us to do so. That, for me, is all I need to know to pour every fiber of my being into learning how to skillfully operate in the lifestyle of my heavenly Father. Isn't the same true for you?

*...All things are possible to him who believes* (Mark 9:23).

*I can do all things through Him who strengthens me* (Philippians 4:13).

Within these two verses is the motto of my life. When I first read these verses over 25 years ago, I realized that no matter what I wanted to do, where I wanted to go, or who I wished to meet, learn from, or give to, I could do so! I instantly, and I mean that literally, believed what I read in those Scriptures. And what I believe, I go after with everything I've got. It was the power locked within those truths that catapulted me into achieving my dreams of a professional circus (Circus Alleluia Ministries), of my first book, of my own network marketing organization, and of all the other aspects of my life that I have pursued.

**Never make excuses—make a difference.** (Anon.)

My Destiny Goals List is filled with goals beyond my ability to accomplish on my own, but I have yet to come up with one of substance that the Lord has told me *He* cannot handle. Notice how often the word *all* is used in the verses just quoted. What does that word mean? It means *all*! Everything you and I will ever attempt to do, the Lord says we can get it done and we can rely on His strength while doing so. It is not by our puny, human strength and abilities, but by the power of Jesus Christ in and through us!

If you are going to live in this realm of godly accomplishment, you will have to do things God's way. That is, after all, the message in Isaiah 55; His thoughts and His ways are above ours. God is not shy about sharing His secrets with His children. He actually exemplifies them continually throughout the Bible. His ways are not hard to understand, nor are His requirements difficult to perform. In fact, they are easy to do. But they are just as easy *not* to do, and that is why many believers never walk in the realm of infinite possibilities. They find it easier *not* to. But such is not the case with you and me.

There are three Master Keys with which you must become skillful. There are just three, and they open every lock on every goal of your life. As I have said previously, I am assuming that you are submitting everything you undertake to the will of the Lord, and so I ask you to study each key from that perspective.

## Master Key #1: See It

**The world of tomorrow belongs to the person who has vision today.** (Robert Schuller)

> *And Jesus answered saying to them, "Have faith in God. Truly I say to you, whoever says to this mountain, 'Be taken up and cast into the sea,' and does not doubt in his heart, but believes what he says is going to happen, it shall be granted him. Therefore I say to you, all things for which you pray and ask, believe that you have received them, and they shall be granted you"* (Mark 11:22-24).

Jesus was teaching His own disciples about faith, at their request. He did not waste words. There have been volumes printed about what

He meant, but He said little to get this point across. If you want to receive something from the Lord, anything at all, it requires your *seeing* it *before* you receive it. That is the simplicity of faith. Verse 22 is explicit; your faith must be in God. Then Jesus proclaims the spiritual law of faith: Believe you have it before you get it, or you won't get it! You must see things as you desire them to be, not as they are, or you will not receive.

Several years ago I was helping my good friend Dr. Charles Shaffer move into a new home. While I was lying under the framework of his bed attempting to attach a long and very heavy solid oak board to the bookshelf/headboard, the weight of the plank shifted and grazed my eyebrow. I barely felt it, but the weight of the board was sufficient to cleave my skin and start a rather profuse flow of blood. Fortunately Dr. Shaffer's office was a short distance from his home, and we walked over to fix my face. As I lay on the examining table in Chuck's office, I began to ask him what it was like sewing someone's skin back together. "How did you learn? What did it feel like?" And then I asked, "Is it hard to see what you are doing sometimes?"

The answer to this question opened a new horizon of understanding for me. Chuck smiled and told me that sewing up a cut such as mine was child's play compared to what medical personnel do in micro surgery. Intrigued, I asked what he meant, and he told me that in order to pass a specific examination in med school, he had to successfully *sew two human hairs together, end to end*! Wow! I guess my jaw dropping to the floor in unbelief and amazement was enough to prompt Chuck to say matter-of-factly, "Greenman, if you can see it, you can do it."

Ding! Ding! Ding! The bells and whistles went off. I saw it! That is what faith is all about. That is what achievement is all about. If you can see it, you can do it! Now I realize that some of you reading this will be saying, "So what, Greenman. I learned that in second grade in finger-painting 101," or something equivalent. But for me it was revelation! It wasn't so much that I didn't already know the principle, because I had used it for many years by that time. It was the articulation of it in such simple terms that captured me. I have taught this principle of "faith sight" through that story ever since. I will never forget it. Now you won't either.

**If you don't know what the end result looks like, you can't get there.** (Vince Lombardi)

## My First Mind Movie

The first time I experienced this "see it" principle, which is now widely taught in just about every success motivational seminar worth its price, I was a senior in high school. We had a new coach for our championship track team at my high school and he was just plain fun. We all loved him. Coach Bill Harvey helped me take my pole vaulting to a new and more rewarding level using this technique. "Harv" taught me how to *see* my self sprint down the runway, plant the rubber tip of my fiberglass vaulting pole in the wooden box, rock back, push with my left hand and pull with my right, pick up my feet, and thrust them over the bar as I rotated my hips 180 degrees, push the pole away, and throw my head back to land in the foam rubber pit on my back.

He told me to play that movie over and over again in my mind before each vault. I had never before heard of doing such a thing, even though I unknowingly did it before almost every vault, just from nervousness. I was just never conscious of doing it until Harv explained that I should do so deliberately. At his bidding I complied. Before every vault I would go through that mental movie again and again. As I continued this routine for several weeks, my skills increased and my confidence grew!

I experienced a new skill level that year. When other vaulters were struggling with the wind or with sun in their faces, I simply played the movie a few more times and vaulted. I cannot remember ever having a problem with the elements. They were there, but they just did not affect me because they were not in my movie! I hit my highest height. I found my best form. I won awards. I was not the best, but I hit my personal best! That is all the Lord is asking of any of us. I took that key principle and applied it to everything I did from then on. It became especially helpful in my circus career.

> *By faith we understand that the worlds were prepared by the word of God, so that what is seen was not made out of things which are visible* (Hebrews 11:3).

God created the universe from something *invisible*. Where was that something before He made it visible? I believe it was in His divine imagination. I believe that the Lord created everything first in His imagination and then applied Master Keys #2 and #3 to bring them into the visible realm. I believe that God painted every detail of every bird, every mountain, every ecosystem, and of course every human, in His imagination first. I also believe that we are to do the same thing and, in fact, always have—even though many of us have not understood the principle. If we truly are made in *His* likeness and image, then we must operate in the same *way* He does. We too should be taking the invisible and making it visible, and we do.

**The most interesting people are those with the most interesting pictures in their minds.** (Earl Nightingale)

Look closely at the cover of this book. The design you see was first seen in the mind, the imagination, of a gifted artist. That artist then took the invisible and made it visible with the help of a printer. The chair you sit in. The room you are in right now. The clothes you are wearing. The pages you have been turning, and even the words printed upon them were first seen in the mind of another. The invisible has become visible to you because it was first made visible in the imagination of someone else. Everything you see around you right now is the purposeful creation of another person. God did it. They did it. You *must* do it!

### Picture What You Want

> *This book of the law shall not depart from your mouth, but you shall meditate on it day and night, so that you may be careful to do according to all that is written in it; for then you will make your way prosperous, and then you will have success* (Joshua 1:8).

Godly meditation and imagination draw the picture in your spirit. Is there a certain person or type of person you particularly enjoy watching or being like? Would you like to act, speak, or walk a different way than what you presently do? Would you like to be someone of noteworthy style? You can! You can look and act and speak like anyone you wish to. It is simply a choice that you make. It must begin in the movie production company of your mind. Simply by imagining with deliberate force the kind of person you wish to act and speak and dress like, you can. It is quite childlike to do so. It does not require great educational degrees; it simply takes a decision.

**Imagination is the mother of creation.** (W.G.)

You can do this with anything you wish to become. If it is within the Kingdom of God and He has not told you to refrain from it, you can do it if you can see it!

Everything begins in the imagination, in the invisible realm where God dwells. Our spirits can connect with the Holy Spirit easily in this dimension and believe what we see. There are no hindrances in our imagination, no one telling us it can't be done. There are no skeptics or dream stealers. There is only pure belief. What we must learn to do is to see exactly what we *want*—what our goals are to be—and then bring those pictures into the reality of this *visible* realm.

When my son was on drugs shooting heroin and snorting cocaine, I had to work very hard at seeing what I wanted and not what I had. I would sit and picture myself standing next to him on a ministry platform sharing the Word of God together and ministering to people. For two years I fed my spirit the Word of God concerning His promises about children. I turned again and again to Deuteronomy 28 to study the curse of the law. I knew that by understanding the *curse* of the law, I could believe God to do the *opposite* according to Galatians 3:13-14.

I studied these Scriptures and found the verse that stated that my children, if I was under the curse, would be taken from me and would be raised by someone else, and I could do nothing about it. I knew that this was the opposite of God's will for me and for my children, so I meditated on this truth and pictured my children always with me until they were grown and on their own. Eventually this constant meditation and seeing it in my mind transferred into the realm of the second key to achievement: the *saying* of what you believe.

## Master Key #2: Say It

Let's go back to Genesis 1. In this chapter the Lord created the heavens and the earth, the entire universe, and all the living things in the earth. God saw His entire creation in the invisible realm of His imagination first. Then, in order to bring it into the tangible, touchable realm of the physical, He *said* what He saw. Every time God created something from the invisible, He spoke it into existence. Isn't that fascinating? I figured that there had to be an explanation as to why this was the case and, upon researching the Bible, I found the answers.

> *But having the same spirit of faith, according to what is written, "I BELIEVED, THEREFORE I SPOKE," we also believe, therefore also we speak* (2 Corinthians 4:13).

This verse is quite simple. It goes hand in hand with Mark 11:22-24, which we discussed earlier. According to Jesus' teachings on faith, there is the requirement both to believe or *see* what you want and to *speak* what you saw or believed. Speaking is not an option for us if we wish to fulfill our God-ordained purpose. Speak specifically and directly what you desire. Leave no question of what you mean. Gain control of your vocabulary and what you believe and put them together to unleash the power of God for whatever you seek to achieve. That is Kingdom of God living! I am not talking about positive affirmation here. I am talking about filling your mouth with words of power wrapped in the belief of your spirit! When you meditate upon the goals that God has shown you, and you get to the point where you can see them clearly and in detail, a miracle takes place.

> *For with the heart man believes, resulting in righteousness, and with the mouth he confesses, resulting in salvation* (Romans 10:10).

> *For the mouth speaks out of that which fills the heart* (Matthew 12:34b).

> *Death and life are in the power of the tongue, and those who love it will eat its fruit* (Proverbs 18:21).

> *For we all stumble in many ways. If anyone does not stumble in what he says, he is a perfect man, able to bridle the whole body as well. Now if we put the bits into the horses' mouths so that they may obey us, we direct their entire body as well. Behold, the ships also, though they are so great and are driven by strong winds, are still directed by a very small rudder, wherever the inclination of the pilot desires. So also the tongue is a small part of the body, and yet it boasts of great things. Behold, how great a forest is set aflame by such a small fire!* (James 3:2-5)

Our words are so powerful that they have the ability to bring us life and death. Our words can set our lives on fire or guide us to safe havens. It is our words, backed by the belief born of constant imagining, visualizing, and seeing—good or bad—that directs our lives' production. We will always speak what we believe. We will always believe what we meditate upon most.

**When we speak, the hosts of Heaven or the hordes of hell go to work to bring it to pass.** (W.G.)

As I mentioned, my son was a drug addict for over two years. I spent much time seeing him as I wanted, not as he was. As my heart overflowed with the visions I saw of him in my mind and spirit, I began to speak them.

- I told everyone whom I felt could understand me that Daniel was a called minister of the gospel and we would someday minister side by side. I told Daniel that too.

He only laughed and said he didn't believe in God. He said he was going to be a street person and leave home when he was 16.

- I told him he would never leave and I would see him grow up with us.

He told me I was an idiot. He ran away.

- I said he would never leave.

He came back. He was arrested and put in juvenile detention with a possible prison sentence.

- I said that he would not be raised by another.

He was sentenced only to probation and came home. He ran away while on probation.

- I said that he would be back and that we would see him grow up with us.

He was recaptured.

- Prison looked imminent, but I said that he would live only with us.

That last time before the judge, all charges were dropped and he came home!

Many miracles took place during my son's drug life. But one day, the greatest miracle of all occurred. He came to me and, with tears in his eyes, told me that he had to give his life to God because he couldn't take it anymore. It was a glorious time to kneel with him as he made Jesus the Lord and Master of his life! But I was puzzled that I shed no tears with him on that day. I asked the Lord if there was something wrong with me. His reply was simple and, as usual, to the point. "You already lived this moment and shed your tears long ago." I realized that He was right in that I had played the scenario in my mind so many times and with such conviction that I spoke it as fact for months. When the event found visibility, I had already been there and lived it. That is the glory of these Master Keys of achievement!

**You can and do have what you say.** (W.G.)

### Word Power

*For the word of God is living and active and sharper than any two-edged sword, and piercing as far as the division of the soul and spirit, of both joints and marrow, and able to judge the thoughts and intentions of the heart* (Hebrews 4:12).

There is power inside the Word of God. It is more powerful than you or I can possibly imagine, for it is God Himself. God is His Word! When we take the Word of God into our spirit and meditate upon it until it permeates our every thought, our words will flow forth in line with His Word. When that happens, you will release His power as you speak. And the power you release is the creative power that formed the universe!

It's not a mysterious or theoretical principle; it's very simple and logical. If we are made in His likeness and image, then we should operate the same way with the same power at work. Jesus said that we would be able to do the exact things He did—and even greater things. That requires the same power. It is developed in you through meditating upon and picturing within your mind and spirit what God's Word says, and in speaking it out your mouth. That includes God's personal words to you, as well as your personal purpose and destiny goals. But catch the reality of Jesus' promise of the "greater works"—they *are* works!

## Master Key #3: Do It!

**Apply yourself. Get all the education you can, but then, by God, do something. Don't just stand there, make it happen!** (Lee Iacoca)

> *And why do you call Me, "Lord, Lord," and do not do what I say? Everyone who comes to Me, and hears My words, and acts upon them, I will show you whom he is like: he is like a man building a house, who dug deep and laid a foundation upon the rock; and when a flood rose, the torrent burst against that house and could not shake it, because it had been well built* (Luke 6:46-48).

> *You see that faith was working with his works, and as a result of the works, faith was perfected... For just as the body without the spirit is dead, so also faith without works is dead* (James 2:22,26).

Deny yourself the deception that mental pictures and spoken words are all you need in order to eat the fruit of your goals. "It ain't so!" If you want to enjoy what you *see* and what you *say*, you must *do* it as well. The planning and strategizing we have spoken of in previous chapters will do you no good if left on the pages they fill. If you are to prove that you can and will accomplish what you believe the Lord has given you as your divine purpose, then *you* will have to *make* it happen. You cannot get by with lip service and dreams. You must put muscle on the move and act on what you believe. That is the final part of the faith equation. If you say you believe and never do it, you will have nothing. *Faith* ***must*** *have works to* ***be*** *faith.* Otherwise it is deception.

Jesus was quite pointed on this issue. If you want to be counted among the wise and those who truly have made Him Lord of their lives, you must go beyond listening and *act.* Seeing the pictures of your destiny come into the view of your mind is wonderful—but useless without action. Your life will be as unstable as the man who built on sand. Storms will come. Tough times will come. Pain is part of life. If you have not acted upon what you believe, you will have nothing to hold on to.

It is our *experience* that gives us the strength to go on in tough times. The key to success with building on the rock is to dig deep into the Word of God and get it into your spirit. By that I mean you must meditate upon the written Word and the word spoken to you personally. There is no other way to get the Word of God to be such a part of your life that, when the storms come, they do not break you. You'll be able to bend with the winds and roll with the tides. Truth is like that. It is unbeatable. The truth for you will be your personal purpose and destiny. Find the written Word of God that supplies strength for you as you perform your purpose. Think on these verses continually until they effortlessly flow from your mouth; then be sure to do exactly what they say.

**Some people dream of worthy accomplishments. Others stay awake and do them.** (Anon.)

> *And Jesus came up and spoke to them, saying, "All authority has been given to Me in heaven and on earth. Go therefore and make disciples of all the nations, baptizing them in the name of the Father and the Son and the Holy Spirit, teaching them to observe all that I commanded you; and lo, I am with you always, even to the end of the age"* (Matthew 28:18-20).

> *And He said to them, "Go into all the world and preach the gospel to all creation. He who has believed and has been baptized shall be saved; but he who has disbelieved shall be condemned. And these signs will accompany those who have believed: in My name they will cast out demons, they will speak with new tongues; they will pick up serpents, and if they drink any deadly poison, it shall not hurt them; they will lay hands on the sick, and they will recover." So then, when the Lord Jesus had spoken to them, He was received up into heaven, and sat down at the right hand of God. And they went out and preached everywhere, while the Lord worked with them, and confirmed the word by the signs that followed* (Mark 16:15-20).

As I have said before, the Great Commission is just that: great! It is filled with actions. It is aggressive and exhorts us to go, teach, preach, make, and baptize. No matter how you look at it, the Great Commission is to be performed, not just spoken. Your part in it, your personal purpose, will be no different. If you dawdle on the sidelines of your life, you will only be disappointed when the game is over. All the coaching, Bible training, and mediating on the Word of God will be meaningless if you do not go do something. If you do not have a strong work ethic, a desire to work hard at something, then you had best acquire it immediately. Without a desire to perform the very things that God lays out to you, there will be little fruit to enjoy.

**The opportunity of a lifetime must be seized during the lifetime of the opportunity.** (Leonard Ravenhill)

## Just Do It!

Nike corporation made that phrase famous worldwide. Why? Because it speaks to something in the heart of every man and woman to go after their dreams and desires and to work until those dreams are accomplished. It is a rallying cry for the sports-minded, but the ones seeking their true meaning in life will embrace it just as strongly. If you are to fulfill your destiny, you will have to adopt the same creed. When you do so, be sure to "go for it" with all your passion! Passionate action should be our heart song. This is exemplified in the Scripture that says to "love the Lord with all your heart, mind, and strength" (see Mt. 22:37). Here are some other verses that emphasize this point.

*Poor is he who works with a negligent hand, but the hand of the diligent makes rich* (Proverbs 10:4).

*In all labor there is profit, but mere talk leads only to poverty* (Proverbs 14:23).

Let me share an example. I spoke earlier of the slackwire act I performed. At Florida State University's Flying High Circus, where I learned my skills, the performer usually walked carefully to the center of the wire and performed different balancing tricks, such as juggling or balancing objects, or even riding a unicycle. It was usually a slower act, with stationary balancing as the primary crowd pleaser.

But I was never satisfied with doing what everyone else did. I wanted a new twist. One day, while thinking about this desire, I had an idea flash into my head: Why not run on the wire? I liked that! No one was doing that, nor had anyone done so before in Flying High, that I knew of.

**Bold, overwhelming action is your passkey to unlimited achievement!** (W.G.)

That night during practice at Calloway Gardens Resort in the mountains of western Georgia, the circus' summer home, I set up my rig and pictured myself running back and forth across the wire. I began to sing a tune in my head that had a very fast beat while simultaneously picturing myself running on the wire from end to end, over and over. I played this mental movie again and again for several minutes and then got up on the wire to give it a go. I took two or three quick steps and fell off with a smack on the wooden stage! (Fortunately for me, slackwire is performed only six or seven feet in the air!) I got back up and tried again. Smack! Same result. And again, smack! And again, smack! And again, smack! Smack! Smack! I must have fallen 40 or 50 times that night, but I never once felt discouraged because I had a *vision* of what I could do and the incentive of being the *first* to do it.

It took me about a week or so to master that new feat of running on the wire. It added an excitement to my act that had not previously been there. It kindled a new confidence in me. I also learned another lesson: Be willing to look foolish while going for your goals!

## Repetition, the Greatest Teacher

As I said in the previous chapter, in every sport, performing art, and ministry endeavor I have attempted, I have found that *constant and repetitive action is what develops skill.*

The story I just told illustrates this truth. It is not necessary to have extreme talent, just extreme patience and fortitude to press through all barriers until you succeed. I must have run on that slackwire thousands of times before I actually had it mastered.

It is repetition that trains us best. As my favorite movie hero, Indiana Jones, said, "It ain't the years, it's the mileage." It's not how many years you've been doing something, it's how many hours, how many repetitions. As you embark upon the journey of achievement, you will need many skills. The first skill you must develop is that of accepting repetition as your instructor, mentor, teacher, and friend. Nothing is free! Be a doer. Be a skilled doer!

## Final Thoughts: Confront Yourself!

**Some people wait so long for their ship to come in that their piers collapse.** (John Goddard)

Taking action on what you believe requires confronting yourself. By this I mean you must be completely honest with yourself about where you are presently with the Lord. Words without actions are merely lies. It is *not* enough to say it! You must honestly assess where you are now in relation to achieving your destiny. Then you need to begin to act in such a way as to *catapult* yourself to the next level of accomplishment.

Your biggest struggle will be with inertia. Inertia is the force that holds a rocket on the pad at Cape Canavaral for those first few seconds after the engines have begun to fire. It takes more power to get the rocket moving upward in those first few seconds than it does to fling it into orbit! Once it's moving, it takes less and less energy to keep it flying. This is true for you as well.

When you say yes to any one of your goals, you will experience the power struggle to get off square one and on the move. Procrastination, distractions, and many other pulls will try to keep you on the launch pad. But you must expend whatever energy is necessary to get moving and stay moving! Do not let yourself buy the lie that thinking and saying is all it takes. It is the truth that sets us free from the gravitational pull of lethargy and unbelief, and the truth is that you must act on what you believe or nothing will happen! So, just do it!

# Chapter 16

# The Law of Increasing Success

**The Law:**
**"To everyone who has shall more be given."**

Matthew 25:14-30 is the story of the man who, before going on a protracted journey, gave several large sums of money to three of his servants. I shared this story in its entirety in Chapter 3 when we discussed our personal giftings, and so will refrain from doing so again. However, the moral of the story is certainly pertinent to our success. It illustrates the first law of increasing success: To everyone who has shall more be given.

It's as simple as that. The real chore here is being someone who "has" and who therefore *can* receive "more" on a continual basis. As you discover, design, and then direct your purpose, destiny, and achievement, you will become such a person. The key is *not* to amass great volumes of things or superlative public accolades, but instead to abound in faithful service to God and others. The servants in this passage in Matthew were given a large amount of financial wealth to look after. By serving their master through faithfully increasing the sum, they were also serving those involved in the transactions and, of course, themselves in the long run. Faithfulness is the key to living in the realm of *increasing* success.

A person who has exemplified faithfulness is rare, but such a person will never lack for opportunities for success. The very nature of a faithful person is to succeed. His motivation is obeying God and helping others, which we have said is the crux of every believer's life purpose. A person so motivated will constantly be accomplishing things of substance and worth. *That* is success. What drives a faithful person is doing the right thing at *all* times, not accumulating vast amounts of money or gaining prestige, though these are often by-products of a faithful life. They believe serving to be the highest form of love and are willing to be a servant in any and all circumstances. Do you want success? Be a faithful servant.

**Success is accomplishing the good thing you attempted and growing better by the work of it.** (W.G.)

This law of success breeding more success through faithful service begins with the *little* you have, not the *large* you will accumulate. You must start where you are in utilizing this law. In your personal purpose and destiny, you can grow far beyond everything you presently believe you can accomplish, because you will reap more than you sow. By simply beginning where you are, you put into motion the law of faithfulness, which states that if you are faithful in the little, you will be given more to be faithful with in the future.

Most of us, myself included, do not want to wait for the "faithful in much" part to take place! We would rather *start* there, but it ain't gonna happen. Everyone has to pay his or her dues somehow at some time. My experience has been that those who are given large volumes to start with usually don't progress much farther. For example, studies done on lottery winners show that many have lost their money and usually their quality of life in family, friends, and health within a year or two of winning. Proverbs tells us that an inheritance gained quickly is not blessed in the end.

My story is that when I first entered the ministry, I wanted to preach before thousands, and yesterday would be too long to wait. Fortunately for me, and for those I would minister to in the future, the Lord placed me under a wise man who had the wisdom to prove my faithfulness in the little things first. I wanted to preach in the main church sessions on Sunday mornings, but Dale gave me the privilege (and I mean that sincerely) of preaching to the children's church group.

Dale told me that if I could preach to children and have *them* understand what I was saying, then I would be able to teach and preach to adults and have *them* understand. I wasn't thrilled, but I was faithful. I gave those little guys and girls everything I knew and, amazingly enough, they seemed to get it. After a few months of children's church, I was graduated to the youth group. I was faithful there for several months as well.

Also during this time, Meg and I were the janitors and grounds keepers. We scrubbed the restrooms, vacuumed the auditorium and classrooms, mowed the acreage, cleaned out the outdoor baptistry, and repaired the church roadside sign on a daily basis. We were *not* looking for strokes. We were simply being faithful servants because we wanted to and because we understood the law of reciprocity. I have no doubt that the success we have enjoyed throughout our ministerial, family, social, and business careers is due to the faithful service we rendered during those early years. "Faithful in little" brings the opportunity to be faithful in much.

One truth about a law is that it always works. Gravity works at all times. Mathematics work at all times. Fire works the same all the time. Each of these can be good or bad, depending on your situation. Laws are impersonal; they just work. This is why corrupt people can use the laws of success and reap seemingly rich rewards. Jesus taught the disciples about faith and told them that whoever believes can move a mountain (see Mk. 11:23). There are no qualifiers other than believing. Jesus followed that by saying we should therefore put our faith in God and receive from *Him*. The implication here is that you won't be asking God for things outside His will and way.

I want to be constantly growing into a more faithful servant. I want the Lord to know I can be trusted with more and more. I let the thinking I've explained here pervade every area of my life and ministry. Continually increasing the value of what He has entrusted to me is of major importance to me and is the cornerstone of the law of increasing success.

Let me illustrate. Quite often during our circus years we were given various items, ranging from vehicles to trailers to toolsheds. Each time we received an item, we immediately began to improve it. We would paint, re-upholster, and repair whatever was most needed. My desire was always to be sure that everything we owned and borrowed was of an excellence beyond normal. No, we did not spend extravagantly, nor could we, but we did give everything a good scrub and polish. We never received a gift or borrowed anything that we did not attempt to improve in some way.

## The Peak to Peek Principle

The phrase Peak to Peek Principle was coined by Reverend Robert Schuller in his book by the same name. Its premise is that the precise moment you accomplish a goal is the most opportune time to peek about you, from that high place of achievement, and view the next "peak" available to climb. In business it may be a five thousand dollar sale that gives you the impetus to see yourself selling a one million dollar item the next time. In ministry you may have traveled to a church across town to minister, and now you can believe for the ability to trek to the next state. An athlete who runs a 10 second hundred meter dash can then see a personal best of 9.8 seconds. One success breeds more success. One achievement gives thought, belief, and therefore power to another.

**Never let your first place ribbons become finish lines.** (Anon.)

As I have continually said, the best way to get your mind actively seeking new ideas is to ask yourself questions.

- When you achieve a goal in your Destiny Master Plan, ask yourself, "What can I do to build upon that goal?"
- Look to the next goal in your plan and ask, "How can I accomplish it in less time and with less effort?"
- "How can I condense my resources to do more?"
- "What did I learn from this accomplishment that will give me more power to accomplish the next?"
- "How can I expand in a new direction that I did not see before?"
- "How can what I've experienced help others as I pursue my next goal?"

Your questioning should extend into all your Life Areas, for you will never accomplish even one of your destiny plan goals without affecting every area in some manner.

### Self-Encouragement

Please read First Samuel chapter 16 before going further.

Another form of the Peak to Peek Principle that I have found extremely helpful is self-encouragement by remembering past successes and victories.

When we remember these, we are encouraged to press on to the next challenge. When young David faced the dreaded giant Goliath on the field of battle, he took the time to *remind* himself and *inform* those about him that he had been in such "life or death" struggles before. A lion and a bear were no match for David's God-guided stones as they flew from his sling, and he assured everyone that this Philistine would suffer the same fate. David *ran* to the battle line fully confident that what God had done in the past, He would do again.

I have used this technique of self-encouragement many times when facing great odds. When my children show symptoms of sickness, I take time to remind myself of how the Lord miraculously healed me of pneumonia, healed third-degree burns on my son's hand, repaired torn ligaments in my knee, and removed countless fevers and sicknesses. This has always served to renew my confidence in the Word of God and to spur me on to win the victory!

It has worked just as well with finances. Many were the times in our past when we were financially broke with no way to pay bills or purchase needed items for our family. We pulled out our memories of past provisions by God's hand and rejoiced that the present circumstances would bow in like manner. The provision *always* came. I strongly urge you to try this technique the next time you get in a bind, and feel the strength that you receive from such encouragement.

**Few things in this life are more powerful than a positive push.**
(Richard M. De Voss)

On the other hand, I also urge you not to rely on your memory. It's a good idea to have a journal or notebook of some sort where you can record your triumphs and learning times. Again, please refer to the *Destiny Planner®* and use the Achievement History Worksheets to keep excellent records of such events. This will be a very valuable asset to you in the years to come when you face your own giants.

Another aspect of the Peak to Peek self-encouragement technique is to actually let yourself re-experience the *feelings* of your past victories. I have no doubt that David did just that as he remembered and told the stories in detail of how he had killed the lion and the bear. His emotions were certainly running high by the time he met Goliath! He *ran* toward the towering warrior and *screamed* his oaths of killing the giant, beheading him, and feeding his carcass to the birds! Try to say *that* without getting emotional. No, I believe that our ability to relive our past triumphs, and even our defeats, with full emotion brings another dimension of our being into play and bolsters our confidence even more.

For example, I have often used such memories when confronted with adverse situations. When my son was two years old and received third-degree burns on his hand, I got *very* emotional about it. I was angry and upset over the accident at first. But then I let that emotion turn on the problem as I consciously reminded myself of the countless times God had healed my family. The anger turned to confidence in God and His Word. Then it turned to praise for His faithfulness in times past. As I began to worship Him for what He *had* done and *would* do in my two-year-old's hand, my son stopped crying and fell asleep in my arms. When he awoke, he had no more pain, and in a few days the scab fell off, leaving no scar! That incident, of course, became another memory to call on in other battles.

**Final Thoughts**

There may be some of you reading this book who have lost your dreams to time and circumstances. I ask you right now to renew your dreams and refresh your goals using these laws of increasing success. First, take the time to list every specific event or goal that you have been faithful to obey the Lord in performing. List them on a piece of paper. Look them over and tell yourself that what the Bible promises is the truth: Being *faithful in little creates opportunity to be faithful in much.* See yourself with more to be faithful with. Believe that the Lord wants to entrust you with more than ever before. If you cannot truthfully say that you have been faithful with the little, admit it and start over! Unlike the master of the servants in Matthew 25, the Lord is much more forgiving. He wants to bless you and will give you more opportunities to prove yourself faithful in the little. Your past is not your future!

Second, encourage yourself with any past accomplishments, no matter how small they may seem to you. Take a peek from the peak. If you have accomplished just one thing, you can accomplish something else. If you learned to ride a bicycle, you *can* learn to drive a car. If you learned how to write in cursive, you *can* learn how to type. Don't let yourself be robbed any longer of the joys and freedom of dreaming and setting goals.

*Your past is **not** your future*. You *can* write your future today! You can begin immediately to take a peek at the peaks around you from the vantage point of your past. Take action *today* toward your goals and dreams, even if it's just taking out a sheet of paper and listing what you really want to do. Encourage yourself in the Lord. Ask the Holy Spirit to bring events to your remembrance that will bolster your confidence and light a path toward your dreams, your purpose, your very destiny!

Success breeds success. It's a spiritual law that works for those who work it. It's waiting for *you* to tap into its vast supply of power so it can propel your life into greater and greater accomplishments. Stand on the peaks of your past victories and peek at the peaks on the horizon of your destiny. They are waiting for you to climb them, so they can show you the peaks that lay beyond them!

**Success is never having to say, "I should have."** (W.G.)

# Section Four

# This Could Be You!

*...I most certainly understand now that God is not one to show partiality* (Acts 10:34).

# Chapter 17

# These Work Every Time

*But now abide faith, hope, love, these three* (1 Corinthians 13:13a).

I realize that some of you may have been seeking the Lord for many months or even years concerning your purpose in life. Perhaps you have even applied the principles we have covered here. You have done all the seeking, praying, and talking with God you feel you can do, yet you still have not heard the first word about what He wants you to do with your life. If you are discouraged, it is understandable but *not* hopeless!

Don't lose heart. I have good news for you. The Lord does have something for you to do, and you don't have to wait ten years to put it into practice. You can do it starting today! It's so simple that you may have already thought of it yourself, yet shrugged it off as just another groping shot in the dark. But this is no desperation ploy; it's God's will.

Here it is: If you haven't yet found your personal purpose, then join yourself with someone who has found his or hers and do anything and everything you can to help that person achieve it. That's right—give yourself to another's vision instead of sitting on your hands waiting for the lightning of revelation to flash for you.

### Be Encouraged!

God knows that you are seeking Him, and He will reveal to you His perfect plan for your life. Don't even question that. But of this you must be assured: Until you hear whatever His plan for you may be, get involved in someone else's purpose. It is very likely that the reason you have discovered little of your personal purpose is because He needs your gifts and abilities to help one of His other children succeed. That is a great privilege.

**We must not only give what we have, we must give what we are.**
(Cardinal Mercier)

We saw earlier in the chapter on the ministry of helps that this is the principle of sowing and reaping, a principle we have continually referred to. That ministry is greatly needed in every local church in the world. I'm sure yours is no exception. I suggest that you speak with your pastor, your elders and deacons, or whomever necessary and let them know you are available for service. Find a need that your gifts, talents, and experience can fill and put your zeal for God to work. No church has too many volunteers. No personal purpose has too much help. Whether it be a ministry, a friend's business, or a family, you will find great fulfillment by giving yourself to others.

When the Lord instructed me to pour the majority of my time into the vision of my pastor, a tremendous phenomenon occurred. Suddenly I began to receive more plans for my vision. It seemed that the more I worked for the church, regardless of what I was doing, the more I heard from the Lord. It was the law of sowing and reaping. It was working for me because I was working it. It will work for you too! In fact, it has been working throughout your life.

Will your plan come to you immediately after you begin to give your time and effort to your local church body or to the purpose of some friend? I honestly don't know. I do know, however, that you will not only be opening yourself up to the return on what you have given but also to the joy and satisfaction of seeing a purpose, a destiny, come to pass before your eyes due to *your* efforts. Such on-the-job training can prove invaluable when it comes to walking out your own plan. You will be able to learn from the mistakes and successes of the church or individual with whom you work and to affect the lives of many at the same time. Also, there is a good possibility that the very people to whom you minister through your church will be the same people who help you with *your* purpose. No matter how you slice it, you always come out on top!

So don't get discouraged if you have yet to discover your personal purpose. Be encouraged instead—encouraged by the possibility of learning from others as you prepare for your own purpose and destiny. But even if you never receive a full-blown purpose of your own such as we have discussed in this book, you will discover that being a part of another's vision is just as rewarding. In fact, the *majority* of Christians' destinies are wrapped up in the purposes of others. How do I know that? Because no one is an island. No believer is destined to a life of singular accomplishment. We all need the whole Body of Christ working together. We need each other. Every purposed believer needs others and is needed by others. It's God's will. It's God's way. Be excited, *you* are necessary for the purposes of God in the earth!

## Harness the Power of Patience

For those of you who do have a vision, a distinct purpose from the Lord for your life, or for those who may have received one since starting this book, I have exciting words for you. If you have been struggling with walking out your purpose and feel that you may never see your destiny fulfilled, here is a rock upon which you can stand!

> *For the vision is yet for the appointed time; it hastens toward the goal, and it will not fail. Though it tarries, wait for it; for it will certainly come, it will not delay* (Habakkuk 2:3).

The Lord promises here that every purpose, vision, and destiny has an appointed time and that it will race toward the finish line. It *will* come to pass. It *will* be done. It *will* see fruition. Just hang on! Sure it can be frustrating, wanting to see the plan unfold a bit faster or the finish tape get a bit closer. But don't let the dark clouds of discouragement hang over you like a guillotine blade. Keep going. Stay excited about your goals. Take a look at how far you've come. Get out your destiny plan and daydream about it some more. It *is* on the way! Your vision *will* happen!

> *Therefore, do not throw away your confidence, which has a great reward. For you have need of endurance* [patience], *so that when you have done the will of God, you may receive what was promised. ... BUT MY RIGHTEOUS ONE SHALL LIVE BY FAITH; AND IF HE SHRINKS BACK, MY SOUL HAS NO PLEASURE IN HIM. But we are not of those who shrink back to*

*destruction, but of those who have faith to the preserving of the soul* (Hebrews 10:35-36,38-39).

Did you get that? God told us *not* to throw away our confidence. What confidence is He talking about? It's your confidence in Him and in yourself. That's right, *yourself*! You see, if you throw away your confidence in you, you have nothing to work with. God has confidence in you. He trusts you enough to give you the purpose and destiny that will steer your life on its appointed course. He trusts you enough to give you a vision that will enlist the lives of others who love Him. If *He* has that kind of trust and confidence in you, you can and must also!

Don't throw away your confidence in God either. He has yet to come up against an obstacle in the life of one of His children that is a surprise to Him or is more than He can handle. You will not be the first! Jesus said, "With God all things are possible" (Mt. 19:26b). Between you and God, your purpose has everything it needs to be a divine success.

**I don't think there is any other quality so essential to success of any kind as the quality of perseverance. It overcomes almost everything, even nature.** (John D. Rockefeller)

Hebrews 10:36 contains the real issue you must deal with: endurance, patience, perseverance, hanging on. Patience is a problem for most of us, especially those with a definite purpose to achieve. We want to please our Father in Heaven so much that we are quite willing to run leagues ahead of Him to accomplish our appointed tasks. Such hasty behavior is not indicative of a life of confidence. The confident person is one who is content to wait for God's timing. After all, it is *His* will we want to accomplish. The reward spoken of in the Scriptures is ours only after a *patient* performance of God's will.

Patience is ours. We don't even need to ask for it. Galatians 5:22 proclaims that it is part of the fruit of the Spirit of God, and as believers in Jesus Christ, the Holy Spirit is in us. Therefore, asking for patience is unnecessary because it is *already* in us. What we need to do is develop our patience through submission to the Lord's timing. Acquiring it in the way He intends is only possible by submitting to His timing. The zealot casts aside his patience and rushes out to perform his vision ahead of God's seemingly tortoise pace. But he will eventually end up waiting for the Lord anyway as he gathers up the pieces of his vision, which was shattered by his haste. There are no shortcuts!

So don't let discouragement overtake you as you work through the steps of finding and living out your life's destiny plan. Each step not only brings you closer to the achievement but also builds within you the fruit of patience. That patience will manifest itself in the joyous reward of your Father's pleasure as you complete His will and help those you touch. Hang on to that promise in Habakkuk 2:3, and you will see the vision God gave you *hasten* to completion.

**Fight the Good Fight!**

I wish I could say that you will *never* face discouragement. But that would be a lie. Discouragement is a chief weapon of the devil, as we have said. But you have far greater weapons and far superior power. Proverbs 4:20-22 explains that the Word of God is *life* to those who find it. Hebrews 4:12 states that His Word is filled with power. When the forces of discouragement close in, take God's Word and push them back into the darkness where they belong! The Bible is our sword and we must be skillful in wielding it for whatever we need. Here are a few verses I use to encourage myself when things seem to be closing in on me, or when my destiny seems to be in peril of washing out. Speak them boldly and out loud. Speak them with *fire* in your heart. If you do this, discouragement will run from you like darkness from the light!

*And Jesus said to him, "'If You can!' All things are possible to him who believes"* (Mark 9:23).

*And my God shall supply all your needs according to His riches in glory in Christ Jesus* (Philippians 4:19).

*But thanks be to God, who always leads us in His triumph in Christ, and manifests through us the sweet aroma of the knowledge of Him in every place* (2 Corinthians 2:14).

*But thanks be to God, who gives us the victory through our Lord Jesus Christ* (1 Corinthians 15:57).

*But in all these things we overwhelmingly conquer through Him who loved us* (Romans 8:37).

*You are from God, little children, and have overcome them; because greater is He who is in you than he who is in the world* (1 John 4:4).

*For whatever is born of God overcomes the world; and this is the victory that has overcome the world—our faith* (1 John 5:4).

*No weapon that is formed against you shall prosper; and every tongue that accuses you in judgment you will condemn. This is the heritage of the servants of the Lord...* (Isaiah 54:17).

## Final Thoughts

With a vision, a purpose, in your heart and a destiny plan in your hands—even if it is that of another believer—you are walking in the realm of the highest form of living. To know that the plan laid before you is the *perfect* will of the Almighty God who created you, and to know that *He* is going to help you and send *others* to assist you in its achievement, is the ultimate experience. It brings peace, joy, and life. Nothing compares to walking with God! Go for it with all you've got, and never, ever give up. *You **can** do it!*

# Chapter 18

# The Birth of a Vision

**The very essence of leadership is you have to have a vision. It's got to be a vision you articulate clearly and forcefully on every occasion. You cannot blow an uncertain trumpet.**
(Father Theodore Hesburgh)

## A Challenging Question

Since 1977, as I began to discover my own purpose and started planning for its fruition, many people have come to me for advice on how they could do the same. I spent many hours in one-on-one sessions, growing increasingly irritated at how long it actually took to explain my system. My frustration was relieved in part with the 1987 publication (reprinted in 1992) of my book entitled, *How to Find Your Purpose in Life*. It was basic, to be sure, but it was the *only* material in Christian circles I could find at the time that dealt directly with *finding* and *doing* one's personal purpose and destiny.

Over the ensuing years, I received many letters and thank you's for the book. Here are some summaries from a few of those letters.

*One woman finally discovered that her purpose was something totally different from what she had been doing. After reading* ***Purpose****, she got on the right track and was bringing her purpose to pass.*

*Another woman told of her desire to commit suicide because she was so distraught over not knowing and doing what she was ordained to do. After reading the book, she discovered her true purpose and decided to live and make it happen!*

*Another man actually came to my office and gave me a substantial check for our ministry because he had read my book and had found his purpose. He had left his home in Michigan with the intention of quitting his business. On his drive to Florida, he stopped in a bookstore and purchased my book. He read the entire book as his wife drove from Atlanta to Tampa. During that time, God spoke to his heart as he read, and he received the direction he was seeking!*

Without a doubt such testimonies are thrilling and rewarding for me. But I still have never been satisfied with that first book's results. It was simply too little effort against too mountainous a problem. While I had hoped to do more with the book and the message, the Lord did not allow me to do so.

Then, in late spring of 1996, I received an interesting word in my prayer time. During my years as an associate minister at Metro Christian Fellowship in Kansas City, Missouri, I became friends with Mike Bickle, who is senior pastor there. Mike related to me a visitation of the Lord in which he heard the audible voice of God say, in essence, "I will change the face of Christianity in the earth in one generation." I had never given that phrase much thought before because it was not spoken to me. But that day in prayer, the Lord reminded me of Mike's divine encounter and asked me, "What does that mean?" After a moment or two of thought, I had to admit that I had no idea. Then He asked me, "If I told *you* to change the face of Christianity in the earth in one generation, how would *you* do it?" Now, I am not so naive as to think He was asking me to accomplish that gargantuan task single-handedly, but it definitely got me thinking! I knew He was challenging me, and I had to find the right answer—His answer.

## More Challenging Questions

I immediately began to ask myself some questions. After much research and prayer, I came up with some enlightening answers. I've listed the questions below, with their answers. These are merely *my thoughts* and are in no way meant to be an exhaustive treatise on the state of the Church of the Lord Jesus Christ.

**Question:** What does the Lord mean by the "face" of the Church?

**Answer:** *Face* has many meanings. After searching the Hebrew, the Greek, and finally Webster's dictionaries, I came up with the following lengthy and rather intriguing list. I believe you will find its variety to be a bit more enveloping than you might have first anticipated. I list them in alphabetical order.

Appearance
Appearance of wealth
Confront
Countenance
Knowledge
Person
Position or state of being
Poverty
Presence
Prestige
Rapid breathing—as in passionate
Reputation
Resemblance
Revealing the inward thoughts and feelings
Superficial judgment
Value
Validity
Worthy

It takes little study of this list to understand that the Lord most probably intends to change *every* aspect of His Church's appearance in the earth. *To change the face of His Body, He will have to address us at the spiritual, personality, intellectual, financial, social, and physical areas of our lives.* That covers the entire spectrum of the human being. That amount of change will guarantee two things: excitement and discomfort!

**Question:** What does the face of the Church look like now, so that I can see the change take place?

**Answer:** I believe that if less than five percent of the Church knows what their personal, God-ordained purpose for existing is, its face must be very immature. Having had the opportunity both to travel and to spend time with fellow ministers who travel even more than I do, I have found the Church to be in need in each of the six areas mentioned above.

- Too little of Jesus' Church resembles His personality in power, grace, humility, knowledge, wisdom, and anointing.
- Too little of Jesus' Church is in a position of social strength.
- Too few in the Church are robust physical specimens.
- Financially, churches are filled with too much poverty and too little wealth.
- Too few Christians practice biblical confrontation of sin.

Please understand, I say these things in a spirit of truth, not condemnation. I sadly admit that I have been found among most of these too much of the time.

We all desire to be conformed to the image of our Lord Jesus, but even with the outpouring of the Holy Spirit that is taking place around the world today, how many believers are truly walking in such conformity? How many Christians have discovered who God created them to be? Discipleship is not an event, but a process of maturity that involves more than becoming filled with the Holy Spirit. It's about being a *specific* stone in the *specific* place in the awesome building of living stones known as the Church! Yes, we, His Church, are in need of a new face.

**Question:** Has God "changed the face" of His people before in one generation?

**Answer:** No, not in one generation, but in two or three. Twice before God *has* changed the *appearance* of His believers: once in the Old Testament and once in the New Testament.

The first was after freeing Israel from Egypt. When Israel departed from Egypt, they were healthy, wealthy, and spiritually and supernaturally alive. It was obvious to the world whose children they were! Word about them spread throughout the earth, and that word was fearsome. The presence of God was visible about them day and night in the fire and the cloud. But it took 40 years—two generations—to confront the sin of unbelief. So, when it was time to go into the Promised Land, only the true believers were left, an entirely *new* generation from those who began the journey. Consequently, the world was never the same.

The second time was when God changed the look of His followers in the ensuing 60-plus years (three generations) after Christ's death, resurrection, and ascension, and the outpouring of His Spirit on Pentecost. They were accused of turning the world upside down! The young Church walked in supernatural, miraculous happenings. They confronted sin and people died. They confronted sickness and death and people lived. They gave of their wealth for the good of all. They resembled Jesus to the point of death. The world has never been the same since.

**Question:** If God did change His people, did He work similarly each time?

**Answer:** The Lord followed a similar, specific plan for changing the look of His people in both instances. Both required intense learning and the retooling of traditions and lifestyles. They were exciting times, as well as uncomfortable times.

The first time took 40 years in the school of "hard knocks," combining deep training in the levitical laws, the covenant, and in understanding the tasks of each tribe and family. These were *published*, and a command to *teach* them to following generations was initiated, which still goes on today.

The second time required a *new covenant* to be taught. *New doctrines* of forgiveness, mercy, and caring for each other were initiated by a *new leadership* of apostles, prophets, evangelists, pastors, teachers, and elders. All this was *published* in the letters of the apostles (written over the 60-plus years after Jesus rose), which became the New Testament. It has been *taught* constantly as, even now, we "gather house to house and in the Temple" (see Acts 20:20).

**Question:** What does God's Word say is the number one ingredient for creating such change?

**Answer:** It is the renewing of our minds that transforms us, according to God's Word in Romans 12:2. Renewing, or more literally renovating, our minds requires new revelation. That means teaching, training, and study, which, as we have seen, God has used twice to transform His believers. It was *this* revelation that opened to me a very wondrous possibility.

## What If!

What if God changed the individual and collective thinking of the Church concerning their purpose and destiny in a single generation? Could you imagine just *one* fellowship of believers in just *one* city who all knew what their individual, personal purpose was and how they were going to fulfill it—and who were actually walking it out? That power possibility astounded me. Make no mistake here. I realize that there are many church bodies who have rallied around the vision of the pastor or the elders who lead them. But I am speaking of something even more dynamic: a *synergism* of collective individual purposes flowing together in unity to fulfill that *body's* purpose.

I happen to believe that God can do anything. I believe such a possibility is attainable. I believe it *can* be done in a single generation. Obviously no one man could reach the millions of believers in the earth with such a message, but by multiplying the vision and effort through as many people, media, organizations, and educational venues as possible, it *could* be done. It's the law of leverage: Anything can be moved with a fulcrum and lever of sufficient size!

## All Things Are Possible to Him Who Believes

Seizing this possibility, I developed an initial strategy based upon the plan God had used twice before in the history of His people: Change their collective appearance through intense learning and training. It must touch every generation alive over a 20-year period (one generation). It will require the use of every available media. It will require the utilization of every form of education, from formal schooling to the Internet. It will require mass media and individual study materials. It will require a lot of work! The main key to success in this vision is duplication of effort by as many people as possible.

## A Request

You will see by the following outline of this vision for changing the face of Christianity in the earth, that it will require much prayer and many laborers. To facilitate such activity, I ask *you* to seek the Lord for any insight and direction He may give you concerning this grand task. If He should give you *anything*, please send it to us. We are more than aware of our need for the input of the Body of Christ.

Also, pray for the many aspects of the vision, as you can commit to do so. Wisdom is our primary request, for with it comes everything else we will need. If you would like further information concerning our vision of purpose, destiny, and achievement, please write or call our offices at the address and phone numbers supplied on page 235.

**Vision without action is merely a dream.**
**Action without vision just passes the time.**
**Vision with action can change the world.**
(Joel Authur Baker)

## The Plan

**I. Create teaching and training materials.** (All materials can be personalized with cooperating organizations' names and logos.)

A. Books, audiotapes, videotapes, computer programs, films.
B. Seminars and conferences.
C. Curriculum for Christian schools grades K-12.
D. College level correspondence and classroom courses.

**II. Enlist every Christian organization and media.**

A. All local, national, and international mass media (television, radio, Internet).
B. Major denominations networking.
C. Parachurch organizations.
D. Christian business organizations.
E. Formal school and home school organizations.
F. Christian Bible schools, colleges, seminaries, and universities.

**III. Enlist established Christian success/motivation experts and speakers to:**

A. Contribute to training materials.
B. Combine with other experts for seminars and conferences.
C. Consult with churches and parachurch organizations.

## IV. Enlist Christian celebrities to:

A. Endorse "purpose, destiny, and achievement" movement (in training materials, seminars, etc.).
B. Create musical and dramatic videos and films.
C. Create themed music albums (various artists contributing).
D. Assemble live touring troupes of dramas and musicals (children, youth, adult).

### Final Thoughts

I did not fully accept this vision of doing my part to change the face of God's people until one night, as I crawled into bed, the Lord powerfully arrested me with a sobering vision. I saw multitudes of people wandering aimlessly about the earth, sad and broken. I knew that they were Christians. The Lord then said to me, "You *must* do this vision of purpose and destiny. There are so many who will *never* fulfill their own destinies if you do not accept My commission to do this." I felt the Lord's broken heart for His people as He spoke with deep pain in His voice. I was overwhelmed by His passionate plea for my obedience, and I promised Him I'd do it.

But a few months later I grew tired of working on this book, its accompanying *Destiny Planner®,* and the first seminar tape series. With no one to help me and little encouragement, I again questioned whether I had actually heard from Heaven. Once more the Lord confronted me with a clear and haunting vision.

This time I was standing next to the Lord's throne. Before Him was a sea of people—Christians. He lovingly, but painfully, asked the man before Him, "Why didn't you do what I created you for?" The man, with total brokenness and sincerity said, "I didn't know how to find out what it was." My heart broke for this man and the thousands behind him who nodded in agreement. Then the Lord turned to me, His facial expression somewhere between anger and anguish, and He said, "Why didn't *you* teach them?" I was pierced in my heart! I was instantly undone with grief at the thought that I had not only missed my *own* purpose but had also denied others the ability to discover and fulfill *theirs* as well. That was the last time I questioned my destiny as it pertains to this commission.

Please believe me when I say that I am not for a moment thinking that the lives of any Christians rest in my hands. I am not God. I am only a son like any other believer. However, He has given me a commission and I will be a foolish, restless, and unfulfilled man if I do *not* obey. I have no idea how God works in the lives of men with such matters. All I know is that I have a part to play in helping His people, believers like you, *Discover Your* ***Purpose****, Design Your* ***Destiny****, and Direct Your* ***Achievement***. I'll do my part as best I can with His help. My daily prayer is that you will be better equipped to do your part because I've done mine well.

# Appendix A

# G.COM International

G.COM International is a nonprofit organization recognized by the U.S. government. Our primary ministry is worldwide evangelism, Christian education, and all related activities. Presently we are focusing on the message of purpose, destiny, and achievement. For an overview of this message, turn to the Introduction to this book. We ask you to consider praying for us and our vision. There is so much to do and so little time!

For further information please write or call our offices at the numbers below. You may also visit our website at www.reapernet.com/di/greenman. Contributions within the United States of America to G.COM are tax deductible.

P.O. Box 1095
Belton, MO 64012
Office: (816) 322-5910
Fax: (816) 322-0930
Gcom@juno.com

# Appendix B

## Seminars

Mr. Greenman has created a training seminar teaching the rudiments of *discovering your purpose, designing your destiny, and directing your achievement*. These seminars can be scheduled as one- or two-day events. Each seminar is filled with the most important and practical information from this book and the newest information hot off the press from the author's research. There is an abundance of audience participation and activities to help you get started immediately in living your God-given purpose. No one will be bored!

In fact, we're so sure that you will receive at least three specific items you will be able to put into practice before leaving the seminar, that we will refund 100 percent of your registration if you are not satisfied!

Registration has been formulated to accommodate everyone who wishes to attend. Our goal is to get this information into the hands of as many people as possible. Financial hardship should not stop anyone. If you wish to attend, we'll find a way for you!

To receive an information package or to secure a spot on our seminar schedule, simply call our offices at the number on page 235, visit our website, or write us. We look forward to working with you!

# Appendix C

## Financial Opportunities

One of the author's personal goals is to distribute over one million copies of this book to Christians around the world. Although he cannot reach everyone personally, he can use mass media to touch more with the purpose message. But he also desires to give fellow Christians a chance to benefit financially from this effort. Together we can touch over one million believers.

G.COM has set up a system for distributors of the purpose materials to make substantial financial remuneration. By helping us get these materials to the Church, you will not only aid those believers in finding their purpose but will also enjoy a new source of income. For information on this and other financial opportunities offered by G.COM and/or its associates, please contact our offices at the address on page 235. We'll send you a complete information package on how to get started.

# Appendix D

## Do You Have a Story?

This book you now hold is only the tip of an iceberg. My vision for this message is much bigger and more far-reaching. But I need the help of dedicated believers like yourself to get it done.

One of my goals is to produce a series of books on how ordinary people have utilized these principles to change their lives and achieve their destinies by God's direction. There are no specific categories. I'm looking not just for ministers but also for housewives, single mothers, blue collar workers, executives, entrepreneurs, schoolteachers, politicians, and movie stars. I want to be sure that no one is left out or feels that his or her specific purpose is not worth discussing. There is always someone who needs to hear from someone else who has triumphed in the same area.

If you have such a story or know of someone who does, please write or call my offices at the number on page 235 and let me know. I'll give full credit in my books to the people involved with helping me find these true stories. I believe that the heroes of the faith will most likely be those who have never graced a TV screen or written a book. I want to hear from those faithful saints!

William D. Greenman

# Appendix E

# Other Available Materials

### BASICS of the Christian Life

A booklet for the new believer, this publication has found its way around the world and into several languages. It covers nine major areas of the Christian life in a concise, yet informative manner. It is easy to read and is used by ministries across America and other nations. This booklet is free and can be secured in bulk orders for the cost of shipping. Donations are accepted to help cover the printing costs.

### Purpose/Destiny/Achievement Audio Seminar

These eight tapes are housed in a handsome binder. A synoptic presentation of Mr. Greenman's seminar covering all the main points, it's a great tool for reviewing your purpose/destiny/achievement studies while riding in the car or working around the home. There are several items on these tapes not found in the book or taught in the live seminars.

### Destiny Planner®

This is the indispensable tool for formulating and tracking your purpose and destiny for the rest of your life. A large, multi-sectioned three-ring binder, it holds all your pertinent information for easy reference. This is a must for all who wish to go onward and upward in their life's achievements.

## Other Authors and Speakers

Our goal is to make available every worthy piece of teaching and training in the areas of purpose, destiny, and achievement. We will constantly seek out and review new materials and let you know what's out there. Through our quarterly resource publication, we will list the best of the best for you to purchase for your personal library or for those of your business, church, or organization. There will also be special sales of materials from time to time, giving you added savings.

Simply call us at the number on page 235 or write for our present catalog of these and other materials by William Greenman and other Christian authors and speakers. Discounted prices on bulk orders are available.